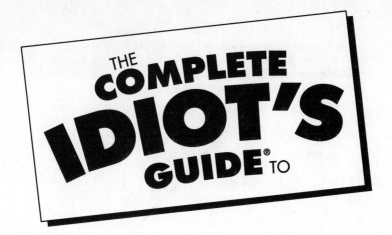

THE COMPLETE IDIOT'S GUIDE® TO

Getting Rich

D1403947

Third Edition

by Stewart H. Welch III, CFP®, AEP, and Larry Waschka

ALPHA

A member of Penguin Group (USA) Inc.

This book is dedicated to the life and memory of Larry Waschka; an extraordinary person whose zest for life and love of people inspired those who came to know him. And to his wife, Jessica, a woman who is beautiful both inside and out.

ALPHA BOOKS

Published by the Penguin Group

Penguin Group (USA) Inc., 375 Hudson Street, New York, New York 10014, U.S.A.

Penguin Group (Canada), 10 Alcorn Avenue, Toronto, Ontario, Canada M4V 3B2 (a division of Pearson Penguin Canada Inc.)

Penguin Books Ltd, 80 Strand, London WC2R 0RL, England

Penguin Ireland, 25 St Stephen's Green, Dublin 2, Ireland (a division of Penguin Books Ltd)

Penguin Group (Australia), 250 Camberwell Road, Camberwell, Victoria 3124, Australia (a division of Pearson Australia Group Pty Ltd)

Penguin Books India Pvt Ltd, 11 Community Centre, Panchsheel Park, New Delhi—110 017, India

Penguin Group (NZ), cnr Airborne and Rosedale Roads, Albany, Auckland 1310, New Zealand (a division of Pearson New Zealand Ltd)

Penguin Books (South Africa) (Pty) Ltd, 24 Sturdee Avenue, Rosebank, Johannesburg 2196, South Africa

Penguin Books Ltd, Registered Offices: 80 Strand, London WC2R 0RL, England

Publisher: *Marie Butler-Knight*
Editorial Director: *Mike Sanders*
Senior Managing Editor: *Jennifer Bowles*
Acquisitions Editor: *Paul Dinas*
Development Editor: *Jennifer Moore*
Production Editor: *Janette Lynn*
Copy Editor: *Tricia Liebig*

Cartoonist: *Richard King*
Book Designer: *Trina Wurst*
Cover Designer: *Bill Thomas*
Indexer: *Tonya Heard*
Layout: *Ayanna Lacey*
Proofreading: *John Etchison*

Contents at a Glance

Contents

Appendixes

Foreword

For over 20 years, I've had the privilege of managing wealth for affluent families and serving on charitable endowment boards with stewardship over endowment funds in excess of $400 million. During this time, I've seen these and other "institutional investors" prosper while the average individual ("retail") investor fails. The national data over many decades supports this assertion. In this book, respected experts Stewart Welch and Larry Waschka share the disciplined steps and effective techniques used by successful investors to accumulate wealth and how to apply them consistently so you, too, can "Get Rich."

I was honored to be asked to write the foreword to this book. I have a tremendous amount of personal and professional respect for both Stewart Welch and Larry Waschka. Larry Waschka was the nicest guy in the world and the world is not quite as sunny of a place since Larry's passing.

Larry craved knowledge that would help his clients and would hop on a plane and fly anywhere to see an advisor who was doing something innovative. I met Larry at the Charles Schwab "Impact" Conference in New York City in 1992. A week after the conference, he called me and said that he wanted to fly up to Detroit with another advisor friend, Stewart Welch of Birmingham, Alabama, to compare notes about our practices and learn from each other.

That meeting started a 12-year friendship and "study group." The three of us, and another advisor who joined our group, Rob Rikoon of Santa Fe, came to regard each other as brothers. With Larry as a driving force, we started an organization called the Council of Independent Financial Advisors (CIFA), which has now grown to include 14 leading independent wealth management firms from major metropolitan areas around the country. These 14 CIFA firms have over $5 billion collectively under management and push each other to practice "state of the art" wealth management on behalf of our clients.

These same wealth management principles form the core of this book, *The Complete Idiot's Guide to Getting Rich, Third Edition.* These principles have been used for generations by affluent families with high-caliber advisors but have been ignored by "ordinary" people. Now you hold in your hand a disciplined road map for building wealth, "getting rich," and achieving your goals.

Ron Yolles
Birmingham, Michigan

Ron Yolles, an attorney and Chartered Financial Analyst (CFA), is founding partner of Yolles-Samrah Wealth Management, LLC, located in Birmingham, Michigan. In 2004, Yolles-Samrah was recognized by *Bloomberg Magazine* as one of the country's 64 leading Family Office firms. Mr. Yolles has written two best-selling books on retirement planning: *You're Retired, Now What?* (1998) and *Getting Started in Retirement Planning* (2000). Visit his firm's website at www.internetinvestmentmanager.com.

Introduction

Too often people believe that wealth is something you can achieve quickly. They look for the lottery win or the windfall that they believe is out there somewhere. However, this approach to getting rich is an illusion for the vast majority of people. Our experience is that most self-made multimillionaires worked hard and smart to accumulate their fortunes.

The book you're holding in your hand is not a get-rich-quick book. It's about strategically building wealth over time that, if cared for properly, can last for years and even generations to come.

Over the past several decades, we've spent countless hours studying wealthy people—and not so wealthy people. What we've learned is that the difference has more to do with decisions and habits than it does with talent, skill, and intelligence. We know multimillionaires who never went to college, and we know multitalented, highly intelligent people who will never become millionaires.

The decision to build wealth is easy to make but may be difficult at times to maintain. It doesn't take a brilliant idea, but it often takes the ability to change your habits and ways of thinking. Old habits are hard to break, and we've seen many times how bad habits ruin a person's chances of ever building significant wealth. The journey takes some effort, and for whatever reason, many people are just not willing to put out the effort necessary to make the change.

What exactly is a strong enough power to change a person's habit? The answer is decision and passion. The decision to build wealth must be accompanied by and aligned with your passion. The first part is easy to do, but the second takes some people a lifetime. You must know your passions. What do you enjoy the most? What excites you? What makes you smile? What would you be willing to do for free? These are the types of questions you must ask yourself. Within the answers you should find several items that will motivate you enough to build the wealth you've always dreamed of. This book will help you find your own passion and motivation.

Let us comment on the concept of wealth, which has many definitions. This book focuses on financial wealth, which may be important to you, but it shouldn't be your only goal. It is a tragedy to be financially wealthy, but personally empty. We've met hundreds of very wealthy people who have spent all their lives trying to get rich with little or no focus on what's really important. They have enough money to buy whatever they want, but their families suffer, they have no spiritual life, they have little or no real friends, they have no social skills, and they are miserable—often depressed. That may be difficult for you to imagine, but we assure you, this is reality for many wealthy people. Fortunately, we've been blessed with very happy wealthy people as clients.

The best advice we can give you before you read this book is that the wealthiest person in the world is someone who has healthy relationships with family and friends, looks for the good in every situation, endeavors to follow his or her passions, and lives well within his or her means. We've also found that a spiritual foundation certainly helps as well—no matter what religion you follow. These are the people you want to follow and emulate.

You can build significant financial wealth with the lessons in this book. We've seen thousands of people do it. However, be sure to focus on the other facets just as much. True wealth involves a balanced life. It's a journey, not a destination.

How to Use This Book

This book is carefully organized to present the tools and techniques you can use to set and reach your goals for wealth. We've defined five levels of wealth to make iteasier for you to plan your journey to wealth, and this book leads you through each level.

Part 1, The Basics of Getting Rich—Wealth Stages 1 and 2, lays the groundwork for getting rich. It breaks down the definition of wealth into five measurable levels and shows you how to design a plan to achieve the first two levels. This part covers the habits and characteristics of wealthy people, as well as how to get rich as an employee.

Part 2, Becoming an Investor—Wealth Stages 3 and 4, shows you how to become financially independent. It focuses on the investment tools and strategies you need to win the investment game.

Part 3, Building Wealth with Your Own Business, explains the basic details of starting, growing, and selling your own business. It also shows you how to achieve the top two levels of wealth using your own business.

Part 4, The Advanced Strategies for Building Wealth, shows you how to make a fortune in real estate; use the tax laws to reduce your taxes and increase your wealth; and how to protect your assets from bad things that sometimes happen.

Extras

The text in each chapter provides full coverage of each topic. However, while we wrote each chapter, certain related topics came to mind that were just too good not to include. We've placed these extras in four different types of informational boxes within each chapter:

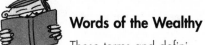

Wealth Warning

If you know what to avoid in your financial life, you can significantly reduce your chances of experiencing problems. These warning boxes help you do just that. Consider these the caution signs on your journey toward wealth. They are common errors or things to be aware of.

Words of the Wealthy

These terms and definitions are part of the language of the wealthy. If you know and understand these words, you are well on your way to building wealth. These terms will also help you have more meaningful discussions with your financial advisors.

Treasure Tip

These helpful little hints make life easier. If you prefer the "path of least resistance," be sure to read them.

That Reminds Us ...

It seems that many lessons we've learned about building wealth have been the result of our own experiences or the experiences of others. These boxes explain such lessons for you in the form of a story or observation so that you get a better understanding of the concepts within this book.

Everything you need to become the financial success you've dreamed of is in this book. You've already taken the first and most important step ... you've made the decision to get started.

Acknowledgments

My Co-author. I first met my co-author, Larry Waschka, in 1992 while attending a continuing education conference. We became instant friends, which as it turns out was characteristic of Larry's personality. Not long after, we met Ron Yolles, who wrote the foreword for this book, and together we founded the Counsel of Independent Financial Advisors (CIFA). CIFA is a collection of well-run practices from around the United States that gets together every six months to share ideas. We have learned a lot from each other—and have helped each other a lot over the years.

I learned a lot from Larry. Never had I met someone who was so full of life. He loved every minute of every day and loved everyone he ever met. All of the CIFA gang was married except Larry so we all took responsibility in helping him find his "soul" mate. We were rewarded when he met and married Jessica in 2003. Jessica is one of the sweetest, most attractive ladies you could ever want to meet and Larry just adored her. Tragically, while celebrating their one-year wedding anniversary in Mexico, Larry drowned while swimming in the ocean. The Governor of Arkansas, Mike Huckabee, gave the eulogy at Larry's funeral and I'll never forget what he said: "Larry is one of the few people I've ever met that has few, if any, acquaintances, but has literally hundreds of close friends." It was true. You always felt like you were Larry's best friend, and in fact you were in the sense that he would drop everything and do anything for you.

This is Larry's book. He conceived the idea and did all the heavy lifting for this project. His goal was to treat you like a close friend and share all of his secrets of financial success with you. I was very honored when Jessica asked me if I would write this revision. My goal is to continue Larry's legacy.

My Associates. As with any project of this magnitude, there are many people behind the scenes who help make it a success. I first want to thank my associates for all of their support. Scott Lee, MBA, is a partner in my firm and, as director of investment research, provided much of the detailed investment research I used in this book. Hugh Smith, CPA, CFP®, CFA, is a partner in my firm and is the director of financial planning. Hugh provided assistance in so many areas, I am not certain where to start. Diana Simpson, CFP®, MBA, is the managing partner of our sister company, Fee-Only Planning Professionals, LLC (www.fopp.net). This is one of the few fee-only companies in the United States that does not have a minimum fee requirement and was set up to work with young professionals throughout the country. Diane proofread all of my work and offered many valuable suggestions. Greg Weyandt, CPA, is my partner and director of operations. Greg always kept the day-to-day operations running smoothly so I could devote maximum time to this project. Kimberly Reynolds, MS, is one of our young bright superstars. As an adjunct instructor at the University of Alabama teaching income tax, she provided invaluable technical research. Chris Hudgins is another of our young Turks and helped with investment research for this project. Roxie Jones is our receptionist and client care person. Roxie always makes everyone feel special, which is a rare talent. She's also the unofficial den mom. Other associates including Woodard Peay, CFP®, MBA, Jeff Davenport, Wendy Weber, Jonathan Ward, Deborah Brown, and Melissa Erikson all helped keep the business running smoothly by taking excellent care of our clients. I also want to thank Lauren Kirby and Marie Gresham for their support of me during these past few months.

My Technical Advisors. Bob Holman, CPA, partner in Donaldson, Holman & West (www.dhwcpa.com), is one of the brightest tax people I know. Bob did the technical review of the chapter on taxes and provided much-needed assistance. Chip Hazelrig is a successful private investor and provided insights regarding our chapter on real estate investing. Mike Priestley is president of The Priestley Company and an expert in disability income insurance as well as other group products. Babs Hart is an expert in long-term care insurance (www.babshart.com) and provided insights into the changing world of nursing care. Sam Watson is not only my nephew, but a math wiz attending college at the University of Mississippi. Sam helped develop the complex mathematical table used to determine your target savings goal.

My Family. Whatever I have chosen to do, I have always received unconditional support from my family. My lovely wife, Kathie, is always the one who pays the highest price for my long hours at work and time away from home. My parents, Stewart and Sally, have always been a guiding light for me. My sisters, Jean Watson and Babs Hart, have been my cheerleaders for my entire life. A brother couldn't have asked for two better older sisters.

Our Clients. In the world of high finance, I'm supposed to be the teacher, but I have learned so much from my clients. Such great people with so many different dreams, goals, and facts. I have had to run like an Olympic sprinter just to stay ahead of them. They have inspired me to seek to improve my knowledge each and every day. They are wonderful people and I am so thankful to have them in my life.

Special Thanks to the Technical Reviewer

The Complete Idiot's Guide to Getting Rich, Third Edition, was reviewed by an expert who double-checked the accuracy of what you'll learn here, to help us ensure that this book gives you everything you need to know about building wealth. Special thanks are extended to Kenneth Kaplan.

Trademarks

All terms mentioned in this book that are known to be or are suspected of being trademarks or service marks have been appropriately capitalized. Alpha Books and Penguin Group (USA) Inc. cannot attest to the accuracy of this information. Use of a term in this book should not be regarded as affecting the validity of any trademark or service mark.

Part 1 The Basics of Getting Rich—Wealth Stages 1 and 2

Wouldn't it be nice to win a multimillion-dollar lottery? It's everyone's dream. You walk in, plop down a buck, and a week later you learn that you're $99 million richer! Then reality sinks in and you realize that the likelihood of this daydream coming true is, well, 99 million to one.

The good news is that you can still become wealthy. The better news is that becoming wealthy is far easier than you might think. Even if you're an employee and are not making a lot of money, you can become financially independent by learning the secrets of self-made millionaires. You simply have to break it down into different levels of wealth and design a plan to achieve the first level first, then the second, and so on. That's exactly what we've done for you in this part of the book. All you have to do is read and implement the steps, habits, and characteristics needed, and you will be on your way to becoming rich!

The Paradigm of Success

In This Chapter

- ◆ Believing you're never too old to start
- ◆ Hearing real-life rags-to-riches stories
- ◆ Having a college degree: will it make you rich?
- ◆ Learning how adversity can build wealth
- ◆ Testing your chances of building wealth
- ◆ Learning some common misconceptions about wealth

So, you want to be rich? Are you prepared to pay the price necessary to get the job done? Buying this book was the first step, and the rest of the steps may not be as hard as you think. You see, achieving wealth is mostly a mindset. It involves making a conscious decision that you're going to be different from the pack—different in your focus and different in your actions.

You remember the old riddle, "How do you eat an elephant?" The answer is astonishing in its simplicity: "One bite at a time!" After you've made up your mind, becoming rich is as simple as taking pre-planned, focused steps that will continually move you toward your ultimate financial goal. However, this "wealth" mindset does require you to make two paradigm shifts in the way you view your world and the world around you.

Paradigm #1: Think of Your Personal Finances as a Small Business

Think of your personal finances as if you're running a business. Your business has income (your salary) and expenses (your monthly bills), and it needs to be managed (budgeting) so that you end up with a net profit at the end of each month. By net profit we mean that when you subtract your expenses from your income, you have some money left over. In the business world this is called your net cash flow. Any good business person will reinvest this to grow their business, so you should do the same with your excess cash. This reinvestment of cash will be your investment program that you will develop as part of reading this book.

All great businesses have a written business plan that outlines their financial goals as well as their strategy for achieving each goal. All great businesses build their own "dream team" of advisors to help guide them along the path to success. Think of yourself as the Chair of the Board (co-chair, if you have a spouse or lifetime partner) of your business and make yourself responsible for monitoring your progress each month.

Many of the wealthiest people we know created their wealth by starting, then building, great businesses. They think in terms of income, expenses, and profits. If you can learn to think like they do, you'll be well on your way to becoming rich. We have designed this book to show you how to do this, step-by-step.

Paradigm #2: Every Dollar Counts

Most people think of money in a frivolous way. They spend without thinking. In the mindset of the rich, you never do this. One wealthy person we know has an interesting take on money: "When I think of my money, I picture each dollar bill as a worker who is working for me. Now, I despise lazy people so I want all my dollars working hard for me. I will either use my dollars to buy something I truly want (a conscious thought process) or I put those dollars to work where they can make me the most money. I have focused financial goals, so I carefully manage my money and don't allow dollars to sit idly by."

Thinking of your personal finances as a business and paying attention to all your money are two themes we will carry forward throughout the rest of this book. For now, let's take a look into the world of self-made millionaires.

Ordinary People Doing Extraordinary Things

Who would you say is the wealthiest person you know personally? How did he or she achieve the wealth? Is it possible for you to achieve similar wealth? It's as possible as you think it is. Most of the wealthy people we know built their fortunes with their own hands. This is self-made wealth: it's not inherited, acquired through marriage, or won in the lottery. It's built with hard work, determination, and passion.

Self-made wealth is often invisible. You don't see it or recognize it because the people who earned it don't flaunt it or talk about it. You can learn a lot from these people, but they aren't often featured in magazines or television. They may live down the street from you without you even knowing it.

Entrepreneurship as a Path to Wealth

When we meet or read about someone who has achieved extraordinary success, we automatically assume that they are unusually gifted people. We believe that they are unusually smart; that they are unusually lucky; or that they had unique opportunities that we'll never have. Certainly this is true some of the time, but more often than not, these are ordinary people who have accomplished extraordinary things based on a laser-like focus to succeed, extremely hard work, and persistence through multiple obstacles.

Take Lisa Renshaw. At age 21, she bought a failing parking garage near the Amtrak station in Baltimore, Maryland. She was determined to turn it into a moneymaking business, no matter what it took. The "what it took" was someone to man the attendant's booth 24-hours a day. Because she had no money to hire employees, she solved her 24-hour staffing needs by moving into the garage herself! Then she needed a marketing plan, but again, she had no money to pay for a marketing plan. Her innovative solution was to make up inexpensive pocketsize fliers offering a free car

Words of the Wealthy

Wealth is defined by *Webster's Dictionary* as an "abundance of valuable material possessions or resources," and the word wealthy is defined as "extremely affluent." The definition of **affluent** sounds even better: "Having a generously sufficient and typically increasing supply of material possessions."

wash after a customer parked in her garage five times. She passed the fliers out herself at the Amtrak Penn Station. First-time customers became long-time customers because of Lisa's superior service. That was in 1983. Today, her company, Penn Parking (www.pennparking.com), owns or manages over 50 garages and Lisa is multimillionaire.

Jake Burton grew up in Long Island, New York, and wanted to surf the ocean, but he could only afford a $10 snurfer—essentially a board with a curved nose that you stand on while sledding down a snow hill. Jake quickly became an enthusiast and entered numerous snurfing competitions. As early as age 14, he dreamed that someday he could make a living out of his favorite sport.

After graduating from college and working for a short period of time for an investment banker, Jake quit his job in 1977 and began pursuing his dream of owning his own business. He bought a saw and some lumber and began to make snowboards. By the end of the first two years he had made more than 100 prototypes and racked up more than $100,000 in debt. His perseverance paid off in 1984 when the first ski resort allowed snowboarding on the mountain. The rest is history. Today, snowboarding is an Olympic event and Burton Snowboards (www.burton.com) commands approximately one third of the snowboard market worldwide with manufacturing plants in Vermont, Australia, and Japan. In the process, Jake Burton has become a millionaire many times over. It's important to note that Jake still manages to get in his 100 days per year of snowboarding. Jake has proven that you can make a great living doing what you love!

Former nurse and aerobics instructor Karen Behnke became a millionaire before her thirtieth birthday by starting a company called Execu-Fit. Her company offered medical screenings of executives and analyses of employee health. She built sales by calling on human resource departments and signing large companies such as Pacific Gas & Electric. When bank loans were impossible, she used credit cards at 22 percent interest. Later, she traded 10 percent of her company for additional capital. In 1991, Karen sold her company to PacifiCare HMO for nearly $5 million.

The people in these stories achieved their wealth by starting their own businesses. Lest you think that this is the only path to wealth, let us share a couple of stories of people who became millionaires simply by saving money every month.

Saving as a Path to Wealth

One day, a retired couple in their 60s came to co-author Larry Waschka's office for some help. They were a tiny couple, both about 5 feet tall, and wore clothes that had to be 10 years old. You couldn't ask for a nicer couple. They asked almost bashfully if Larry would take a look at their "little" portfolio and make some suggestions. They both apologized for the "small" size of their holdings. The husband said, "I know that you are accustomed to dealing with much larger amounts, but would you please give us some advice?" Larry explained that size didn't matter and that he would be glad to help them in any way he could. He nearly fell out of his chair when he opened the portfolio to find more than $1 million in stocks, bonds, and mutual funds! By looking at them and talking to them, you'd never have thought that these people had any money. Larry asked them a little about their background. They said that the most they ever made in income in one year was $27,000 and that they didn't inherit anything. We're willing to bet that you know people just like this in your neighborhood, church, or synagogue. They are the salt of the earth, and if you can ever get them to tell you their story, you may learn more than you ever thought you could.

Here is another true story, this one involving a modest couple who attended Larry's investment workshop in 1993. This couple, let's call them Mr. and Mrs. Post, met with Larry after the workshop to discuss some specific questions they had regarding their *no-load* fund portfolio. As usual, Larry asked some questions and found that Mr. Post had worked all his life for the United States Postal Service and was considering retirement the next year. His wife raised their children and had never earned any additional income. Mr. Post told Larry that the most they had ever made in one year was $30,000. They were conservatively dressed, simple in their ways, and almost shy about talking to him.

Words of the Wealthy

No-load funds are mutual funds that can be purchased, sold, and owned without any commission charges (or loads). The only charges involved are yearly management fees. A commission-paid broker or salesperson would never offer to sell you a no-load fund because there is no commission available for the salesperson.

They wanted Larry to review their no-load mutual fund portfolio to see if he thought anything needed to be sold. As Mr. Post began to open his portfolio, Larry was prepared to see a small selection of funds.

Wrong! Their portfolio had more than 35 different no-load mutual funds worth more than $800,000. He was dumbfounded. How could this couple have so much money? First, he asked if any of the money was inherited. They replied quickly and firmly, "No, not one dime." He asked if they owned any real estate other than their home. They replied "No." He was impressed.

They told Larry that they had also purchased homes for each of their two daughters as wedding presents, both of which cost $120,000. They paid cash, of course. They had also prefunded their four grandchildren's college education with a total of $100,000. If you add that up, the total is $1,140,000. Larry gave up and asked how they did it. They came to him for advice, and he turned the appointment around and asked for theirs. What he learned from them that day he will never forget. We share their secrets of wealth in Chapter 6.

> **Treasure Tip**
>
> One of the best books on the subject of the "quiet" self-made millionaire is *The Millionaire Next Door*, by Thomas J. Stanley, Ph.D. Dr. Stanley's extensive research sheds light on how hundreds of thousands of ordinary people achieved extraordinary financial results simply by effectively managing their finances and money. His follow-up book, *The Millionaire Women Next Door*, highlights women who have achieved extraordinary results as well.

There are literally thousands of stories just like these: people who have built fortunes on their own starting from nothing. Some built businesses, some simply were systematic investors.

Wealth Is Relative

It is important to note that you don't have to become a multimillionaire to be wealthy. Wealth is a relative term. It is not based on the absolute dollars you have in your bank and investment accounts, but rather the amount of money you have relative to your lifestyle needs. If you lead a modest lifestyle, one that you're happy with, you can achieve relative wealth with far less money than the people in our stories have accumulated. Based on their $30,000-per-year lifestyle, $800,000 of investments qualified our postman and his wife (Mr. and Mrs. Post) as wealthy.

You're Never Too Old to Start

Most people in their 50s and 60s, and even people in their 40s, think it's too late to build wealth. They claim they don't have the energy they once had. They feel as if their peak earning potential is behind them, that they've missed out on too many opportunities. Our response to these people is simply, "Have you ever had a piece of Kentucky Fried Chicken?"

Harland Sanders was born on September 9, 1890. At the age of 6, his father died and his mother had to go to work to support the family, leaving Harland to take care of his younger brother and sister. In addition to the house chores, Harland learned to cook and by age 7 he had mastered a number of recipes. He got his first job at age 10 and bounced around from one job to another for the next 55 years. These jobs included working as a farm hand, streetcar conductor, soldier, railroad fireman, justice of the peace, insurance salesman, steamboat ferry operator, tire salesman, and finally, service station operator. It was as a service station operator that he first began serving his now famous fried chicken. As his fame grew, he left the service station and moved across the street to a hotel and restaurant and continued to serve his fried chicken dinners to a growing customer base for another nine years. In 1935, the governor of Kentucky made Harland an honorary Colonel because of his contribution to the state's cuisine.

Wealth Warning

In spite of the fact that the chances of winning the lottery are worse than a million to one, all too many Americans use lottery tickets to plan for their retirement. The irony is that a large percentage of people who win the lottery end up in serious financial trouble, if not dead broke.

Things took a turn for the worse in the early '50s. A new interstate highway bypassed his town and Colonel Sanders auctioned off his establishments to pay off his debts. By age 65, he was broke and living off of his $105 monthly Social Security check. Undeterred and confident that he had a winning recipe, in 1952 he began traveling from town to town cooking his chicken dinners for restaurant owners across America. If the owner was favorably impressed, the Colonel worked out a handshake deal where he provided the secret recipe and they would pay him 5 cents per piece of chicken sold. By 1964, Colonel Sanders had more than 600 franchised outlets across the United States and Canada. That same year he sold his company for $2 million. Colonel Sanders continued to be a spokesperson for the company until his death at age 90.

Bob Montgomery, who went on to become a successful banking executive, traveled with Colonel Sanders. He recalls what the Colonel said at his ninetieth birthday celebration in response to this question: "Colonel, what keeps

That Reminds Us ...

Most of the millionaires in this country are not recognizable. They lead simple lives far away from the glitz of the stereotypical Hollywood millionaires. You would never think these people had any more money than the average citizen. As a matter of fact, they often go to great lengths to keep their wealth confidential.

you going?" The Colonel smiled and said, "Don't 'ya see, I'm still dreaming!" The life lessons in the Colonel's words of wisdom are that you're never too old to dream and you're never too old to accomplish great things.

Is a College Education Necessary?

Contrary to popular belief, you don't need a college education to build great wealth. In fact, some of the wealthiest people in the world never finished college.

Michael found his entrepreneurial streak at the age of 7 when he started his first business … selling candy. He bought his first computer when he was in high school and immediately dismantled it so he could figure out how it worked. He figured out how to upgrade computers and began modifying them and selling them to high school friends for a profit. He went off to the University of Texas but continued to sell his customized computers from his dorm room, now expanding his customer base. His little business was thriving and he was having so much fun with it that he dropped out of college and began selling upgrade kits for computers full-time. Michael admits that he was woefully undercapitalized and made lots of mistakes, but he always remained focused on his core principle: Always do right by your customers. Today, Dell Computer is the hands-down leader in direct, just-in-time PC computer sales and Michael Dell has become one of the wealthiest men in America. In fact, at age 40, he is reportedly worth more than $14 billion!

> **Treasure Tip**
>
> No matter what your education or resources, the key to building financial wealth is to compose and follow a plan of action you design to meet your specific needs and goals. Your plan should identify and combat your weaknesses.

Did you realize that the wealthiest man in the world never finished college? Bill Gates dropped out of college and began the forerunner of Microsoft in the garage of his parents' home. Okay, it was Harvard College that he dropped out of, but he recognized that a college degree was not a requirement for success.

Please hear us clearly. If you have the opportunity to go to college, by all means go. The college experience teaches you many important lessons that will serve you well later in life. Just don't let the fact that you never attended or finished college serve as an excuse not to pursue your dreams.

Wealth and Adversity

It's strange how adversity can change people's lives for the better. Loggers know that the strongest pine lumber comes from trees that have been subjected to windy environments. The same is true for people. The strongest people we know have struggled the most in life. Some of the wealthiest people we know have done the same, often having faced financial bankruptcy more than once. The difference between them and most people is their perseverance. The value of courage, persistence, and perseverance has rarely been illustrated more convincingly than in a list of key failures and successes in one man's life:

Event	Age
Failed in business	22
Ran for legislature—defeated	23
Again failed in business	24
Elected to legislature	25
Sweetheart died	26
Had a nervous breakdown	27
Defeated for speaker	29
Defeated for elector	31
Defeated for Congress	34
Elected to Congress	37
Defeated for Congress	39
Defeated for Senate	46
Defeated for vice president	47
Defeated for Senate	49
Elected president of the United States	51

Today, Abraham Lincoln is one of the most celebrated presidents in our history.

Don't Be a Hodaddy!

Just because someone makes a lot of money, it doesn't mean they're wealthy. If their expenses equal or exceed their income, they don't qualify as wealthy. Just because someone works hard, earns a great salary, and has nice things, it doesn't make him or her wealthy. The person may look like wealth and smell like wealth, but it's all a big show. In the world of surfers, these people are called Hodaddy's. This is the guy who, to impress the girls, straps a surfboard to his car but is not a surfer. In Texas, they refer to such posers as "Big hat, no cattle."

Words of the Wealthy

Hodaddy is a slang word used to describe someone who is a fake or phony. They are the guys who ride around with the surfboard on top of their car but don't know how to surf. It's all a ruse to impress the girls. They may look like the real thing but they aren't.

You know people like this. They are all egos and no substance. They need people to envy them and treat them as VIPs. Somewhere along the way, these seemingly wealthy people didn't learn the habits and characteristics necessary to build real wealth. No one taught them the concept of saving for a rainy day, much less retirement. They don't have what it takes to be wealthy. Don't YOU be a hoddady!

Treasure Tip

Research suggests that less than 5 percent of Americans ever achieve financial independence. Research also indicates that only about 5 percent of Americans develop and follow a written financial plan. If you want to achieve financial independence, a written financial plan must be a basic part of your strategy.

The Wealth Quiz

Most everyone we know would like to be rich, although not all of them are willing to admit it. So why do so few people actually get rich? What do people do to become rich? Why can't everyone do it? We're going to discuss the answers to all these questions throughout this book, but first, we must ask the most important question.

Do You Have What It Takes to Be Rich?

We have designed a mini quiz to help you determine if you have what it takes to be rich. It's based solely on our own experience and the experiences of wealthy people we have met, almost all of whom share certain habits and characteristics.

The purpose of the wealth test is to give you a picture of yourself today based on what you've learned in the past and what you're doing now to achieve wealth.

Remember, your chances will increase after you've finished this book and implemented what you've learned. For now, let's focus on the "old" you. After the test, we'll focus on the "new" you.

The Wealth Quiz

1. Do you enjoy your work?   Yes   No

2. Do you often visualize yourself achieving something bigger than what you are currently doing?   Yes   No

3. Do you save money every month?   Yes   No

4. Do you invest at least some of your money directly in the stock market either through a 401(k) or other retirement plan, individual stocks, or mutual funds on a monthly basis?   Yes   No

5. Do you shop before you buy most of the time, especially for big-ticket items?   Yes   No

6. Do you take care of your home or apartment, performing regular maintenance as well as repairs?   Yes   No

7. Do you perform regular maintenance on your car and other expensive items?   Yes   No

8. Do you pay off the full balance on your credit cards each month?   Yes   No

9. Do you buy used, big-ticket items such as cars?   Yes   No

10. Have you ever started your own business? (Even a lemonade stand counts.)   Yes   No

11. Have you ever estimated how much money you would need in a portfolio to produce enough income to cover your current living expenses?   Yes   No

12. Do you measure the performance results of your investments at least yearly?   Yes   No

13. Do you maximize your personal contribution to your IRA or company's 401(k) plan?   Yes   No

14. Is your mortgage payment less than 20 percent of your take-home pay? (If you do not own a home, is your rent less than 20 percent of your take-home pay?)   Yes   No

15. Do you spend less than you make each year?   Yes   No

16. Have you ever read a book about building wealth or an auto-biography about someone who was wealthy?   Yes   No

17. Do you have your own business now that produces a positive net income?   Yes   No

18. Have you ever worked 18 hours or more on a single (personal or work-related) project without stopping?   Yes   No

For each question that you answered yes, give yourself one point.

Total these points and then compare the total to the following scale to find out your probability of becoming wealthy.

Score	Probability of Becoming Rich
1–5	Low
6–10	Average
11–15	Very likely
16–18	You're on your way!

Even if you scored low on the test, don't worry about it. A low score simply means that if you don't make changes in your life, the probability of becoming wealthy is low. All you have to do is make some changes. Regardless of your score, you can achieve wealth. Take a moment and look at the questions to which you answered "No." These are your areas of weakness. By identifying these areas now, you will be able to recognize the solutions as you read this book.

Why Are Most People *Not* Wealthy?

Why is it so difficult to become rich? Most people lack the willingness to change their ways. As we explained in the beginning of this chapter, building wealth is a way of life. It's a mindset or paradigm that few people are willing to accept. Achieving the mindset often requires only a few simple changes in the way we think about and view life, followed by some simple changes in our actions.

Most people also lack the discipline to maintain the changes. It's not easy to change, much less make the change permanent. Most people don't have the tenacity or "stick-to-it-ness" necessary to build wealth. They give up too easily.

The Misconceptions of Wealth

People often misunderstand what wealth is and how it is achieved. We call the following popular misconceptions about wealth the fallacies of wealth:

♦ If I had a lot of money, my problems would go away.

♦ If I were rich, it would be easy to decide how to spend my money and whom to leave it to.

♦ More people would like me if I were wealthy.

♦ Getting rich is something that only happens to other people.

♦ If I just had a little more money, I'd be happy.

♦ If I were wealthy, I could buy anything I wanted.

♦ I wish I were wealthy so I wouldn't have to worry about money anymore.

♦ I'm young; I've got plenty of time to become wealthy. Why save money now?

♦ I'm too old to start saving money.

♦ There's no chance of me ever becoming wealthy. I only make $20,000 a year.

♦ The only way to get rich is inheriting the money, winning the lottery, or marrying someone who is rich.

♦ If I were really wealthy, I wouldn't care how much I paid in taxes.

♦ I'm not smart enough to become rich.

All these misconceptions boil down to one thing: most people aren't willing to make the decisions or sacrifices it takes to become wealthy. The whole process seems too overwhelming. Admittedly, if you're starting with little or no money, this process of building wealth might seem overwhelming. *But it can be done!* If you think becoming wealthy is impossible, well, you can bet it will be. You'll never make it. Someone once said, "Argue your limitations and they're yours." Therefore, if you want to get rich, stop arguing your limitations and get busy taking the actions necessary to achieve your goals.

Wealth Is a Journey

Building wealth is basically a lifestyle change, just like losing weight or starting a new hobby. It's a journey, not a destination. We change our lives by changing our attitudes, our perceptions, and our actions. Whether you believe you *can* or you *can't*— you're right. In the end, we become exactly what we think about. If you think about what you lack, you will always lack. If you have an attitude of abundance, you will have abundance.

That Reminds Us ...
Try this exercise. Make a list of three things you would choose to accomplish if you knew you would not fail. It might be to complete a marathon, get a promotion at work, or become debt-free. Now write a simple action plan for achieving each goal. With your goals and action plans in place, what's holding you back from accomplishing these goals?

You will often get trapped in a comfort zone that could ultimately stalemate your efforts. Remember to be aware of these zones and don't get too comfortable. Don't be afraid of making mistakes. Mistakes will teach you everything you need to know if you're willing to learn from them.

Occasionally, you'll have setbacks. You can plan for some of them in advance, but others will blind-side you. However, if you find yourself off course, all you have to do is retrace your steps, make the necessary adjustments, and continue your journey. Remember that wealth is a journey, not a destination. When you make the decision to seek wealth, you have taken the first step on a lifelong journey.

Let's get started.

The Least You Need to Know

- Wealth can be built by anyone at any age who is willing to learn and develop the necessary habits and characteristics.

- Start identifying the common misconceptions about wealth, and don't let them hold you back from achieving your fortune.

- To build real wealth, you have to believe that it can be done.

- Wealth is a journey that requires a high level of tenacity and determination to overcome the occasional setbacks.

Eleven Tools for Building Wealth

In This Chapter

- Learning how to think like an investor
- Using the enormous power of time
- Using geometric growth—the eighth wonder of the world
- Using debt as a tool
- Understanding what net worth is

Before you start any project, you must know what tools you'll need and how to use them. After you've identified the proper tools and mastered their use, the project is much easier to finish. This chapter teaches you the basic tools you need to build wealth. These tools are easy to understand and easy to use.

Tools to Build Your Wealth

Here's a list of the 11 tools you'll need for building wealth:

Investments	Tax minimization
Time	Debt
Geometric growth	Target savings goal (TSG)
Living expenses	Salary or income
Risk management	Net worth statement
Inflation awareness	

Every industry has its own unique language, which consists of the jargon and concepts that are used every day. Because almost everyone deals with at least some financial issues, most of the terms should already be somewhat familiar. Even so, it's important to make sure that we're all using the same language for our discussions. If you don't understand how we define these tools, you'll have trouble understanding the logic of the next chapter. So let's start at the top of our list—investments—and work our way down.

Investments

An investment is something you buy with the expectation of it growing in value. Therefore, before you buy an investment, you want to learn to think like an investor. Your biggest concern should be the amount of money you'll get back in the future from the investment. The second biggest concern should be the risk of volatility in the investment's value while you're holding it. Will the price fluctuate over time? Can you handle that? What's the risk of the investment becoming worthless? When you're considering whether to buy an investment, these are the questions you must ask.

An asset is considered *liquid* if it can be easily sold for cash within an established financial market. This includes publicly traded stocks and bonds, CDs (certificates of deposit), and mutual funds. The most common liquid assets are checking and money market accounts. You can sell or liquidate these assets and get your money within 24 hours.

A portfolio could also include *illiquid assets*, such as privately held securities or commercial real estate—assets that may take weeks, months, or even years to sell. However, there is abso-lutely nothing wrong with illiquid assets. For example, the most commonly held illiquid asset is a home. It can be sold and converted to cash, but the process can take some time. Another example of an illiquid asset is *privately held stock* (which is not listed on an exchange such as the New York Stock Exchange).

Many wealthy people have built their fortunes using illiquid assets such as land, commercial buildings, and privately held company stock. However, these people understood the characteristics and risks unique to each particular illi-quid asset. Do not attempt to get involved with illiquid assets without doing some serious homework. If you understand what you own and the market you participate in, you can make money by investing in illiquid assets.

> **Words of the Wealthy**
>
> A financial asset is something that you own that has financial value and can include stocks, bonds, savings accounts, and real estate. **Liquid assets** include those assets that can be converted into cash very quickly. **Illiquid assets** are just the opposite; they are not easily converted into cash.

> **Words of the Wealthy**
>
> A privately held company is one in which its shares are not publicly traded. **Privately held stock** is issued to a small number of shareholders, and the value or price of the stock is usually not readily determined.

The Value of Time

Most people don't realize the value of time and its effect on an investment. Time is a powerful tool. If you're in your 20s or 30s, you have an advantage over someone in her 40s or 50s. Given enough time and the right tools, you can build a fortune. The opposite is also true. The less time you have, the more difficult it will be to build any significant wealth.

> **Wealth Warning**
>
> The tool of time can also work in reverse. The longer you wait to start your portfolio, the harder it is to build any significant wealth. A good place to start your investment portfolio is a $4,000 IRA, which can grow tax-deferred until the money is drawn out during retirement. This account allows you to combine the tools of time, compound growth, and tax deferral.

Let's take a closer look at how important time is in the accumulation of wealth. The following table illustrates the progress of a portfolio for an early saver versus a portfolio for someone who starts saving later.

The Early Saver Advantage (at 10% Annual Return)

	Early Saver		Late Saver	
Age	Savings	Total Savings and Return	Savings	Total Savings and Return
25	$4,000	$4,400	0	-
26	$4,000	$9,240	0	-
27	$4,000	$14,564	0	-
28	$4,000	$20,420	0	-
29	$4,000	$26,862	0	-
30	$4,000	$33,949	0	-
31	$4,000	$41,744	0	-
32	$4,000	$50,318	0	-
33	$4,000	$59,750	0	-
34	$4,000	$70,125	0	-
35	0	$77,137	$4,000	$4,400
36	0	$84,851	$4,000	$9,240
37	0	$93,336	$4,000	$14,564
38	0	$102,670	$4,000	$20,420
39	0	$112,936	$4,000	$26,862
40	0	$124,230	$4,000	$33,949
41	0	$136,653	$4,000	$41,744
42	0	$150,318	$4,000	$50,318
43	0	$165,350	$4,000	$59,750
44	0	$181,885	$4,000	$70,125
45	0	$200,074	$4,000	$81,537
46	0	$220,081	$4,000	$94,091
47	0	$242,089	$4,000	$107,900

	Early Saver		Late Saver	
Age	Savings	Total Savings and Return	Savings	Total Savings and Return
48	0	$266,298	$4,000	$123,090
49	0	$292,928	$4,000	$139,799
50	0	$322,221	$4,000	$158,179
51	0	$354,443	$4,000	$178,397
52	0	$389,887	$4,000	$200,636
53	0	$428,876	$4,000	$225,100
54	0	$471,764	$4,000	$252,010
55	0	$518,940	$4,000	$281,611
56	0	$570,834	$4,000	$314,172
57	0	$627,917	$4,000	$349,989
58	0	$690,709	$4,000	$389,388
59	0	$759,780	$4,000	$432,727
60	0	$835,758	$4,000	$480,400
61	0	$919,334	$4,000	$532,840
62	0	$1,011,267	$4,000	$590,524
63	0	$1,112,394	$4,000	$653,976
64	0	$1,223,634	$4,000	$723,774
65	0	$1,345,997	$4,000	$800,551
	$40,000		$124,000	

Both investors invest $4,000 per year in an S&P 500 stock index fund using a Roth IRA. Our Early Saver wisely begins his investment program early, at age 25, and continues until age 34 (a total of just 10 years). Our Late Saver waits until age 35 but continues to invest each year until age 65 (30 years). You would expect the second investor to accumulate a lot more money, right? After all, he invested a total of $124,000 as compared to the meager $40,000 invested by the first investor. The results will shock you. Our Early Saver accumulates $1,345,997 while our Late Saver only accumulates $800,551. That's a difference of $545,446! How is this possible?

Our Early Saver simply had the advantage of more time to compound the growth. Notice that by the time the Late Saver began saving money, the Early Saver's yearly gain exceeded the Late Saver's deposit. Time is powerful stuff and is often completely overlooked. The lesson here? Use the power of time.

Time is also important during times of volatility. In a bear market, many investors lose sight of the value of time; they focus on the short term and forget all about the long term.

Geometric Growth

Geometric growth occurs when you invest in certificates of deposit, bonds, stocks, real estate, or anything that appreciates in value, and then you reinvest the interest, dividends, and capital gains back into your original investment or another investment that is expected to appreciate over time. The key concept here is to keep your money constantly working. This may seem simplistic, but the results will amaze you. You see, most people think in linear terms when it comes to investing their money. Visually, they believe that regular investing (say monthly) produces a result similar to the following chart.

Linear growth.

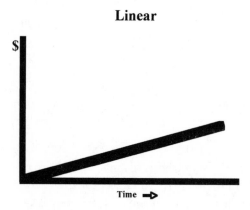

But because of the effect of geometric growth, the growth line bends upward as depicted in the following chart.

Geometric

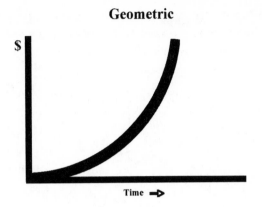

Geometric growth.

A not-so-obvious lesson to learn from this is that in the early stages of your investment program, the rate of return that you earn on your investments is not nearly as important as is the consistency of systematic investing. In the later stages, your rate of return becomes more important than continuing to add new money to your investment program. The following table illustrates this concept.

The Power Curve

Year	Annual Investment	at 10%	Earnings	Ending Balance
1	$10,000		$1,000	$11,000
2	$10,000		$2,100	$23,100
3	$10,000		$3,310	$36,410
4	$10,000		$4,641	$51,051
5	$10,000		$6,105	$67,156
6	$10,000		$7,716	$84,872
7	$10,000		$9,487	$104,359
8	**$10,000**	1 × 1	**$11,436**	**$125,795**
9	$10,000		$13,579	$149,374
10	$10,000		$15,937	$175,312
11	$10,000		$18,531	$203,843
12	**$10,000**	2 × 1	**$21,384**	**$235,227**
13	$10,000		$24,523	$269,750
14	$10,000		$27,975	$307,725

continues

The Power Curve (continued)

Year	Annual Investment	at 10%	Earnings	Ending Balance
15	**$10,000**	3 × 1	**$31,772**	**$349,497**
16	$10,000		$35,950	$395,447
17	**$10,000**	4 × 1	**$40,545**	**$445,992**
18	0		$44,599	$490,591
19	0		$49,059	$539,650
20	0		$53,965	$593,615
21	0		$59,361	$652,976
22	0		$63,298	$718,274
23	0		$71,827	$790,102
24	0		$79,010	$869,112
25	0		$86,911	$956,023
26	0		$95,602	$1,051,625
27	0		$105,163	$1,156,788
28	0		$115,679	$1,272,466
29	0		$127,247	$1,399,713
30	0		$139,971	$1,539,684
31	0		$153,968	$1,693,653
32	0		$169,365	$1,863,018
33	0		$186,302	$2,049,320
34	0		$204,932	$2,254,252
35	0		$225,425	$2,479,677
36	0		$247,968	$2,727,645
37	0		$272,764	$3,000,409
38	0		$300,041	$3,300,450
39	0		$330,045	$3,630,495
40	0		$363,050	$3,993,545

Notice that it takes this investor eight years of systematically investing to reach what we call 1 to 1. By this we mean that the portfolio is now increasing in value each year as much as the investor is contributing each year. Because of geometric growth, it only takes an additional four years to reach 2 to 1; three more years to reach 3 to 1; and two more years to reach 4 to 1. In year 17, the earnings on the portfolio are producing $40,000 per year while the investor is still only contributing $10,000 per year. When geometric growth really begins to bend the line, typically 8 to 12 years out, we call it the power curve.

Obviously we have oversimplified this illustration to point out the importance of both systematically investing and reinvesting your interest, dividends, and capital gains. In reality you will not earn a constant 10 percent per year and, therefore, your geometric growth line will not be smooth, but jagged. However, if you understand and follow this concept, you'll be well on your way to becoming rich.

That Reminds Us ...

The Rule of 72 estimates how fast money can compound over time. Divide the number 72 by the rate of return you expect to receive. The result is the number of years it will take for your money to double. If you get 6 percent, your money would double in 12 years. If you get 8 percent, your money would double in 9 years; if 10 percent, 7.2 years; if 12 percent, 6 years. The rule also works in reverse. Divide the number 72 by the number of years you have to invest. The result is the percentage of total return you need to double the portfolio. This equation measures pure compound growth without the effect of any taxes. Therefore, it works best in measuring the growth of tax-deferred accounts such as 401(k)s and IRAs.

The Rule of 72 can work in your favor or against you. If you have $5,000 in credit card debt at 18 percent interest, your debt will double in 4 years.

Living Expenses

There are many different categories of living expenses. Variable expenses cover entertainment, clothing, and travel. Fixed expenses include rent or mortgage payments. Living expenses might seem like a relatively boring subject, but most people don't understand just how important the expense component can be in building wealth. When you're just beginning to build your portfolio, the amount of money you spend monthly for expenses directly affects the speed of your journey to wealth. If you're accustomed to a high standard of living and aren't willing to be flexible, your chances of saving money in the early years are small.

The main reason people don't save money is that they're unwilling to limit their standard of living. As financial advisors, we often see this unwillingness in young couples but also notice it in older retired couples as well. In the later years, especially during retirement, if you spend more than your portfolio produces, you may deplete your capital source or principal, which can leave you in financial peril if you live too long. It's important to understand that systematic measurement of your monthly expenses is vital to the wealth-building process. We'll show you how to do this in Chapter 3.

> **CAUTION**
>
> **Wealth Warning**
>
> You must be willing to make some sacrifices now to build wealth in the future.

Risk Management

We discuss the many different types of risk in more detail later. For our purposes in this chapter, the two basic types of risk are portfolio and situational. Portfolio risk can be defined as the volatility (the potential to rise or fall quickly) of the total portfolio value. Some investors are willing to accept higher levels of volatility for higher rates of return. Return is your reward for your willingness to assume risk. In general, risk can increase your potential for return, but it can also lead to more potential for loss. Setting proper return goals involves determining your acceptable level of risk.

Situational risk is the chance you'll experience health problems, premature death, a disability, an automobile accident, or another liability. Each of these risks has the potential of ruining your journey toward building serious financial wealth and will be discussed in Chapter 20. A wealthy person understands these risks and manages each type by efficiently using the right insurance tools.

Inflation Awareness

Inflation is what happens when too many dollars chase too few goods. It takes place when the economy is growing strong, wages are high, and consumers are spending a lot of money. For example, during a time of increased consumer spending, retailers can easily raise prices a little without bothering the consumer much. The opposite is also true. If the economy is not growing strongly, wages are low, and consumers are not spending a lot of money, then retailers may have to drop prices. This latter situation is called deflation.

Inflation is simply an increase in the price of goods and services. The most important thing to remember about inflation is that it will affect your future living expenses.

What costs a dollar today may cost five dollars in the future. You must take inflation into account when making projections about the future. A common way to measure and project inflation is to use the *Consumer Price Index (CPI)*, which is the yearly growth rate of the total price of a basket of consumer goods. All financial publications show this rate as the CPI. It isn't a perfect measurement, but most economists use it. You'll need to use this index in Chapter 3 when we show you how to project your future living expenses.

Words of the Wealthy

Tabulated by the U.S. government's Bureau of Labor Statistics, the **Consumer Price Index (CPI)** measures the cost of a representative basket of consumer goods, which might include a loaf of bread, a gallon of milk, or a new car. The price of the basket is not that important. The most important aspect of CPI is the rate of change from one month to another. The amount of change from month to month in the cost of this basket of goods is stated as a percentage of the CPI for the previous month. This percentage is known as the rate of inflation and is usually quoted as an annualized percentage.

Tax Minimization

When discussing taxes, we're referring to all federal, state, and local income taxes. Specifically, in Chapter 3, you will need to know your overall income tax rate. An easy way to calculate this is to add the federal, state, and local taxes you paid last year and divide that amount by your gross income. This will give you your effective income tax rate. If you need help calculating this, ask your CPA.

(Federal + State + Local Taxes) ÷ Gross Annual Income = Your Effective Income Tax Rate

For example, if you had a gross income of $30,000 with federal taxes of $3,540 and state taxes of $1,344, your effective income tax rate equals 16.28 percent. In other words, you're paying an average of 16.28 percent in taxes on every dollar you earn.

Taxes can be avoided or deferred using certain investment vehicles. However, the primary goal of an investor should be to make money, not avoid taxes. If you focus primarily on avoiding taxes, you might accomplish that goal, but you may miss opportunities for greater accumulation of wealth in the process. Later in this book, we discuss ways you can defer taxes without sacrificing total return.

Debt

Debt is simply a loan, which can include a home mortgage, personal loans, business loans, and lines of credit. Debt can be the proverbial double-edged sword—it can be a very good thing or a very bad thing. If you want to build serious wealth, you need a good relationship with a banker who can service your needs properly. The most common healthy debt tools include mortgage loans, business loans, and lines of credit. All of these tools can help you leverage your wealth (or cash flow) to buy a home or other real estate, invest in a business, or cushion cash-flow problems.

One type of debt investors sometimes use is a margin loan against a brokerage account. A margin loan is simply a loan against the securities in your account. For a variety of reasons, we recommend that you avoid margin debt. We also don't recommend loans for purchases that improve your self-image, such as fancy cars and boats. Our hope is that this book helps you look at everything you buy, especially when you borrow money to buy it, as an investment. As previously stated, your biggest concern is the amount of money you'll get back in the future from the investment. The risk gets worse if you get upside down. You're upside down when you borrow money to buy something and it falls in value so much that the money you owe exceeds the value of the item.

Target Savings Goal

An important concept for building wealth is the amount of money you save every month or every year. The two terms we use in this book are *target savings goal (TSG)* and actual savings. Your target savings goal is the amount of money you need to save every year to build a portfolio large enough to produce a total return by a certain date (usually retirement) that will sustain your standard of living plus keep up with inflation. We realize that this definition might be a mouthful, but don't worry, it's simpler than it seems. We discuss this concept step-by-step in Chapter 5 and make it easy for you.

Your actual savings amount is just what it says: the difference between your total household income and expenses. This surplus is what goes into your investment account. If there is money available for savings, you're living within your means and that's great. If you have a negative actual savings amount, you're living beyond your means, and that's a problem you must solve.

The actual savings amount is important in the early stages of your life. Therefore, your focus should be on saving and investing as much as you can when you're young. During the first years of saving when your portfolio is small, total return is relatively less important than the amount of money you save (the deposits you make). The deposits you make at first will dwarf the amount of money you make on your investments. Therefore, your early years of saving are a great time to learn about investing. When you're new to the game of investing, you tend to make a lot of mistakes. If you can make those mistakes early, when the returns have less effect on your overall portfolio, you save your portfolio from harm later when your return really counts.

Salary or Income

Before you can save any money, you have to be making money, which we refer to as cash flow. The most common source of cash flow is a salary. The idea behind this book is that you spend less than your salary so that after taxes, you have some excess cash flow to save and invest. Your salary is a key tool in the wealth-building process.

Most people believe that your salary is the most important tool. The bigger the salary, the more you have to spend and invest. This is certainly true. However, many people get caught up more in the spending rather than the investing. Increasing your salary is wonderful for the wealth-building process if you can discipline yourself to save more as you make more. As we illustrated for you in Chapter 1, a hefty salary is not necessary to build significant wealth. Don't get discouraged if your salary isn't as high as you want it to be. By all means, do what you can to maximize your salary, but don't get so caught up that you lose sight of other tools such as compound growth, time, and controlling expenses.

Net Worth

Building your net worth is the goal of this book. The definition of net worth is the value of your assets minus your liabilities (debts):

Assets – Liabilities = Net Worth

The general idea is to increase assets and decrease liabilities. However, this definition of net worth is flawed because we often see cases where a client's financial statement is filled with nonproductive assets and not enough of the right kind of liabilities. We'll discuss this subject in more depth in Chapter 3. Also, you may find yourself increasing liabilities temporarily to increase assets at a future date. The key is to focus on assets that grow over time and the use of "good debt" versus "bad debt." We'll expound on this concept in the next chapter as well.

Ultimately, the most powerful tool for building wealth is your own business, which we discuss in Part 3. The second most powerful tool is investment real estate because of the opportunity to use leverage, which we'll cover in Chapter 18. The third most powerful tool is stock in someone else's business, which we'll discuss in the next few chapters.

The Least You Need to Know

- To build significant wealth, think like an investor and focus on the amount of money you'll get back from your investment in the future.

- We consider the "eighth wonder of the world" to be geometric growth, which suggests that you start a systematic investment program as early as possible and continue for a long time.

- If you're accustomed to a high standard of living with no willingness to be flexible, your chances of saving money in the early years are small.

- You must understand and manage both portfolio risk and situational risk to continue your journey toward wealth.

- To build your net worth, your long-term focus should be increasing assets and decreasing liabilities.

The Five Stages of Wealth

In This Chapter

- ♦ How to calculate your current net worth
- ♦ How to calculate your stage of wealth
- ♦ What you should focus on when attempting to achieve each stage
- ♦ How to get through these stages faster
- ♦ When saving money becomes less important

Everyone's definition of financial wealth is different. To make things simple, we've defined five specific, measurable stages of wealth. These stages reduce the confusion surrounding the concept of wealth by breaking down the definition into easy-to-understand pieces.

The first thing you must realize in your search for a personal definition of wealth is that your definition will always be a relative term. Relative to what? A poor immigrant family might say that being rich means having an apartment with running water and a roof overhead. You might be wealthy relative to your neighbor or friend. If you use peers as your benchmark, you're likely to find that the benchmark becomes a moving target as you continue to meet new and wealthier friends. Your idea of wealth should be defined relative to your desired standard of living—not your neighbor's or your friend's. Be realistic about this standard and focus on what income stage makes you happy. Your life will be a lot easier and you will feel more fulfilled in the process.

What Is Your Net Worth?

The most common way to define your current stage of wealth is to measure your net worth. When you go to a bank and apply for a loan, one of the first things they want is a statement of net worth, sometimes referred to as your financial statement. This statement lists both liquid and illiquid assets, subtracts your liabilities (debts you owe, such as your mortgage), and results in a bottom-line net worth amount. Take a moment and copy the following Net Worth statement. Fill it out and calculate your net worth today. Be sure to date it so you'll be able to look back and compare in the future.

Net Worth Statement

Assets	Total Value
Cash	_____
Money market funds	_____
Savings account	_____
Real estate (estimated current market value)	_____
Residence	_____
Farm	_____
Other	_____
Investments	
Individual stocks	_____
Individual bonds	_____
Mutual funds	_____
401(k)	_____
IRA	_____
Other retirement plans	_____
Closely held business (estimated current market value)	_____
Equity interest	_____

Assets	Total Value
Personal Assets	
Automobile	_____
Jewelry	_____
Other	_____
Total Assets	_____
Liabilities	
Personal line of credit (short term)	_____
Home mortgage(s)	_____
Automobile loan(s)	_____
Other	_____
Total Liabilities	_____
Net Worth (Total Assets Minus Total Liabilities)	_____

If part of your strategy for building wealth includes the use of debt, then it's essential that you maintain an up-to-date Net Worth Statement because virtually all lending institutions will require one. However, a traditional Net Worth Statement can be deceiving and cause you to think you're better off financially than you really are. This is because many things that you list as assets aren't assets at all. In fact, they're liabilities. Take, for example, that fishing boat with its 200-horsepower motor. Is it really an asset? More than likely it is a sinkhole for precious cash.

To remove the typical clutter from the traditional financial statement and focus on assets that really count toward real wealth, we have developed a concept called the Investment Net Worth Statement and the Wealth Index, a tool used to measure where you are on the path to becoming rich.

More Importantly, What Is Your Investment Net Worth?

The concept of investment net worth focuses on building true wealth—the kind of wealth that will set you free to pursue life on your terms. It distinguishes between assets that create wealth and assets that don't. Many people get confused about this and end up owning lots of assets that may suggest that they're wealthy, but that have very little value in achieving goals of financial freedom.

To simplify your understanding of investment net worth, we have created a few terms to identify real assets versus nonproductive or counterproductive assets. A *financial asset* is any asset expected to appreciate over time that can produce cash flow for you either now or in the future. A *doodad* is everything else. A couple of examples should make this clear. Stocks, bonds, investment real estate, CDs, and money market accounts are all examples of financial assets. They are expected to grow in value over time and either currently produce cash flow in the form of interest, dividends, capital gains, or rents, or can be converted to do so at a later time. Automobiles, boats, four-wheelers, jewelry, and home furnishings are all examples of doodads. In most cases, not only do doodads not increase in value over time but, more often than not, they also require current cash flow to maintain.

Most people seem to grasp the idea of financial assets versus doodads easily with one exception: their home. Is your home a financial asset or a doodad? We normally consider the home a doodad for a couple of reasons. Although it meets the first test—it is expected to appreciate over time—it rarely meets the second test. In most cases, it is never going to be converted into cash flow because most people's goal is to live in a home for the rest of their life. It also tends to be a sinkhole for cash due to costs of repairs and maintenance. In reality, your home could be considered an appreciating doodad and, in most cases, is the best doodad you will ever own. Now don't get us wrong. We're not saying doodads are bad. Often, they're part of what makes life's journey fun. We simply want to be clear that you should not count them as assets when measuring your progress toward your goal of financial freedom.

Words of the Wealthy

A **financial asset** is an asset that is expected to appreciate over time and that can be used to produce cash flow for you either now or in the future. A **doodad** is an asset that typically depreciates in value over time and produces no cash flow.

Now that you know the difference between financial assets and doodads, take a few minutes to complete the following Investment Net Worth statement. In Chapter 5, we will show you how to use it to determine where you are along the path to your wealth accumulation goal.

Investment Net Worth Statement

Assets	Total Value
Personal Investments	
Money market accounts	$_____
CDs	$_____
Stocks	$_____
Bonds	$_____
Mutual funds	$_____
Investment real estate (equity)	$_____
Other	$_____
Retirement Plan Investments	
IRAs	$_____
SEPs	$_____
401(k)s	$_____
Other	$_____
Total Financial Assets	**$_____**

If you're using debt to purchase financial assets, show your net equity. Notice that this Investment Net Worth statement does not include any liabilities. All your personal debt will be accounted for when we calculate your Wealth Index in Chapter 5.

Building on what you learned from Chapter 2, let's discuss the five stages of financial wealth.

Wealth Stage 1

The beginning of your journey is Stage 1. At this stage, you're able to maintain your standard of living and save enough money to achieve your target savings goal (TSG). This stage usually involves only a simple mindset change. When you live within your means and your actual savings amount equals or exceeds your TSG, you've made it to Wealth Stage 1. It's the easiest stage to achieve and can be your wealth safeguard if you fail at other stages.

Wealth Stage 1 has nothing to do with looking wealthy or building a financially wealthy outer image. In fact, in many ways, it means doing just the opposite. If you really want to achieve Stage 1, you may have to simplify your life and reduce expenses to achieve your target savings goal. Building wealth is not about buying fancy cars and clothes. It's about living within your means. If you can't handle this concept, you're unlikely to achieve significant wealth.

Most people would love to build wealth. However, many get caught up in the glamour and excitement of spending rather than saving. The end result is that they don't live within their means, and they constantly struggle to be at Stage 1.

In fact, our observations are that the people who breeze through Wealth Stage 1 have a sense of purpose about them. They understand what they need to do financially and exercise discipline regarding their spending.

What's Your Focus Here?

To make it to Wealth Stage 1, the most important thing is your actual savings amount. This will affect the portfolio much more than the compound growth on your portfolio. For now, growth is of secondary importance. The most common mistake made by neophyte investors is that they focus too much on growth. Consequently, many of them end up taking too much risk and losing their money. To achieve and maintain this stage, you should focus on maximizing your actual savings amount as much as you possibly can.

During your journey toward Wealth Stage 1, you should also focus on learning as much as you can about investment management and learn from your mistakes now. These mistakes, if made now, will not have nearly the effect they will later when your account is larger and the mistakes are harder to recover from.

It may be easier to conquer Stage 1 in steps. Let's say your minimum goal is to save 10 percent of your gross income. We've found that virtually everyone can save this much simply by cutting expenses. We'll show you how in our next chapter. In every case we have reviewed, people are wasting at least 10 percent of their income.

You might find increasing your savings above 10 percent to be more challenging. One easy way to accomplish this is to commit 50 percent of every bonus and every pay raise to your wealth-building strategy. This allows you to apply half of your additional income toward improving your lifestyle while at the same time continuing to make progress toward your long-term financial goals.

Treasure Tip

You don't need a college education to earn a high income, but it does help. According to the Census Bureau, the median income of a high school graduate is $36,853 while the median income of a college graduate is $73,446.

Wealth Stage 2

As you cross into Wealth Stage 2, your portfolio is large enough to produce, on its own, compound growth each year equal to your TSG. That means you have now, in essence, doubled your TSG—one part comes from your monthly TSG deposit and the other part from portfolio gains. You've really harnessed the power of geometric growth. The combined effect of your TSG deposit and geometric growth produces enormous portfolio growth power for you. This is what we referred to in Chapter 2 as 1 to 1.

What's Your Focus Here?

Because at this stage your actual savings amount and geometric growth are equal, they become equally important. You must focus on both components. This is also the stage of wealth where knowledge of risk becomes vital to the remainder of the wealth-building process. Unfortunately, most people wait until this stage to begin learning about risks. Bad investment decisions made in Wealth Stage 2 are more costly than they would have been in Stage 1.

Stage 2 continues as your portfolio produces a compound growth equal to two times your TSG. Therefore, your portfolio is growing by three times your TSG. One part is your actual TSG deposit, and the other two parts come from portfolio performance. The most important component becomes geometric growth. Your actual savings amount still helps speed the process, but geometric growth is more important and powerful. If geometric growth is twice the size of your actual savings amount, then your downside risk is also twice as big, making large losses more difficult to recover from. At this point, making the right investment decisions becomes paramount, as does risk management.

When your portfolio produces a geometric growth equal to three times your TSG, the compounding effect is expanding your portfolio three times faster than your own deposit. Now the relative effect of an additional deposit equal to your TSG has little influence on the growth of the portfolio. That doesn't mean you need to stop saving money! It just means that geometric growth is vital, and investment management has never before been so important.

Wealth Warning

Our Social Security system has produced a population of citizens who believe in their right to a subsidized comfortable retirement. Approximately two thirds of retirees depend on Social Security as the foundation of their retirement income and an astonishing 50 percent depend on Social Security as their sole source of income! Government sources tell us the Social Security system is in financial jeopardy. You should not depend on Social Security as part of your wealth management plan.

Wealth Stage 3

If your portfolio produces annual cash flow large enough to cover your desired lifestyle and inflation, then congratulations! You've made it to Wealth Stage 3 and have created *financial independence* for yourself. Employment is optional, and your money is working hard for you. According to our research, only about 5 percent of the population achieve this stage of wealth.

Words of the Wealthy

Financial independence is that point in time when the cash flow from your investments is sufficient to cover your inflation-adjusted lifestyle costs for the rest of your life.

Financial independence is often not about retirement but about creating choice. People who are financially independent can now choose to do what they have always wanted to do. Many will choose to continue working but with a fresh attitude. They know they're working because they want to and are fulfilled by what they're accomplishing. Others will choose to do something else. We know people who have gone into full-time missionary work. One couple left their jobs and moved to Colorado, where the husband joined the ski patrol while his wife became a ski instructor, a fulfillment of their life's dream. Hopefully, retirement is only a transition into another passion. After people make the decision to retire, or at least slow down, their living expenses often decrease. For others, their expenses actually go up because they like to travel and have more time for leisure activities, but they still live within their means. They built their wealth over a long period of time by living well within their means, and they maintain their wealth by continuing to do the same.

What's Your Focus Here?

If you plan to retire and give up all sources of earned income, you should shift your focus from rapid accumulation to preservation of capital with conservative growth. There are a number of ways to accomplish this, which are covered in Chapter 12.

If you don't plan to retire at this time, you can simply continue as you have but keep in mind the importance of risk management. Large losses at this point may take years to recover. At this stage, we strongly urge you to seek the advice of a professional advisor. We'll discuss how to choose an advisor who is right for you in Chapter 11.

Wealth Stage 4

You have accumulated enough assets to produce annual cash flow sufficient enough to substantially increase your desired lifestyle, while at the same time keeping up with inflation. The minimum target here is annual cash flow equal to two times your lifestyle requirements. We define a person who reaches Stage 4 as wealthy. You now have the option not to work and, at the same time, raise your standard of living. You might buy a second home, travel more, or just spend more money. You not only have enough cash flow to cover your desired lifestyle, but you also have the opportunity to continue to build your Net Worth.

That Reminds Us ...

There is a crisis brewing in our Social Security system as the 80 million Baby Boomers head for retirement. There will be fewer and fewer workers supporting more and more retirees. One of four things must happen: We must raise taxes, raise the official Social Security retirement age, radically change the existing Social Security system, or radically change our own personal retirement savings program. The only option we completely control is the last one.

Only about 1 percent of the population makes it to Wealth Stage 4. Most people aren't willing to take the time to plan, make the sacrifices, or take the risk. That's right: this stage involves planning, sacrifices, and risk. There's that word risk again! After reading this book, you will understand more about risk and how to manage it properly.

Many of the individuals who make it to this stage are business owners. Their wealth was built from net income, the sale of the business, or both. However, you can certainly make it to this level without having your own business. This book shows you how.

What's Your Focus Here?

Your two master components are geometric growth and risk management. The portfolio is very large, and you might want to focus on reducing volatility. You can do this yourself, but it must be a hobby you enjoy. Most Wealth Stage 4 people hire professionals to help in the investment management process. Chapter 11 shows you how.

Wealth Stage 5

You have accumulated enough assets to produce an annual cash flow well beyond what you would ever spend. The minimum target here is five times the amount of cash flow needed to cover lifestyle expenses. We define this person as rich. You have the option not to work, raise your standard of living, and bestow large gifts to family members and favored charities. After you reach this stage, you need some serious estate planning help.

CAUTION

Wealth Warning

Many of the teenagers and 20-year-olds today who are living with their parents to save money are actually spending what they save on their image by buying cool clothes and nice cars. This makes them look and feel successful, but does nothing to put them on the path to wealth.

What's Your Focus Here?

What do you think Wealth Stage 5 people focus on in regard to their money? The master component is risk and, more specifically, management of risk. When you make it to this stage, you tend to focus on protection of principal. It doesn't matter whether you make 5 percent or 15 percent on your portfolio. Your needs are covered either way. Therefore, you tend to focus on maintenance instead of geometric growth. First, you want to reduce the possibility of a substantial loss. Second, you want to maintain an adequate rate of return.

Certainly, it's great to achieve this stage of wealth, but most people would be content with Stage 3 or 4. Therefore, this book focuses primarily on the first four stages. Most people who achieve this stage of wealth focused on their passion and not necessarily on getting rich. This idea is important, and we discuss it later. Following your passion is an important element in the wealth-building process.

How Can You Get There Faster?

You can skip some stages completely by following one of two paths. You can either invest in investment real estate or start your own business. If you take one of these routes, get ready for an exciting ride. Expect to spend long hours learning what you need to know to succeed. Expect setbacks as your best-laid plans fail to produce your desired results. Throughout this book we'll give you insights regarding planning strategies and pitfalls to watch out for.

Your fastest and least risky path to riches may be the use of multiple strategies. For example, if you're an employee, you should be contributing to your company's 401(k) at least to the extent that your company provides a matching contribution. Next, you could use savings to gather the down payment to buy a small piece of rental real estate and finally, begin to develop and implement a business plan that will convert your hobby into a small business. If you find yourself frozen by the fear of failure, re-read the story of Abraham Lincoln in Chapter 1. We will show you how to tackle these more challenging strategies. All you need is courage, a good game plan, and a willingness to commit the time, effort, and discipline to see your dreams become a reality.

The Least You Need to Know

- Your idea of wealth should be based on your desired standard of living, not your neighbor's.

- If you really want to build wealth, don't buy the fancy cars and clothes; keep things simple and live well within your means.

- Take one wealth stage at a time and focus on what's important in each stage.

- In Stage 1, focus primarily on having a consistent savings program whereby you are investing money every month.

- In the later stages, focus on managing the risk in your portfolio.

Chapter 4

Eliminating Bad Debt: Wealth's Greatest Roadblock

In This Chapter

- ◆ Determining the reasons people get into debt problems and solutions for each of them
- ◆ Setting guidelines for keeping debt under control
- ◆ Finding the best strategy for eliminating your debt

If you were to ask us "What is the single biggest reason people don't achieve any significant level of wealth?" our answer would be misuse of debt. We live in a society where it is easy to borrow money. This is a good thing if you're borrowing to invest in assets that will help you obtain wealth. However, the vast majority of Americans use this access to easy debt as a way to purchase things that destroy their chances of obtaining financial freedom for themselves and their family.

Do you have a debt problem? Take this simple test to determine if your debt load is too much.

- Do I spend more than 30 percent of my take-home pay on debt repayment (including home mortgage or rent)? Y__ N__

- Do I have to borrow to make ends meet? Y__ N__

- Do I have to borrow to pay off old debt? Y__ N__

- Do I find it impossible to consistently save money? Y__ N__

- Do I use my checking account overdraft protection to pay expenses? Y__ N__

- Am I unable to pay off my credit charge balances each month? Y__ N__

If you answered yes to any of these questions, it should serve as a wake-up call that you need to get your debt under control. In this chapter, we not only shine a spotlight on 'bad' debt, but we provide appropriate guidelines for debt and give you a system to eliminate bad debt forever.

Understanding and Controlling Debt

Some advisors suggest that all debt is bad. This simply is not true. In fact, you may need to incur debt to reach your long-term goals. It is important, however, to distinguish good debt from bad debt.

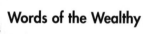

Words of the Wealthy

A **depreciating asset** refers to something you own that goes down in value over time. For example, most automobiles are worth less every month that you own them.

Treasure Tip

The Debt Rule: Never borrow money to purchase something that will depreciate in value.

Bad debt is any debt used to buy a *depreciating asset;* meaning something whose value is expected to decline over time. Examples include automobiles, clothes, food, and appliances. Good debt, then, is just the opposite. Good debt is debt used to purchase something that is expected to appreciate over time. Examples include your home, investment real estate, and buying or starting a business.

If you're serious about achieving Wealth Stages 3, 4, or 5, you must understand the difference between bad debt and good debt. The key concept is that if you must borrow to buy something, make sure that what you buy is always worth at least what you owe. We've turned this concept into what we call The Debt Rule: Never borrow money to purchase something that will depreciate in value. That way if you get into financial trouble, you can sell the item and raise enough money to pay off your loan. Some items, such as clothing, have very little value after they're purchased and should not be bought using borrowed money. Other items, such as automobiles, depreciate rapidly and therefore will require that you save for a larger down payment to make certain that the underlying asset (the car in this case) is worth more than the pay-off on the loan associated with the asset.

You may have already broken The Debt Rule. Now, you're going to learn to do something about it. First you need to understand the causes of debt problems, so let's review the most common areas of abuse.

Debt Problem #1: Credit Cards

The potential to misuse credit cards is enormous. It's easy to get credit. You probably receive credit card offers through the mail regularly. Credit card companies know that the more credit cards you own, the more you will spend. Then, if you only make minimum monthly payments, you've got a debt disaster. You simply have to avoid the credit card trap. Here are some solutions:

- The first thing you should do is reduce the number of credit cards you own to one or two. All retail stores will accept either a credit card or a personal check, so it's not necessary to have a retail store charge card. By reducing the number of credit cards, you automatically reduce the risk for misuse. The key is to control their use and avoid abuse.

Treasure Tip _____

You should own one or two credit cards for these reasons:
- To help establish your credit
- To use as a source of cash in case of an emergency
- To provide identification (i.e., for boarding airlines or cashing checks)
- To avoid carrying large amounts of cash

- One problem with using credit cards is that it's very difficult to keep track of how much you've spent. To keep better records, enter charges directly into your checkbook just as you would if you had written a check. Subtract the charge from your balance. Why? You just spent the money, so you must account for that expense immediately. Later, when you get your credit card statement, don't subtract the payment to your credit card company from your balance because you subtracted it earlier. See the following table for an example.

Enter Credit Card Charges in Your Check Register

Date	Check Number	To	Amount of Deposit	Amount of Check	Balance
9/25	107	Power Company		$127.50	$1075
9/25	108	Gas Company		$25	$1050
9/27	VISA	Best Department Store		$150	$900
9/29	109	Best Grocery		$67.75	$832.25

Debt Problem #2: Keeping-Up-with-the-Joneses Mentality

Undoubtedly, you feel pressure to keep up with your peers. When your friends buy new sports cars, you think you should have one, too. If they can afford it, surely you can, right? Such an attitude only leads to more debt. We want everything *now*, and this makes it hard to stay focused on our long-term financial goals. Here's what to do:

♦ Develop an "attitude of contentment" with your financial situation. When you're considering a large (or small) purchase, ask yourself, "Is this something I need or something I want?" If it falls into the want category, try postponing the decision for a week or two. By giving yourself a cooling-off period, you will often find that logic will win over your emotional desires.

♦ Your neighbors who spend wildly likely have no long-term goals. You must focus on your long-term goals and resist excessive spending today. Keep your written long-term goals somewhere where you will see them every day. Visualize what life will be like after you've achieved these goals. Visualize it so clearly that you can feel what it is like.

Debt Problem #3: Monthly Payment Mentality

When considering financing the purchase of a car, boat, furniture, or any other big-ticket items, most people are only concerned with the amount of the monthly payments. This mentality is a shortcut to financial disaster. You cannot become financially independent by frequent borrowing. Solutions to this frame of mind include:

- Postponing purchases until you have the cash to pay for them. This is called delayed gratification. For example, you want to purchase a bedroom set that costs $6,000. The finance company offers you "no money down" with payments of $213 a month for 36 months. This brings the total cost to $7,668! It would be better if you delayed buying the set while you begin your savings plan. Then, when you have the cash, buy the set. Also, when you pay with cash, you are in a much better position to negotiate a lower price.

Treasure Tip

The payment plans that many furniture companies offer include no money down and no interest payments. This "free" interest is built into the price of the furniture. If you're prepared to pay cash, you can negotiate a much lower price (10 to 20 percent).

- Before you borrow on an installment plan, have the salesperson do three things. First, have the salesperson tell you the interest rate being charged. Often, you will find it is 18 percent or more. Second, have him or her calculate the total interest you will pay over the term of the loan. Finally, have the salesperson calculate the total of all payments you will make and then compare it to the original price of the product. After you have all these numbers in front of you, buying this product on installment payments will likely be less appealing. If you'll take one week or at least a couple of days to think about how hard you'll have to work to earn the money "after taxes" to pay for it, we can almost guarantee you won't think it is worth buying.

Debt Problem #4: Failing to Plan for Major Events

Most people tend to focus only on the short-term—tomorrow or next week. This inevitably leads to many financial surprises because expenses such as home repairs, a new car, a child's wedding, or a child's education haven't been considered.

Good planning requires that you look ahead one to five years to anticipate known and unknown expenses. Here's what you need to do:

- Start with the known expenses. Sit down and make a list of nonmonthly expenses that you know you will owe. A good example is semi-annual auto insurance premiums.

♦ Next make a list of future major purchases. For example, you know your car will eventually need to be replaced. If you ignore the inevitable, your only choice will be to borrow to meet your needs.

♦ Finally, make a list of expenses that you think "might" occur, along with an appropriate amount of money to cover them. For example, if your furnace is 25 years old, you might reasonably expect to have to replace it over the next 5 years. The key is to have a list with dollar values to work from. Now you at least have a sense of the size of the problem and can begin to address solutions.

Treasure Tip

A major key to financial success is to apply the self-discipline necessary to keep your financial house in order.

♦ Now that you have your list in place, begin to build cash reserves to cover the expenses using a money market account. If you have concerns about being laid off from work, you should build additional reserves to cover lost income until you could reasonably expect to get another job. Begin by setting up automatic monthly deposits of 2 to 5 percent of your take-home pay directly into a money market account at your bank, brokerage firm, or credit union. Continue until this account reaches your target amount.

Guidelines for Borrowing

To get a firm handle on the destructive power of debt, it is vital that you learn the true costs of debt. Invariably, this is something that we don't think about. The true cost of borrowing not only includes the effort it takes to repay the loan, it also includes the opportunity costs of your money. In other words, if you hadn't borrowed, you could have used those funds to enhance your wealth by investing.

True Costs of Debt

To achieve Wealth Stages 3, 4, or 5, you must put your money to work for you. When you borrow money for purchases, your money is working for someone else (the bank, for example) because you must repay the loan and also pay interest. The amount of interest you pay over the life of a loan can be enormous. For example, a $100,000 mortgage loan at 6.5 percent interest over 30 years requires a total payment of more than $226,000! Fortunately, your home will likely increase in value over time.

Consider two additional examples:

◆ **Financing the purchase of a car.** If you borrow $20,000 at 12.5 percent interest over 60 months, the total cost of your loan would be $26,719. Your $6,719 of interest payments represents an increase in the total cost of the automobile of approximately 33 percent. If you repeat this process every five years over the next 40 years, you would buy eight cars at a total cost of $213,752, of which more than $50,000 is interest. If you can buy these cars without borrowing, that $50,000 of interest payments could be put to work for you in an investment program. Properly invested, that $50,000 could grow to more than $750,000. This $750,000 is the true cost of borrowing. Note that most people are spending more than $20,000 on their car and are trading cars more often than once every five years, so our example understates the true effect.

◆ **Overspending.** If you spend more than you make, you must borrow money to make ends meet. This borrowing often shows up in the form of increasing credit card debt.

The following table shows you what overspending $1,000 per year over 10 years really costs you.

The Costs of Overspending

Year	Overspending	Debt Accumulation	Interest at 18%
1	$1,000	$1,000	$180
2	$1,000	$2,000	$360
3	$1,000	$3,000	$540
4	$1,000	$4,000	$720
5	$1,000	$5,000	$900
6	$1,000	$6,000	$1,080
7	$1,000	$7,000	$1,260
8	$1,000	$8,000	$1,440
9	$1,000	$9,000	$1,620
10	$1,000	$10,000	$1,800
Totals	**$10,000**	**$10,000**	**$9,900**

To get out of debt over the next five years, you must first stop the $1,000 overspending per year. To repay principle and interest will cost an additional $3,000 a year, or approximately $333 per month. The total reduction in cash flow is $4,000 each year. The point is that it is much easier to get into debt than it is to get out of debt.

Before borrowing money, you should answer these five questions:

♦ Does it make economic sense? At a minimum, anything you borrow money to buy should be worth at least what you owe. That way, if you find you cannot make the payments, you can sell the item and pay off your loan. Never borrow money for intangible things like vacations. Always make certain you have a guaranteed way to repay your debts.

♦ Does my spouse agree with taking on this debt? It is essential for couples to discuss financial issues openly. When you're considering taking on new debt, be certain you both agree it is the right thing to do.

♦ Will borrowing this money result in achieving a personal goal that cannot be met any other way? Look for alternatives to borrowing. Could you raise cash through a garage sale? Do you have a boat or car that you could sell to raise cash? Could you wait 12 to 24 months while you save the money to pay cash? Remember, consumer debt always reduces your future lifestyle. Avoid it if you can.

♦ Is what I'm borrowing money to buy going to satisfy a need or a greed? A greed can be defined as something you want rather than need. Be careful about borrowing money to satisfy your wants. Because wants are unlimited, you could never borrow enough money to satisfy them.

♦ Do I have a guaranteed way to repay this loan? The best solution here is to be sure that what you buy has economic value. If not, make sure you have something of economic value that can guarantee the debt. For example, you borrow $5,000 to buy a bedroom set. Used furniture has little economic value so you need a substitute. Say you have $5,000 in a Certificate of Deposit that you can earmark to cover this debt. Now you have a guaranteed way to repay the loan.

Specific Guidelines for Debt

If you must borrow money for purchases, stay within the following guidelines:

Debt Guideline #1: Your Total Debt Payment

Your total debt payments, including your mortgage payment, should not exceed 30 percent of your take-home pay.

Debt Guideline #2: Buying Your Home

One of the biggest mistakes you can make is buying a home that is too expensive. Typically, mortgage bankers will allow your mortgage payments to equal approximately 35 percent of your take-home pay. This is considered the maximum amount banks can safely lend without eventually having to foreclose on the home. However, spending 35 percent of your take-home pay on mortgage payments will strain your budget and not leave enough free cash flow to easily meet other living expenses or investing goals. Therefore, your total house payment, including taxes and insurance, should not exceed 25 percent of your take-home pay. The ideal home mortgage payment is actually a range between 15 percent and 25 percent of take-home pay. Use 25 percent if you have a high degree of job security and you expect your income to steadily increase. If you use 20 percent, there should be plenty of money left over to meet other lifestyle expenses as well as savings and investment needs. Use 15 percent if you are more conservative and cautious or are uncertain about your job security.

Debt Guideline #3: Buying Automobiles

Most people spend more money on automobiles than on any other consumer purchases during their lifetime, including homes. You must avoid the lifetime of debt most people acquire when buying cars. Here are the guidelines for automobile debt:

1. Do not finance automobiles for more than 24 months. Let the payments you can afford over 24 months determine how much you can afford to spend on a car.

2. At the end of that 24 months, continue to make your "car payments." But now make payments to yourself in an investment account. Continue to make payments and drive your existing car until you have accumulated enough money to pay cash for your next car. By continuing this process throughout your life, you will never have to make another car payment. Generally, the longer you own a car, the better off you will be financially.

You can own the car model of your dreams by buying a used car or truck. Consider purchasing one that is 2 to 3 years old. The greatest amount of depreciation occurs during this time period, yet the car will likely still be covered under the manufacturer's warranty.

Debt Guideline #4: Installment Debt for Consumer Purchases

Avoid installment payments on things such as furniture, appliances, and home repairs such as a new roof, and so on. Instead, start putting money in an emergency fund for home maintenance and repairs. If it's not an emergency, wait until you can pay cash for the item. When you must use installment debt, your payments should not exceed 12 to 36 months. Smaller purchases such as a washer/dryer should be paid off within 12 months. Larger items such as a new furnace or roof may take 24 to 36 months.

Debt Guideline #5: Credit Cards

Credit cards are easy to get and to use but they're very hard to pay off! You cannot afford to pay 18 to 21 percent interest on any amount of money. Therefore, you must pay off your credit charges at the end of each month. As discussed earlier in this chapter, the best way to avoid credit card problems is to enter your credit card charges directly into your checkbook register and subtract the balance just as you would a check. Think of your credit cards as part of your overall checkbook system.

Your Overall Debt Load

Okay, we've covered a lot of ground related to guidelines for various kinds of debt. Let's do a quick overall summary. To achieve Wealth Stages 3, 4 or 5, you must take control of your debt by staying within these guidelines:

- Home mortgage payments should not exceed 25 percent of your take-home pay.

- Other debt payments should not exceed 15 percent of your take-home pay.

- Total combined debt payments (mortgage + consumer) should not exceed 30 percent of your take-home pay. For example, if your mortgage payment equals 20 percent of your take-home pay, you must limit other debt to 10 percent so that total debt payments do not exceed 30 percent of your take-home pay.

Explode Your Way out of Debt

If you feel like you're in a debt vortex with no escape route, rest assured that help is on the way. Co-author Stewart Welch developed one of the fastest ways to get out of debt by using The Debt Pyramid Reduction Strategy. The first step you must take is to decide to get out of debt. By now you're aware that getting out of debt is a lot harder and more painful than getting into debt, but you are ready to make the necessary sacrifices. For what is your alternative? More of the same will not get you to Wealth Stage 3, much less Wealth Stages 4 or 5. Our strategy will make this process both less painful and very fast. Soon you'll be speeding on your way to Wealth Stage 3.

Before continuing, let's take a look at the debt pyramid:

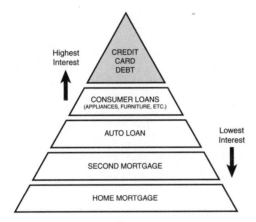

Debt pyramid.

If you have debt problems, you'll probably find that you have "stacked up" (pyramid style) various kinds of loans, from mortgages which usually carry the lowest interest rates, to credit cards which usually carry the highest. You must commit yourself to the task of becoming debt-free. You must also have a focused plan, get organized, and prioritize if you are to be successful.

Step 1: Stop Borrowing

The first step to getting out of debt is to make a commitment to not create any new debt. You must discontinue credit purchases and go on a strictly cash basis. This will require close budgeting (see Chapter 5).

Step 2: Prioritize Your Debts

Complete one Form A for each individual debt you have. Begin by completing only the shaded areas.

Form A
Priority Code _____

Individual Debt Information Report
(Use one page for each debt)

Account _____

Account Number _____

Current Balance $_____ as of _____ (date)

Interest Rate _____%

Current Month	Minimum Payment +	Additional Payment =	Total Payment	Balance or # of Payments Remaining
_____	$_____	$_____	$_____	$_____
_____	$_____	$_____	$_____	$_____
_____	$_____	$_____	$_____	$_____
_____	$_____	$_____	$_____	$_____
_____	$_____	$_____	$_____	$_____
_____	$_____	$_____	$_____	$_____
_____	$_____	$_____	$_____	$_____
_____	$_____	$_____	$_____	$_____
_____	$_____	$_____	$_____	$_____
_____	$_____	$_____	$_____	$_____
_____	$_____	$_____	$_____	$_____
_____	$_____	$_____	$_____	$_____
_____	$_____	$_____	$_____	$_____
_____	$_____	$_____	$_____	$_____

Organize your Form A's in the following sequence: highest interest rate to lowest interest rate. In the priority code section of Form A, number your debts beginning with #1 which represents the debt you owe with the highest interest rate to the lowest. Note: at this point you should decide if you want to accelerate the payoff of your home mortgage. For many people, the goal is to be debt-free except for their home.

Step 3: Organize Your Payment Plan

Complete the Debt Summary Worksheet (Form B) to determine what your total payment on all debt will be each month.

Form B

Debt Summary Worksheet

Priority Code	Account Name	Interest Rate	Current Balance	Minimum Payment
1	_____	_____	_____	_____
2	_____	_____	_____	_____
3	_____	_____	_____	_____
4	_____	_____	_____	_____
5	_____	_____	_____	_____
6	_____	_____	_____	_____
7	_____	_____	_____	_____
8	_____	_____	_____	_____
9	_____	_____	_____	_____
10	_____	_____	_____	_____
11	_____	_____	_____	_____
12	_____	_____	_____	_____
13	_____	_____	_____	_____
14	_____	_____	_____	_____
15	_____	_____	_____	_____
Totals			_____	_____

Amount available for extra monthly payments
(for example, $100/month)   +_____

Total amount allocated to debt reduction each month $_____ *

This is the amount you will apply toward all your debt until you are completely debt-free.

Add up all your minimum payments. Determine if your budget will allow you to pay an additional amount each month above the minimum monthly payments (say $100 a month). This additional amount plus the total amount of your minimum monthly payments becomes your total debt reduction payment amount. Note: *this amount will not change until you are completely out of debt.*

Step 4: Raise Cash

Do an asset review. What assets do you have that can be sold to raise cash? For example, you can raise hundreds or even thousands of dollars by having a garage sale. Not only do you benefit from the cash but you also feel good about cleaning out your closets and garage. Do you have boats, bikes, or motorcycles you can sell? Do you have an extra car, or do you really need two cars? You might even consider buying a less expensive home. Raise all the cash you can from the various sources. The cash raised should be paid on your highest-priority debt.

Step 5: Improve Your Interest Rate

If you can get a lower interest rate, consolidate your debts into a single loan.

Treasure Tip

Before you attempt to consolidate your debts, check your credit history by contacting one or all of the three major credit bureaus at www.annualcreditreport.com. Any potential lender will review your credit history before giving you a loan, so you want to know in advance the information they will see. If your credit history is bad, you'll want to discuss it with potential lenders before they find out on their own. Also, it is not unusual to find a mistake in your credit history file. If you do find a mistake, correct it before you apply for your loan.

Here are some possible loan sources:

- **Cash Value Life Insurance.** You may have a life insurance policy that has built-up cash values. Normally, this money can be borrowed at very low interest rates of 5 to 8 percent. If you do have such a policy, contact your agent to get the details on how much you can borrow and the interest rates. It may also be advisable to replace it with inexpensive level term life insurance (see Chapter 20).

Treasure Tip

Rates on home equity loans vary greatly from bank to bank. Be sure to check with at least two financial institutions before committing to a lender.

- **Home Equity.** If you own your home you may be eligible for a home equity loan. Interest rates on these loans are usually very favorable and the interest is deductible. However, the major disadvantage is that if you can't make your payments, you could lose your home to foreclosure.

◆ **Retirement Account.** Many retirement account plans have provisions for loans to participants. Typically, you can borrow up to 50 percent of your vested balance to a maximum of $50,000. Normally, the interest rate is favorable. Also, the payback schedule is often as long as 60 months. Normally, we don't recommend borrowing money from your retirement plan, but if you're using the funds to pay off 18 percent debt, this might make good sense.

◆ **Loans from Family Members.** Family members with idle cash not earning much interest may be willing to loan you money if they are confident you will re-pay it. There are laws governing loans between family members so be sure to consult your tax advisor.

◆ **Low Interest Rate Credit Cards.** Many credit cards feature hefty 18 to 21 percent interest charges. But today, competition has driven interest rates down on many cards. To find the best deals, go to the Resource Center at www.welchgroup.com. Find a low interest rate card and swap your balances over.

Treasure Tip

Most credit card companies allow you to transfer your account balance from your old card to your new card.

Step 6: Implement

Pull out your Debt Summary Worksheet (Step 3). Pay the maximum that you can pay on your priority #1 debt while paying the minimum required payment on all other debts. When your #1 debt is paid off, take the amount you were paying on #1 and add it to the minimum payment on #2 on your Debt Summary Worksheet. Continue this strategy until all debts are paid off.

IMPORTANT! The total amount you pay each month will not change even though your minimum payments may be going down and individual debts are being paid off. This is *the key* to the Debt Pyramid Reduction Strategy.

Getting out of debt is a worthy goal. By applying discipline and implementing the Debt Pyramid Reduction Strategy, you can put yourself on the fast track to becoming debt-free.

The Least You Need to Know

- Too much debt is the single biggest reason people are unable to achieve financial independence.

- There are many reasons people have too much debt. Understanding the "why" is one of the keys to solving debt problems.

- The Debt Rule says you should never borrow money to buy a depreciating asset.

- Debt always mortgages your future.

- The true cost of borrowing is much higher than we initially think.

- You can use the Debt Pyramid Reduction Strategy to explode your way out of debt.

How to Become a Super Saver

In This Chapter

- How to develop your Wealth Stage 1 formula

- How to increase your income

- How to decrease expenses

- How to calculate how much money you need to achieve financial independence

- How to stay on track with your plan

Mark Twain once said, "The secret of getting ahead is getting started. The secret of getting started is breaking your complex overwhelming tasks into small manageable tasks and then starting on the first one." Most people never achieve any significant wealth because they have no idea how to build wealth or even how to get started. There's no class or television show that really shows you how to do it. You might find a few late-night infomercials that sound pretty convincing, but they're really working on their own get-rich agenda by selling you a product. You might find books on the subject, but rarely will you find an actual formula that works. If you do find a formula, it's probably either too complicated or too ambiguous. Therefore, we sat down and designed an easy step-by-step formula that would help others get to Wealth Stage 1. It's simple to complete, and it should be your first step in your journey toward wealth. Let's get started.

Wealth Is a Journey, Not a Destination

We've learned that wealth achieved over a long period of time tends to be greatly appreciated, whereas wealth acquired suddenly tends to be squandered. This is especially evident among lottery winners. According to Ellen Goodstein, a writer for BankRate.com, Evelyn Adams won the New York lottery not once, but twice (1985, 1986) for a total of $5.4 million. Today, Adams is broke and living in a trailer. Or take William "Bud" Post, who won more than $16 million in the Pennsylvania lottery in 1988. Within one year he was out of money and $1 million in debt. Today, Post lives on his Social Security retirement check. A growing body of evidence suggests that wealth suddenly achieved is often fleeting. It's interesting that so many people play the lottery against overwhelming odds of failure, yet the few winners often meet with tragic results.

> **Treasure Tip**
>
> Looking back at all the wealthy people we've met, it seems that the ones who built their own wealth slowly over time seem to appreciate and maintain it better than those who inherited it, married it, or won it.

Why do these lottery winners end up in so much trouble? Think about it a minute. They win the lottery, they suddenly they feel like they're rich, they begin spending money like they are rich, and they pay little attention to planning for the future. Who cares about the future when you're rich and you have all this money coming in? That's the problem. These winners see wealth as a destination, and they feel as if they've definitely arrived. What they don't understand is that wealth is a journey, not a destination. You can't get to Wealth Stage 3 and go nuts. You have to continue to be a good steward of your money, which requires what we have termed "money responsibility."

If you want to achieve and maintain wealth throughout your lifetime, you must see wealth as a journey. How most people view wealth is that you hit it big somehow (get rich quick) and then live the good life. If that's your view, stop right now and erase this vision from your mind. Wealth is a way of life. It is a set of beliefs and habits, rather than something material that you attain and then sit back and relax. For example, wealth is born from the initial habit of living within your means. As you saw in Chapter 3, this journey has many levels and transitions, and most people don't understand them. If you take the time to plan and prepare for each step or transition, you improve your chances of becoming and staying wealthy. It also helps to be patient along the way, especially at the beginning of your journey.

Let's begin your journey by focusing on accomplishing the first level of wealth. To do this, we're going to take a rather unconventional approach. Here are the steps to follow:

1. Begin with the end in mind. Determine your ideal income.

2. Estimate your target portfolio goal (TPG).

3. Estimate your target savings goal (TSG).

4. Develop your success game plan.

5. Monitor your progress and make adjustments as needed.

What you're about to embark on is a simple process that will give you a good sense of how much wealth you need to accumulate based on your dreams and your goals. It will also help you determine which investment strategies are most appropriate for you.

Step 1: Begin with the End in Mind

Answer this question. If you were to retire today, how much income would you need for the next 12 months to support your ideal lifestyle?

Think before you answer this question, because your answer here will be the primary driver for all your future financial decisions. This is where you should visualize exactly what you want your life to look like. Some of you may be very content with your life as it is now and just want to make sure you're adequately preparing for your future, especially retirement. Others will have dreams of a much higher lifestyle and will be willing to take more risks and work harder to achieve it.

There is no right or wrong answer here, just the answer that will serve to motivate you to action. In developing your answer, don't be concerned with inflation at this point. We will handle inflation later. One obvious way to establish your income goal is to determine what your current expenses are, including income taxes, and how they might change when you retire. The following worksheet helps you determine your desired income.

Retirement Income Worksheet

	Estimated Current Expenses	Retirement Expenses (Today's $)	Increasing Expense?	
Contributions	$_____	$_____	Yes	No
Home				
Mortgage	$_____	$_____	Yes	No
Insurance	$_____	$_____	Yes	No
Real estate taxes	$_____	$_____	Yes	No
Maintenance/repairs	$_____	$_____	Yes	No
Utilities				
Electricity/gas/water	$_____	$_____	Yes	No
Phones	$_____	$_____	Yes	No
Cable TV	$_____	$_____	Yes	No
Security system	$_____	$_____	Yes	No
Insurance				
Medical	$_____	$_____	Yes	No
Personal care	$_____	$_____	Yes	No
Children				
Clothing	$_____	$_____	Yes	No
School tuition/expenses	$_____	$_____	Yes	No
Gifts	$_____	$_____	Yes	No
Other	$_____	$_____	Yes	No
Debt Payments				
Autos	$_____	$_____	Yes	No
Personal loans	$_____	$_____	Yes	No
Other	$_____	$_____	Yes	No
Income taxes	$_____	$_____	Yes	No
Total	**$_____**	**$_____**		

Exercise 1

If I were to retire today, I would need $_____ per month for the next 12 months to meet my ideal lifestyle goal.

Example: you determine that you would need $60,000, including income taxes, to cover your living expenses for the next 12 months.

Step 2: Estimate Your Target Portfolio Goal

Based on your answer in Step 1, Exercise 1, you will need to determine the amount of investment capital you must accumulate to reach your goal. For now, don't worry about inflation—we'll tackle that topic later in this chapter.

Exercise 2

Divide your answer in Step 1, Exercise 1 by .05.

$_____ ÷ .05 = $_____

In our example:

$60,000 ÷ .05 = $1,200,000

Your answer here represents your target portfolio goal or TPG. Now we need to decide how much money you need to be saving monthly to achieve your TPG.

Step 3: Estimate Your Target Savings Goal (TSG) Necessary to Achieve Your TPG

This exercise will require that you make some assumptions about how much you can invest and how many years before you would like to retire (or could reasonably expect to retire). In addition, you will need to refer to Appendix D, where you will find a table titled "Annual Target Savings Goal Factor."

The formula for estimating your target savings goal is:

TPG ÷ Annual Target Savings Goal Factor = TSG

Or stated another way: the target portfolio goal divided by the appropriate Annual Target Savings Goal Factor from Appendix D equals your target savings goal.

You might need to run through this exercise several times before arriving at an answer you're confident that you can accomplish.

Exercise 3

Using the Annual Target Savings Goal Factor table in Appendix D, calculate the annual savings required to achieve your TPG.

$ _____ (your TPG) ÷ ____ (your chosen Annual Target Savings Goal Factor) =
$ _____ (your TSG)

For example, if your target is to earn 10 percent return on your investments and your goal is to retire in 30 years, you would select factor 164.49 from Appendix D. Now $1,200,000 divided by 164.49 equals $7,295. This represents your *annual* target savings goal. To convert this to a monthly savings amount, simply divide $7,295 by 12 ($7,295 ÷ 12 = $608 per month).

Simple enough? This $7,295 represents about 12 percent of the total $60,000 annual income in our example. Saving 12 percent should not be a problem, and we'll show you how later in this chapter. If you ended up with a much higher percentage, don't be discouraged.

Step 4: Develop Your Success Game Plan

In our example, you could achieve your 30-year investment goal by investing in stocks or stock mutual funds, ideally inside a retirement plan. But what if the goal was to retire in 20 years, or 15 years? How might that affect your investment strategy? Here is the answer if retirement in 20 years is the goal:

$1,200,000 ÷ 57.27 = $20,953 required annual investment. This $20,953 represents more than one third of the $60,000 annual income. Using 15 years as the retirement goal would look like this: $1,200,000 ÷ 31.77 = $37,771 investment required or more than 60 percent of the $60,000 annual income in our example. Impossible, you say? Well, the solution is to invest in ways that will earn you a much higher return than can be achieved through traditional investments. For example, using a 20-year retirement goal and investing $7,000 per year, you would achieve your $1,200,000 TPG by earning 19 percent. (We will show you how to do this beginning in Chapter 8. Pay particular attention to the section on leverage.) At this point, you simply need to re-run this exercise until you determine the rate of return needed to accomplish your goal based on what you can afford to invest now. After you finish reading this book, you will need to come back and run through these exercises again after you have determined what type of investments you're willing to use. Ultimately, you must match the type of investments you're willing to invest in with the possible return for that type of investment and your stated rate of return goal.

Step 5: Monitor Your Progress

After you've finalized your game plan and put it into action, you will need to periodically review your results to make sure you're on track. At times you'll find that you are, in fact, off track. When this happens, don't give up! You will need to regroup and decide what steps you need to take to get you back on track.

Monitoring your progress is a vital element to ultimate success. Mainly, you want to be certain that you're investing based on your target goals, but you should also spend some time anticipating potential problems on the horizon. Review your budget for the past month to determine how much you earned and spent compared to your estimates. Then, review your expected income and expenses for the next month, in detail, as well as the next several months. One key progress monitoring tool is your Investment Net Worth statement (see Chapter 3), which should be updated at least once per year.

Your success in maintaining your plan depends a great deal on the following factors:

- **Your flexibility and creativity.** You must be willing to respond to the inevitable changes that life brings. You must be able to handle adversity.

- **Your organizational skills.** You must keep current, at least yearly, with all the elements of your plan.

- **Your willingness to work on your plan.** Your journey toward wealth will take some time, so be certain you enjoy the journey; the payoff will be worth it.

Dealing with Inflation

The formula we devised for determining your TSG accounted for *inflation* during your retirement years, but you will also need to address the effects of inflation between now and when you retire. Your TSG ($1,200,000 in our example) is likely to creep up as inflation pushes the costs of goods and services to higher levels between now and your retirement. To resolve this, you will need to do two things.

First, convert your TSG into a percentage of your income by using the following formula:

TSG ÷ Total Income Before Taxes = TSG as a % of Total Income

Your answer will be a mathematical percent. Simply multiply it by 100 to convert it to a stated percent. To apply this formula to your own situation, complete Exercise 4.

> **Words of the Wealthy**
>
> Most people think that **inflation** is the simple rise in prices. The technical definition is an increase in the volume of money and credit relative to available goods, which results in a substantial and continuing rise in the general price level. The rate of inflation is measured by the month-to-month percentage change of the Consumer Price Index (CPI).

Exercise 4

$ _____ (TSG) ÷ $ _____ (your total income before taxes) = ___%

In our example:

$7,295 ÷ $60,000 = 0.1216 or 12.16%

The percentage you get in Exercise 4 becomes the percent of your income you should invest going forward. The assumption is that your income will rise over time, allowing you to commit an increasing number of dollars to your investment plan. The assumption is also that your pay raises will be greater than the rate of inflation. If not, you have some decisions to make—decisions we will discuss later in this chapter.

The second thing you'll need to do to account for inflation is to rerun Steps 1 through 3 every 12 months to determine how your answers might change over time. By doing these two things, you'll remain focused on what you need to do to meet your retirement goal.

Increase Your Cash Flow

Having completed the preceding analysis, you're probably in a mild state of shock over how large the task before you is. Don't become discouraged. We have both gone before you and know what can be accomplished after you set your mind to it. One thing that is almost certainly clear is that you could use more cash flow. The only way to increase cash flow is to produce more revenue and/or reduce expenses. Let's look at how you might accomplish this.

Strategies for Increasing Your Income

Write down on a piece of paper your current yearly salary or income before tax. Under that amount, write this question: What can I do to increase my income now and in the future? Set aside some time and come up with 20 answers to this question. If you can't come up with 20 answers, ask a friend to help you. Here are a few ideas to get you started:

- Ask the boss for a raise; prepare a proposal that illustrates what you would do for the raise.
- Offer to take on more responsibility for more pay.
- Consider achieving a higher level of education. Ask your boss for his or her recommendation. Often your employer will pay all or part of the costs of additional education and will reward successful completion with increased pay and responsibilities.
- Start a small income-generating business on the side.
- Consider a second job.
- Present an idea at work that will make the company more profitable.
- Find another job that will pay you more.

Afterward, select the best answers and make an effort to implement them. If building wealth is really important to you, you'll take the time to complete this step. As we mentioned in Chapter 1, your journey toward wealth doesn't require a huge salary. However, if you at least attempt to maximize your income, you might shorten the distance you have to travel. There are so many different ways to do this. If you're creative and proactive by nature, you'll have no problem. In Chapter 7, we discuss several techniques you can use to maximize your salary if you work for others. In Part 3, we discuss ways to maximize your net income if you're self-employed.

Your ultimate goal is to maximize your income by becoming more valuable to your employer and being paid what you're worth.

Strategies for Reducing Your Current Expenses

It will be difficult to cut your expenses if you don't know what they are to begin with, so the logical place to start is to determine what you spent over the last 12 months. Start by reviewing your checkbook and credit card statements from the prior 12 months. Use the Retirement Income Worksheet at the beginning of this chapter to itemize your expenses into appropriate categories. (For a more detailed budget analysis, go to the Resource Center at www.welchgroup.com.)

Next, review your expenses and decide where you can cut out waste. When we review the expenses of a client who is having cash flow problems, it's typically like inspecting a sinking boat. Rarely do we find big holes. Rather, what we find is a boat with hundreds of pinholes that are allowing water to seep in. You have to plug all the tiny holes. A good way to do this is to track everything you spend every day for a month with your goal being to cut out all waste. This sounds like a lot of trouble, but remember, we're talking about building your wealth. We have always found that whatever is measured seems to improve. If you take the time to do this, you'll learn a lot about yourself and quickly see where your money is going.

Treasure Tip

"All work and no play makes Jack a dull boy." Don't forget to plan a reasonable amount for entertainment as a regular expense.

Now use what you learned by this exercise to construct a budget for the next 12 months. Be sure to account for any nonmonthly expenses such as auto insurance payments, life insurance premiums, and so on.

If you prefer a more structured approach, the Weekly Expense Worksheet is designed for you to copy four times, one for each week of the month. (Make five copies if the current month spans five weeks.) Take a sheet with you and begin recording now. Record every penny you spend for one month. This includes all cash, credit, and checkbook expenditures.

Weekly Expense Worksheet

Expense Items	Mon	Tues	Wed	Thurs	Fri	Sat	Sun	Total
Auto: Gas	___	___	___	___	___	___	___	___
Auto: Maintenance	___	___	___	___	___	___	___	___
Children: Tuition/Childcare	___	___	___	___	___	___	___	___
Food: Dining Out/Credit Card	___	___	___	___	___	___	___	___
Food: Grocery	___	___	___	___	___	___	___	___
Fun:	___	___	___	___	___	___	___	___
Fun:	___	___	___	___	___	___	___	___
Fun: Vacation/ Entertainment	___	___	___	___	___	___	___	___
Home: Furniture	___	___	___	___	___	___	___	___
Home: Housekeeper	___	___	___	___	___	___	___	___
Home: Pest Control	___	___	___	___	___	___	___	___
Home: Rent	___	___	___	___	___	___	___	___
Home: Repair/Maintenance	___	___	___	___	___	___	___	___
Home: Security Monitoring	___	___	___	___	___	___	___	___
Home: Yard Maintenance	___	___	___	___	___	___	___	___
Insurance: Auto and Liability	___	___	___	___	___	___	___	___
Insurance:	___	___	___	___	___	___	___	___
Insurance: Disability	___	___	___	___	___	___	___	___
Insurance: Health	___	___	___	___	___	___	___	___
Insurance: Life	___	___	___	___	___	___	___	___
Loan:	___	___	___	___	___	___	___	___
Loan: Home Mortgage	___	___	___	___	___	___	___	___
Membership: Athletic Club	___	___	___	___	___	___	___	___
Membership:	___	___	___	___	___	___	___	___
Membership Dues:	___	___	___	___	___	___	___	___
Misc:	___	___	___	___	___	___	___	___
Misc:	___	___	___	___	___	___	___	___
Misc: Clothing	___	___	___	___	___	___	___	___
Misc: Contributions/Gifts	___	___	___	___	___	___	___	___

continues

Weekly Expense Worksheet   (continued)

Expense Items	Mon	Tues	Wed	Thurs	Fri	Sat	Sun	Total
Misc: Laundry/Dry Cleaning	___	___	___	___	___	___	___	___
Misc: Medical/Dental	___	___	___	___	___	___	___	___
Misc: Parking	___	___	___	___	___	___	___	___
Misc: Personal Care	___	___	___	___	___	___	___	___
Misc: Transportation	___	___	___	___	___	___	___	___
Retirement Accounts: (SEP, 401[k])	___	___	___	___	___	___	___	___
Taxes: Income (out of paycheck)	___	___	___	___	___	___	___	___
Taxes: Property	___	___	___	___	___	___	___	___
Taxes: Quarterly Federal	___	___	___	___	___	___	___	___
Taxes: Tax Account to Pay April	___	___	___	___	___	___	___	___
Utility: Electric	___	___	___	___	___	___	___	___
Utility: Gas	___	___	___	___	___	___	___	___
Utility: Phone	___	___	___	___	___	___	___	___
Utility: Water	___	___	___	___	___	___	___	___
Other	___	___	___	___	___	___	___	___
Other	___	___	___	___	___	___	___	___
Other	___	___	___	___	___	___	___	___
Other	___	___	___	___	___	___	___	___

After you've completed this exercise, consider using one of the personal financial software packages that are available, such as Quicken (www.quicken.com). This program will help you perform an expense analysis in great detail. For those who don't have a computer, old-fashioned notebook paper works just as well; it just takes longer.

Increasing cash flow by reducing expenses is largely a mindset. It begins by focusing every morning on what your goal is, then being conscious about everything you spend money on. About every purchase, you should ask yourself this question: "Do I really need or want this?" It may only take you a fraction of a second to go through this exercise on every purchase, but after you make it a habit, you'll be surprised at how much money you can save. Think about it. How much money would you save if today you drank coffee from the office coffeepot rather than buying a latté on the way to work? What would you save if you brought your lunch instead of going out with the gang at work? Plugging pinholes will add up to big money over the course of a year and a lifetime. Wealthy people understand this.

Eliminate Bad Debt

Review the strategies we discussed in Chapter 4.

Our Best Money-Saving Strategies

Do you want a little help thinking of ways to cut expenses and save money? Here are our favorite strategies:

◆ If you're dead serious about getting out of debt, consider using an equity line of credit against your home to consolidate your consumer loans. Your interest rate should be lower and your interest will be tax-deductible. Make sure you don't incur any additional debt.

◆ If you owe money on your credit cards, transfer your balance to a card with a lower rate. If you don't owe money, get a no-fee card. To find the best deals, go to the Resource Center at www.welchgroup.com.

◆ If your employer offers a matching contribution to the company retirement plan, be sure to take advantage of it. Not only will you save money on taxes, a 50 percent matching contribution is the equivalent of a 50 percent return, guaranteed!

◆ Raise the deductibles on your auto and homeowner's insurance. Raising your deductible to $500 or $1,000 can easily cut your premiums 20 percent or more.

◆ Take advantage of company-sponsored reimbursement plans. These plans allow you to set aside money on a before-tax basis for expenses such as childcare, unreimbursed medical expenses, and education expenses.

Wealth Warning

People who turn in small claims on their homeowner's and automobile insurance often find that the insurance carrier will raise their rates or cancel their coverage. You're better off in the long run to carry higher deductibles and pay smaller claims out-of-pocket.

◆ Buy term life insurance instead of cash value insurance. This will cut your premiums by 75 percent or more. (For more on life insurance, see Chapter 20.)

◆ Quit smoking. A two-pack-a-day habit at $3.50 per pack adds up to $213 per month. If a 25-year-old invested this money in stocks or stock mutual funds (averaging a 9 percent return) until age 65, he or she would have more than $1,000,000! Smokers also pay a lot more for life insurance. For example, a $1 million 30-year level term policy for a 30-year-old who smokes costs about

$3,000 per year while a nonsmoker would pay only about $900 per year. This $2,100 difference invested in stocks or stock mutual funds would produce another $300,000 by age 60.

◆ Bring your lunch to work.

◆ Hold a garage sale. The rule of thumb should be, "If you haven't used it or worn it in two years, you don't need it."

◆ Plan your purchases and then shop at discount stores and buyers clubs such as Sam's Club or Costco. You can easily cut the costs of your purchases by 5 percent to 50 percent.

◆ Buy a used rather and than a new car. A car depreciates most during the first two years. Look for one that is at least two years old, but is still under warranty.

◆ Cut the costs of eating out. Begin by eating out less often. Instead, have dinner parties at home and have guests each bring a dish. When you do eat out, gather for cocktails at someone's home, eat out, and then meet back for dessert at someone else's home. Cocktails and dessert significantly add to the costs of eating out.

◆ Give up the health club membership. There's nothing there that you can't do at home with a decent set of dumbbells, a flat/incline bench, and a good set of jogging shoes.

◆ Use regular gasoline rather than premium. Today, virtually any vehicle will run on regular gas and you'll save about 20¢ per gallon or more.

◆ When choosing your next car, check with your auto insurance agent to make sure it doesn't require high premiums.

◆ Keep up the maintenance on your car and keep your car for a long time. Today, cars are built to last 100,000 to 200,000 miles. If you take care of yours, it will last a long time and can save you a lot of money.

◆ Develop a holiday budget for gifts. People tend to overspend during the Christmas holidays. Determine how much you can afford to spend without borrowing; make a list of everyone you plan to give a gift; divide your gift budget among those on your list; then take your list with you as you shop. Stick to your budget.

◆ Terminate magazine and paper subscriptions that you don't read. Most will offer a pro-rated refund.

◆ Use the public library for free access to books and movies.

- If you put down less than 20 percent when you bought your home, you're likely paying Private Mortgage Insurance (PMI). If your home's value now exceeds 80 percent of your mortgage balance, request termination of PMI.

- Avoid ATM machines that charge a fee for withdrawing cash.

- Avoid divorce. We can think of a lot of nonfinancial reasons to avoid divorce, including living up to your marriage vows. Financially, divorce will set you back more than just about anything we can think of. Marriage counseling, if necessary, is much cheaper.

- When purchasing appliances, autos, and so on, go for energy-efficient items. It may cost you a bit more initially, but it will save you money in the long run.

- Save money at home. Cut back your thermostat. Two degrees will noticeably reduce your monthly heating and cooling bill. Run only full loads in your laundry and dishwasher. Use the phone book or the Internet (www.whitepages.com), not Directory Assistance, to look up phone numbers.

- Don't wait until the end of the year to invest in your Traditional or Roth IRA. By investing at the beginning of the year, you will benefit from additional months of deferral. A 25-year-old investing $1,000 per year until age 65 would accumulate $442,000 (assuming 10 percent earnings) if he or she invested at the end of each year. By investing at the beginning of each year, that person would accumulate $486,000, or $44,000 more!

Can all this penny-pinching really make a difference? Remember our sinking boat analogy? It's the small things that add up to a big difference. Saving money is really a mindset—something that the wealthy do almost intuitively. Think of it like this: If you look in your wallet and have a dollar, you have two choices. You can spend it or you can save it. "Well, a dollar is not much money," you say. "Au contraire," we say. If you're age 25 and decide to invest that dollar in, say, a Roth IRA, at age 65 your dollar would be worth more than $45. The paradigm shift for you should be, "Do I really want that soft drink enough to spend $45 dollars?" If your answer is yes, then go ahead, enjoy! But at least you will have made a conscious decision to spend instead of save. If you acquire a wealth mindset, in many instances, you will decide to save.

> **Wealth Warning**
>
> Associate with other people who share your ambitions and aspirations and who are willing to share ideas and support you in your efforts. Look for win/win relationships. Avoid those people who pull you down and drain your enthusiasm.

That Reminds Us ...

To achieve real wealth, you must be open minded enough to recognize and break down the self-imposed barriers that keep you in your present financial condition. These barriers are usually mindsets that need a little adjustment. Normally, the adjustment requires a catalyst or disruption to get it started. Often catalysts and disruptions come from reading and discussing ideas with others. Take some time to understand your own barriers about building wealth. Then discuss them with others who have achieved the level of wealth you desire. How do these people think? How did they overcome their barriers? Did they have similar barriers or different ones? This meeting might be just the catalyst you need.

The Wealth Index: Measuring Your Success

By completing the exercises in this chapter, you have determined the size of the task before you. We designed The Wealth Index as a tool to help you easily measure your progress as you move toward your financial goals and beyond. We begin by completing the Investment Net Worth Statement. In our case example for this chapter, it might look like this:

Investment Net Worth Statement

Personal Investments

Money market accounts	$7,000
CDs	$0
Stocks	$30,000
Bonds	$0
Mutual funds	$17,000
Investment real estate (equity)	$90,000
Other	$0

Retirement Plan Investments

IRAs	$75,000
SEPs	$0
401(k)s	$120,000
Other (Roth IRA)	$37,000
Total Investment Net Worth	**$376,000**

Now we're ready to calculate the Wealth Index for our sample case:

$376,000	Total Investment Net Worth
÷1,200,000	TPG ($60,000/yr. ÷ .05)
0.31	
× 100	Wealth Index Factor
31	**Your Wealth Index**

Finally, go to the Wealth Index Scale to see where you are relative to your goal. Note that your minimum goal should be to achieve Wealth Stage 3. Many people will achieve Wealth Stage 4 and a few will also achieve Wealth Stage 5.

Wealth Index Scale

< 100	Wealth Stage 1 and 2: You must continue to work and invest.
100	Wealth Stage 3: You are financially independent.
200	Wealth Stage 4: You are considered wealthy!
> 500	Wealth Stage 5: You are considered rich!

With a Wealth Index score of 31, clearly the person in our case example has a long way to go before he or she achieves his goal. Now it's your turn. Go through the Wealth Index Analyzer and determine your Wealth Index score.

Wealth Index Analyzer

Personal Investments

Money market accounts	$_____
CDs	$_____
Stocks	$_____
Bonds	$_____
Mutual funds	$_____
Investment real estate (equity)	$_____
Other	$_____

continues

Retirement Plan Investments

IRAs	$_____
SEPs	$_____
401(k)s	$_____
Other	$_____
Total Investment Net Worth	**$**_____

Calculate Your Wealth Index

$ _____	Total Investment Net Worth
÷ $ _____	Target Portfolio Goal (TPG)
= _____	
× **100**	Wealth Index Factor
= _____	**Your Wealth Index**

Did you experience a similar result to our case example? Does this now seem like Mission Impossible? Determining how far you are from achieving your goal is an important step in creating a sense of urgency to get moving *now* toward accomplishing your goal. For if not now, when? Waiting will only make the task more and more daunting. You can achieve wealth if you're determined enough and are willing to develop and execute a game plan geared to achieve your goals.

The Least You Need to Know

- Wealth is a way of life—a set of beliefs and a mixture of habits that begin by living within your means.

- To live within your means, you must be willing to measure your spending habits to understand your means and maximize your savings capacity.

- With a little practice, anyone can become a good saver. There are a number of ways to cut your expenses to increase available cash for your investment plan.

- Along your journey, focus on what you have the most control over—which is the amount of money you spend and the amount of money you save.

- Determine where you are now in relation to accomplishing your desired financial goal and let this serve to motivate you into action.

Chapter 6

The Secrets of Millionaires

In This Chapter

- Saving money systematically each month
- Making money by shopping
- Learning the characteristics of very wealthy people
- Having passion is key to the wealth-building process
- Avoiding debt and paying cash

If you want to be great in a particular area of your life, identify people who are already the best at what you want to do and imitate them. First, identify their habits. What are they doing on a consistent basis that enables them to achieve their results? Second, what are the key characteristics that enable them to achieve their results? Be willing to approach them, share your own goals with them, and ask for their advice. Most will be more than happy to talk with you.

Remember the couple we mentioned in Chapter 1, Mr. and Mrs. Post, who never made more than $30,000 per year, yet their portfolio was worth more than $800,000? Not to mention the $240,000 in homes they had paid cash for as gifts for their two daughters and the $100,000 college education account! How could this couple have so much money with so little income? When asked, they said, "We saved it and invested it in no-load mutual funds." Then they sat back and shared some simple truths that every investor should follow. We call them the seven habits of wealthy people.

The Seven Habits of Wealthy People

The seven habits for building wealth include saving every month, staying out of debt, shopping before you buy, buying used when you can, taking care of your stuff, investing in stocks, and taking time to plan your future.

1. Be a Consistent Saver

The Posts said that each month, no matter what they made in salary, they put money in savings and invested in no-load mutual funds. They said, "No matter what happens, pay yourself first and make it a habit." The combination of systematic savings and compound growth is incredible. Here are several ways you can start saving money now:

- **Maximize your 401(k).** This is the easiest thing to do because the deposits are usually automatically deducted from your paycheck, and you only make an investment decision once in a while. If your company or employer offers one of these plans, take advantage of it now and maximize your contributions. Millionaires are made of these plans. The assets grow tax-deferred, and you get the benefit of using Uncle Sam's money in the compounding process.

- **If you are self-employed, consider starting your own Simplified Employee Pension (SEP).** You'll be able to shelter up to 25 percent of your net income until you retire. This powerful step is simple to implement. All you have to do is fill out an application, make a deposit, and you're on your way.

- **Maximize your Traditional IRA or Roth IRA contribution.** An IRA is an Individual Retirement Account into which you can deposit a maximum of $4,000 of earned income each year. If you're age 50 or older, you're allowed to make an additional "catch-up" contribution of $1,000 each year. The true benefit of the IRA is that all interest, dividends, and capital gains are tax-deferred until they're withdrawn. The second benefit is the flexibility of investment alternatives that are available. You can invest in CDs, stocks, bonds, and mutual funds. Because there are thousands of different mutual funds, your alternatives are almost endless. The third benefit is convenience. An IRA is simple to start. All you have to do is fill out an application and make a deposit. The Traditional IRA is deductible from your income, which lessens your tax burden. You can withdraw money from this IRA after you are $59\frac{1}{2}$ years old without penalties, but all distributions are taxable as ordinary income. With a Roth IRA, you don't receive a tax deduction for your contributions, but your withdrawals after you're $59\frac{1}{2}$ years old are tax-free.

◆ **Write yourself a check.** Before you start paying your bills each week or each payday, write yourself a check and deposit the check in a separate account. The whole idea is to pay yourself first. Your 401(k) works the same way; it comes out of the check before you get it. Your goal should be to save your target savings goal and then use the remainder to budget your spending. Act as if the TSG amount doesn't even exist and budget accordingly.

◆ **Let a mutual fund direct-debit your account.** Most mutual funds offer a direct-debit feature that automatically withdraws a predetermined amount from your checking account each month. This is one of the easiest ways to save money. Each month at bill-paying time, just record the withdrawal in your check register. Don't be afraid of this feature. Try it for a year and cancel if you don't like it.

CAUTION

Wealth Warning

Internal Revenue Service rules govern whether you qualify to contribute to a Traditional or Roth IRA, so be sure to check with your financial advisor.

Treasure Tip

If you're not eligible for a tax-deductible Traditional IRA or you are in a low-income tax bracket, consider investing in a Roth IRA. The assets grow tax-deferred (you don't pay tax on any interest or other income), and you get to make tax-free withdrawals during retirement. With the freedom to invest in almost any liquid security, the Roth IRA is a powerful tool.

◆ **Save your raises.** Another trick is to ignore any raises in income when budgeting for expenses. When you get a raise, save the entire raise. Instead of increasing your spending habits, increase your saving habits. Let the raise boost your saving percentage.

2. Pay Cash When You Can

Debt is a tool, and it works just like a lever. The word *leverage* is often used when people refer to debt, and that's exactly how debt can operate. The more debt you have, the more buying power you control. However, many people in today's world have gone crazy with debt, and the result is a record number of bankruptcies. Debt is okay if you know how to use it. We have a few simple rules to live by when it comes to debt. It's okay to leverage your home, and it's okay to leverage investment real estate or a business venture as long as you can afford to cover the payments. However, it's not okay to leverage your self-image. Using debt to live in a lifestyle you can't afford will be counterproductive to your long-term wealth-building strategy.

Many wealthy individuals pay cash for everything and avoid debt (except for their home mortgage). Instead of borrowing money to purchase an item, they wait until they save enough money to buy the item with cash. Save money for the things you want and pay cash.

Here's what you should do. Have your bank or credit union set up an automatic transfer into a savings account that you will use exclusively for future purchases. It is what we call a "saving to spend" account. If you have something specific you're saving for, determine how much you need to save each month and for how many months. If you don't have anything specific in mind, save 2 percent to 3 percent of each paycheck. Then wait until you have the cash before you buy. This is what we call "delayed gratification," and it is good for the soul!

3. Smart Shopping Saves You Money

Our society today is known for its impatience. Our attitude has become, "We want it right now, and we get what we want!" This attitude doesn't help motivate anyone to shop around for the best deal. We're talking about doing your homework before you buy anything of significance.

The Posts said that they shopped extensively before they bought anything. This is a simple concept, but few people take the time. Analyze yourself. Do you take the time to shop around for the best deal on a particular item? Are you an impulsive buyer? Start the habit of shopping for the best deals on all purchases. Here are some shopping tips:

◆ **Plan on saving money.** To avoid impulse buying, make a list of what you need before you leave home, then do your shopping at discount retailers.

- **Buy seasonal items out of season.** When you do shop, think opposite of the crowd's thinking. Most people buy their boats in the early spring. Avoid the buying pressure, and get it cheap later in the summer. You can say the same thing about lawn mowers, convertible automobiles, and landscaping materials. If snow is a problem in the winter, buy a snow blower in the late spring. If you time your purchases right and negotiate properly, you might pay only a fraction of the normal in-season price. Try to postpone buying an item until the off season so you can buy it cheaper. Have you ever been to Disney World during the month of September? It's great! All the kids are back in school, and the place isn't crowded.

> **Words of the Wealthy**
>
> The word **haggle** comes from the Old English term *heawan*, which means to beat or cut. Haggling is the process of negotiating the lowest price possible in a purchase transaction. The United States is one of the few countries where haggling is not a normal part of everyday shopping.

- **Learn to *haggle*.** The United States is the only country we know where people accept paying the full price on merchandise without negotiation. Teach yourself to always ask, "What is the best price you can give me on this?" Contrary to popular belief, this is not rude, and you will be surprised at how often merchandisers will give you a lower price.

- **Delay purchases of items you don't need.** Before you rush out to the store or pick up the telephone to buy that widget you just have to have, write it down, and think about it for a week. Then ask yourself whether you still want it as much. How many things do you have in your closet, storage room, or drawers that you used only a few times? If you adopt this practice, you'll find you will cut your spending by as much as 90 percent. This habit really cuts down on the amount of stuff you'll be selling in your next garage sale! Remember that the more stuff you have, the more responsibility you take on.

Don't confuse shopping with saving money. How often have you said, or heard someone say, "I saved a fortune at the close-out sale!" Just because it's a good price doesn't mean you're saving money. If you're buying something you don't need, any price is too much.

Treasure Tip

If possible, sell your car on your own instead of trading it in. You have a better chance of getting a higher price than a dealer will offer you on trade.

4. Consider Previously Owned Merchandise

The Posts often bought previously owned merchandise, especially if they could find good quality at lower prices. They spent a lot of time shopping for used items in the local want ads. They said they saved a lot of money over the years by focusing on used instead of new cars. They bought quality used cars from previous owners and eliminated the commission paid to the salesperson, along with the heavy depreciation incurred in the first two years.

Wealth Warning

Over a lifetime, most couples will spend more money on automobiles than any other single recurring purchase. We estimate that the typical couple will spend in excess of $1 million on auto purchases during their lifetime! People are concerned with driving the "right" car and they're often willing to overpay for this status symbol. However, cars depreciate in value as soon as you drive them off the dealer's lot. What you should do now: Commit to keeping your current auto until your loan is paid off. Then continue to "make payments" to a new car purchase account until you have enough money to buy your next car with cash. In the future, buy a car that is at least two years old but still under manufacturer's warranty. This will allow you to own a nice car, free of debt. Generally, the longer you own a car, the better off financially you will be.

5. Be a Great Steward

Another pearl of wisdom the Posts shared involved a sense of stewardship, where they took care of what they owned. They said that it is amazing how long things will last if you take good care of them. They bought great quality items and took great care of them. More than likely, the largest "machine" you have is your automobile. If you want it to last a long time and hold its resale value, you must conduct regular maintenance. The Posts had both of their automobiles serviced every 4,000 miles, which included an oil and filter change. They also waxed their cars every six months. These simple steps helped keep their cars running better and helped maintain the resale value.

Home maintenance is also important. Have your heating and air-conditioning system checked once a year to prolong the life of your equipment. Pay for a good pest control service now so you don't have to pay later for termite damage. Prevent exterior damage to your home by regularly cleaning out your gutters. Try to think about owning fewer things but taking excellent care of them.

6. Learn the Basics of Investing

The Posts also taught themselves a basic understanding of the stock and bond markets. They studied the basics, knew the benefit of owning stocks, and invested in stocks through no-load funds. They learned a great deal from the mistakes they made and understood that investing money in the stock market involves occasionally making mistakes. In spite of all that, they kept learning more each day and stayed the course.

If you feel uncomfortable with your investment knowledge, get proactive and do something about it now. There is no excuse for ignorance. Books and classes can teach you everything you need to know. Part 2 is a great start. Do yourself a favor and learn all you can now.

The best way to learn is to start investing. You'll want to learn because your money is at stake. The next best way to learn is to join an organization dedicated to educating investors. One of the best organizations we've found is the American Association of Individual Investors (www.aaii.com). Contact AAII and ask for an information packet. You might also read some books on stock investing. Here are some of our favorites:

Beating the Street, Peter Lynch, retired manager of Fidelity Magellan

One Up on Wall Street, Peter Lynch

Value Investing, Ben Graham (This may get a little technical, but Ben is the father of value investing.)

Bogle on Funds, John Bogle, past chairman of Vanguard Funds

That Reminds Us ...

When you purchase a bond or bond mutual fund, you are essentially buying IOUs of companies or the government. The total interest paid each year is your reward for loaning the money. Additional reward comes when interest rates fall and the price of the bond increases. The reverse is also true. If rates go up, the price of the bond will fall. A bond is simply a source of future cash flow that can be bought and sold at different prices until maturity. However, at the bond's maturity, the bondholder is paid only the face amount or maturity value of the bond along with the appropriate interest amount.

7. Do Your Homework

Finally, Mr. and Mrs. Post also did their homework. They took time to research their options before they made an investment, and they understood that quick decisions get you hurt in the market. Rumors get started and before you know it, a "hot tip" turns out to be a cold nightmare. They recognized and avoided the traps.

Don't forget to measure the results of your portfolio. Not measuring results is one of the most common mistakes individual investors make. They invest for years, never actually knowing their portfolio's true performance on a monthly or yearly basis. They might estimate it, but they rarely do it accurately, and they almost never compare it to the proper benchmark indexes.

Each year, you should reevaluate your progress toward your wealth goal. Do the calculations in Chapter 5. This will help you stay on track. Did you know that planes that fly on autopilot from the continental United States to Hawaii are off track almost 95 percent of the time? It's because of wind. The autopilot resets the plane's course every few minutes because the wind keeps knocking it off course. The plane makes it because the autopilot mechanism continues to repeatedly reset the compass bearing. Your journey toward wealth is similar. You'll get blown off course along the way. Don't forget to reset your compass bearing at least once a year.

Do You Have What It Takes to Be Wealthy?

What does it take to be wealthy? Is there a trick? If you want to improve your odds of achieving your desired level of wealth, you have to adopt the thought process of the self-made millionaires. Over the past several decades, we've had the opportunity to speak with hundreds of wealthy individuals. They are all different but they also share some common traits. The rest of this section presents the six most common traits. If you incorporate them into your life, you will have little difficulty getting to Wealth Stage 2.

Follow Your Passion

People who have achieved wealth based on their own hard work and wits are invariably dreamers and passionate about their life. When you focus on your dreams and passions, you live from your soul. Unfortunately, not many people do this. When you live from your soul, you become like a magnet, drawing everything you need into your life that will help you accomplish your goal. That might sound a little like hocus-pocus, but we speak from experience.

The great irony today in society is that most people are really afraid of following their dreams. If people would let themselves focus on what they're passionate about in life, they would not only live a happier life, but they would also be able to accomplish more. They would naturally be more competitive. And they would achieve greater accomplishments than they thought possible.

The world is so competitive now that markets around the world have opened up their doors to outside consumers. To compete in any business today, you have to work harder and be smarter than your competition. In the long run, the winners in any industry will be those companies and individuals who were passionate enough about their work to spend the time and effort it takes to produce outstanding products and services. Without this passion, a company or individual will be less likely to make the effort to meet a deadline or make certain they provide the highest quality product or service.

The happiest wealthy people we know have a passion for what they do, which seems to naturally create a certain level of tenacity and perseverance toward achieving their goals. They have a vision, and they are enthusiastic about life. Their enthusiasm is sincere, and it comes from deep inside. However, they don't necessarily have a passion for building wealth. Wealth, for them, is a result of their passion and effort for the work they do.

> **Treasure Tip**
>
> Great dancers are not great because of their technique; they are great because of their passion.
>
> —Martha Graham

When you love what you do, your chances of great achievement improve dramatically. If you're unsure about where your passion lies, the following questions will give you some ideas to consider. These questions could change your life for the better. It all depends on how honest you are with yourself when you answer each question. There are no right or wrong answers, so relax and enjoy yourself. Write down exactly what comes to mind. Do not judge any answer! Let your mind go and list anything that comes to mind, no matter how impossible it might seem:

◆ Your doctor calls and tells you that in exactly six months, you will die a peaceful death due to a weird, incurable virus. What would you do during this six-month period? Whom would you spend time with? What activities would you spend time doing? What would be important to you? (List at least 20 answers.)

♦ An unknown relative dies and leaves you $2,000,000. What would you do? Whom would you spend time with? What activities would you spend time doing? What would be important to you? Would you quit work? How would you spend your money? (List at least 20 answers.)

♦ What three great endeavors would you dare to attempt if you were guaranteed you could not fail?

♦ What do you want more of in your life? (List at least 20 answers.)

♦ What do you want less of in your life? (List at least 20 answers.)

The answers to these questions give you insight into your most important values in life. They illustrate what's really important to you and, in the case of the final question, what you want less of in your life. They should act as a guide in your search for what you really want in life. Use these answers not only to find your passion, but also use them as parameters against which you compare any major endeavor in life.

Wealth Warning

Remember that no matter what you do in life, you will always reap what you sow. In your journey toward wealth, make sure your work helps others or improves the world in some way. If not, your efforts will eventually backfire and reverse the wealth-building process.

If you really take the time to list 20 or more answers, you might find some things you enjoy doing that you haven't participated in for a long time. One of your answers could be something you're passionate about that you can use as a business idea. It might be another position within a company or your own company.

If you can't figure it out now, put the questions away and try this exercise again in a week. Be sure to change your surroundings next time. Sit in a comfortable spot with no interruptions. Try it a third time if necessary.

Be a Decision Maker

The wealthiest self-made millionaires we know are good decision makers. They don't procrastinate or live in denial. They take the time to identify all the issues, research the alternatives, and select the best answers. They don't waste too much time worrying about things they have little control over. They also look carefully at all the possible consequences of each decision. They list the pros and cons, take time to think about all the options, and finally ask themselves, "What is the worst thing that can happen?" If they can accept the worst possible outcome, they press forward. If not, they hold back. They understand zero-based thinking, which we cover in Chapter 12.

Develop Discipline

Discipline is simply sticking to a decision. If you make decisions based on your passions and reasoned research, the discipline should come naturally. The clients we have who built their wealth from the ground up have a certain discipline that helps them adhere to the simple habits necessary to build wealth. Climbing the social ladder is unimportant to them. They focus instead on what they're passionate about.

Discipline is simply a subconscious habit that is established by repetition. It's difficult to form a habit, but research suggests that after 21 days, it becomes part of your life. Here's an idea. For 21 days, take 15 minutes in the afternoon to plan tomorrow. This will give your brain time to think about what you have to do, which will help you get closer to your vision.

Be Patient

Wealthy people are patient and maintain a long-term outlook. They plan for the future and do what it takes to build wealth, and over time, they naturally know they will succeed. When they're faced with failure, they get right back on track again and go for it. They understand that wealth building is a journey, not a destination. It's a practice of patient habits that naturally produces riches.

Have Faith

Having faith may be the most powerful tool in this book. All great accomplishments require faith. We're talking about faith in yourself, faith in your dreams, faith in others, and spiritual faith. You must have faith in yourself and your abilities. The wealthy people we know approach life with an open mind. What they don't know or understand, they commit themselves to learn. Numerous books, classes, and counselors can help you develop more faith in yourself.

Treasure Tip

Along with faith in yourself, faith in others is almost as important. One of the most common characteristics among wealthy people is their belief in the inherent good in others. With few exceptions, all great accomplishments require the help of other people.

Most wealthy people we know also have a strong spiritual faith. Regardless of your beliefs or religion, it is difficult to imagine that we're not all connected in some way. All that you do in life affects the world in some little way. Like the ripples from a rain drop in a pool of water, what you do in life has some effect on the world. You matter, and your life is important. If everyone lived his or her life with this belief, the world would have much more faith to work with. Our hope is that this book, in some way, gives you faith and that you're able to make a greater difference in this world.

Be Willing to Sacrifice

Every great accomplishment involves a sacrifice. To achieve any great endeavor, you must first decide exactly what you want. Then you must be willing to make the sacrifices necessary. You can only focus on one thing at a time, and that means you have to sacrifice your focus on other endeavors. If you have several passions in life, you know how difficult it is to choose one passion to focus on. The bigger the endeavor, the bigger the sacrifices. Most people aren't willing to make the sacrifices. Don't be like most people!

The Least You Need to Know

- The basis of all the habits of wealthy people involves maximizing income, minimizing expenses, and making your savings work for you.

- If you want to achieve anything great in life, find the people who are already the best at what you want to do and imitate them.

- If you delay most major purchases by writing them down, filing them away, and not thinking about them for a month or more, you may save a lot of money and prevent a lot of mistakes.

- Buying used cars can save you a fortune in commission and depreciation expenses.

- To be really wealthy in life, you must have enough passion for what you do that you lose yourself in your work.

- Building wealth requires certain habits that are easy to implement and maintain.

Chapter 7

An Employee's Guide to Getting Rich

In This Chapter

- How to get the job you've always wanted
- How to design a job proposal that really works
- Why you need a role model
- How to design the automatic savings plan as an employee

Passion produces enthusiasm, which is a powerful tool. It's all about living your life with a purpose—doing what you enjoy doing. If you're enthusiastic about what you do, you have a better chance of being the best at it and people will want to hire you. Every employer in your field will want to have you around, and they might be willing to pay you a lot of money to get you on their team. Enthusiasm is contagious, and employers look for it. They know that it's the one thing they can't teach. If they can find sincere enthusiasm, they can teach everything else.

Some people are naturally enthusiastic, and that's great. However, if you put a naturally enthusiastic person in a job he or she hates, you'll kill the enthusiasm. Therefore, to maintain your enthusiasm and get paid what

CAUTION

Wealth Warning

Wealth is never worth sacrificing your happiness, family, or integrity.

you're worth, you must love your work. It might take some time to figure it out, but to maximize your salary, you have to be very good at what you do. As we said in Chapter 6, to be good—we mean *really* good—at what you do, you have to be passionate about it. To be passionate, you have to love what you're doing.

Design Your Own Dream Job

How many people do you know who are enthusiastic about their work? Many people live their lives in frustration and are unhappy working at jobs they despise and for people they don't respect. They stay in this self-imposed prison, locked in by their own fear of change, their inflexible standard of living, or procrastination. Often it takes something dramatic or life threatening to break them out. What they don't realize is that this situation eats away at their self-confidence and self-worth. Don't let this happen to you.

Five Questions Revisited

If you don't know what you like to do, or if you lack the vision or ability to see yourself advancing from your current position, don't get discouraged. That's a common problem that you can solve, and here's how to solve it. Return to the five questions in the Chapter 6 section titled "Follow Your Passion." Follow the instructions and list your answers. If you've already done this, try it again if you need to. Your answers will give you insight into your values and passions. Find something you can focus on that will make you money. It doesn't have to involve owning your own company.

If you think you can't make money doing what you love, you might be right. If nothing else, you could write a book about it. As we said, if you're passionate enough about your work, you will be the best at it and people will want to be a part of your world. Whatever your chosen career, determine that you are going to be the very best.

We know several professional artists. They took the hobby they were the most passionate about and made it into a business. One of them travels the world and sells his paintings to people in many different countries. One of his paintings recently sold in an auction for more than $5,000. His wife manages his business affairs and schedules his appearances. No matter what your passion is, find a way to make money doing it.

What Are You Doing Now?

Take a look at what you're doing now, and ask yourself these questions:

- Do you find yourself stressed out on Sunday night before work on Monday?

- Do you have a vision of what you want in life?

- Is your current job part of that vision? Do you feel as if you're wasting time in your current position?

- Do you see yourself working at your present job for a long time?

- Does your employer treat you with respect?

- Is your job a stepping-stone for what you really want to do?

- Do you have a plan for the next step?

Your answers should tell you whether you're in the right job now. If you're not, why waste your time, your life, or the money you could be making? Develop a plan and move on.

 Treasure Tip

One of the most common characteristics of happy, wealthy people concerns their attitudes every Sunday night before work. Most of them enjoy their work so much that they don't know the difference between a weekday or weekend night.

Design the Perfect Day

Next, find an hour of peace and quiet where you can think clearly. Take a piece of paper and write a vision of you at work doing what you love to do. Title it "The Perfect Day at Work." Make sure you have no interruptions, and let your imagination run. Don't worry about grammar, spelling, or order. Just write whatever comes to your mind. Get as specific as you can. Imagine yourself in your dream job doing exactly what you love to do. Where are you? Describe your surroundings, the people you work with, your boss, and the company. Fill at least one page, if not several.

After you complete this exercise, take some more time to brainstorm how you can make this dream a reality. Believe it or not, you can make your perfect day a reality if you believe it's possible. Your disbelief may be the only obstacle between you and your dream day. Don't accept defeat by saying, "This is only a dream. I can't really do this." That's what most people would say, and it's a self-imposed limiting thought. If you can think it and believe in it, it's possible. But if you don't believe in your vision, you'll never get there. Brainstorm for a minute on how you can make this dream a reality. Remember the words of Vincent van Gogh, who said, "If you hear a voice within you saying 'You are not a painter,' then by all means paint … and that voice will be silenced." After you finish brainstorming, design a plan to get there. If the dream is really worthwhile, it may take some time to accomplish it. If it's what you really want, you won't mind the effort it takes to get there.

Don't believe this technique works? Stewart Welch, one of the co-authors of this book, can vouch for it. In 1983, he had experienced 10 years of success in the life insurance business but he intuitively knew it was time for a change. He took a day off and went through the exercise described previously and committed to not quit until he had designed not only the perfect day, but the perfect career. What he envisioned that day was a fee-only financial advisory practice with a national reputation. It took him three years to execute his action plan, but in January 1987 he launched his fee-only practice and has never regretted a minute of the effort.

What Are Your Options?

Now that you have a better idea of what's important to you, think about all your options. They are unlimited. Here are the four basic directions you can take:

- Stay with your present employer and design a job proposal to move into the position you want or a new position that might not even exist.

- Look into other companies or employers within your industry who might have more appreciation for your work and give you more opportunity. Find the best firm in the industry and submit a job proposal, which is outlined later in this chapter.

- Study other fields of interest. Find the best companies or employers in that industry and submit a job proposal.

- Start your own company. This can be part-time or full-time. We discuss this in Part 3.

Each option involves some homework on your part. For now, focus on role models and job proposals.

You Need a Role Model

Spend some time identifying the people who do what you want to do. Then find the best in the business. Ask everyone you know in that field, "Who's the best at this?" Find at least three people who are successful at what you want to do. If you can, find out in advance what makes them different or special. Call these people, or write them a letter. First, compliment them by saying, "I've been told that you are one of the best in the country at what you do." Compliment them further by mentioning what you think makes them so special and unique. They will be impressed with what you know.

Second, tell them that you're enthusiastic about learning more about their industry and business. Third, ask them if you can talk with them about their success for a few minutes. Just say, "I'd like to hear your story. Would you have a minute to meet with me now or next week (over the phone or in person) for a few minutes?" If you're sincere with your compliments and in asking them about their story, most of them will meet with you. If you have to travel to meet them, go for it. Do what it takes. When you do meet with them, ask them specific questions and let them talk (don't forget to take notes!). Here are some questions to choose from:

Treasure Tip

We can't emphasize enough the power of having a role model in your life. A good role model can change your life and give you hope for your passion. Most successful people have an innate desire to help others and are generous with their time. Identify your role model and ask them for help.

- Tell me the story of your company.
- What are the five most important things that have contributed to your success?
- What do you love about your work?
- What do you dislike about your work?
- What are your biggest concerns each day?
- What do you focus most of your time on?
- Describe a typical day.
- If you had to do it all over again, what path would you take?
- Where would you start?
- Would you share with me your 5- or 10-year vision?

Take some time and review their answers. Did you find what you expected? Are you still as excited as you were? After the appointment, be sure to write them a thank-you note. Mention in the thank-you note the one thing that excited you the most. Call their secretary to find something they really like and have it delivered from a store in the area. They will appreciate your attention to detail and welcome another contact from you, which could prove to be valuable later.

The Job Proposal

If you've designed your dream job, why not put it into the form of a proposal? This simple tool is one of the most powerful job search tools you'll ever find. It's a simple idea that can get you the job you want. The first step in building the job proposal is to know what you really want to do. The job for which you're making the proposal must be your dream job or a stepping stone toward your dream job. Otherwise, you will not have the enthusiasm you need to get the job.

Second, you must find a company that can offer you the opportunity you're looking for. Give your current employer a chance if possible. If your present employer is out of the question, then look elsewhere. There are several ways to find company candidates for your proposal. First, checking the Yellow Pages is the easiest way because it categorizes listings by industry and service. Second, you should find a corporate directory, which is normally produced by the local Chamber of Commerce. Third, try the Internet.

Wealth Warning

The job proposal is a unique and powerful tool. If you use this just to get a job, with no attention to your values or interests, you may get a job you eventually dislike. Before using this technique, make sure you have an idea about what you enjoy doing.

You must make certain that your vision matches the vision of the company or the duties of the position you want. To ensure this, interview the companies you've selected. Just ask whether you can talk to someone about his company. If the company is small, ask whether you can see the owner. If the company is larger, ask to see the person in charge of hiring. If all else fails, ask to speak to someone in sales. Salespeople like to talk and generally know a lot about their company.

Fourth, conduct interviews with the companies you've selected. Study everything you can, and make sure this is where you want to be. Use the same questions from the "Role Model" section to find out all you can about the company. Don't ask them whether they need anyone! They might not even know they need anyone yet. It's your job later to convince them they do. Your goal here is gathering information. You want to know all about the company so you can decide whether this is where you want to work.

Upon graduating, Hugh Smith spent nine years with a "Big Eight" accounting firm before joining a private company and spending six years as their Chief Financial Officer. He went through an exercise similar to the one described previously and decided that what he wanted to do in life was be a personal financial advisor. Further, he knew he wanted to work for a fee-only firm and then decided that he specifically wanted to work for co-author Stewart Welch's company. Hugh recalls riding past The Welch Group offices and telling his wife that this was the company he was going to work for.

Hugh called the Welch Group in June of 2001 asking what he would need to do to get hired by the firm. Stewart Welch was a bit taken back by Hugh's directness but was also impressed. Even though Hugh was a CPA, Stewart told him he would not consider hiring him unless he had his Certified Financial Planner™ certification. Stewart assumed that would be the last he heard of Hugh. But about two months later Hugh called to say he had taken the exam. Stewart's surprised response was, "Did you pass?" He said he had not heard yet. Stewart told Hugh to call him back when he heard, knowing that the pass rate was barely above 50 percent and very few people passed on the first try. In January 2002, Stewart received an excited call from Hugh to say he had passed the exam. The Welch Group hired him in February of 2002, and in January of 2005, he became a partner in the firm. Hugh is a perfect example of someone creating a clear vision of what he wants, mapping out a game plan to achieve it, and then executing that game plan.

Finally, design the employment (job) proposal. In this proposal, describe the position you want on paper and be as specific as you can. What are you willing to do? What are you willing to be responsible for? What are you willing to accept in salary and benefits? Focus on the information you found in the interview. Match your strengths with their weaknesses. Match your talent with their needs.

The following proposal was used by an electrical engineer who wanted to work for a small software company. He interviewed for the job first and was told they were going to hire someone else. He was discouraged but still wanted the job. We wrote a job proposal that he submitted later that week. A week later, he got the job.

There are no rules here, and your proposal may be completely different from his, but this example might help you design yours.

> **Treasure Tip**
>
> If the company shows no interest in your job proposal, go to the company's competitor and offer the same proposal. Don't waste your efforts on someone who doesn't appreciate your enthusiasm and talent.

The proposal should be done with a word processing program on a computer and printed on high-quality paper. It doesn't have to be fancy; it just has to look good, including using correct grammar and spelling. Be sure to present this proposal in person and go over it if you can. Bring several copies in case you must present it to several people. If you cannot arrange a face-to-face meeting, send it via registered mail. Then call within two days of receipt. Don't ask what your contact thinks of your proposal. Instead say, "I'd like to stop by next week on Wednesday to discuss the proposal. Would 10 in the morning be good, or would 2 in the afternoon be better for you?"

Employment Proposal for XYZ Company

I. Why I want to work for XYZ Company

    A. I want to work for a small, growing company.

    B. More opportunity for growth and experience.

    C. Opportunity to work in a team-oriented atmosphere.

    D. I admire the management's philosophy and vision.

II. What I'm able to offer XYZ Company

    A. Sales assistance in the marketing department as new clients are acquired.

    B. Project assistance.

    C. Hardware design, development, and installation.

    D. Programming assistance in producing the best software available.

    E. Troubleshooting and maintaining the highest-quality service in the industry.

III. What I expect to be paid initially

    A. Hourly pay of $X per hour.

    B. $X per hour after 40 hours in a one-week period.

IV. Available working hours

    A. Regular working hours (8 A.M. to 5 P.M.).

    B. After hours.

    C. Weekends.

    D. Moment's notice.

V. Future compensation expected

    A. To be negotiated in two months.

    B. Subject to the value you think I can add to your business. (*You could be more specific here if you want.*)

    C. Bonuses based on a percentage of net profits.

    D. Full benefits including health insurance and retirement plan.

VI. Trial period

    A. Two months.

    B. If things do not work out, I will walk away with no questions asked.

VII. Vision for the future: My goal is to be the chief engineer for XYZ Company and, if possible, stockholder/partner in the firm. I would like to develop new product services that complement existing ones and participate in strategic planning and development for XYZ.

Proposal conclusion: The best thing that can happen is that you get a good engineer with education and experience who adds more value to your company than you pay him. The worst thing that can happen is that you get a good electrical engineer at an annualized salary of $XX,000 ($X per hour) for two months.

Getting More Life out of Your Job

When searching for a job, you need to understand a few key concepts. First, your salary is negotiable (unless you work for the government). Second, if you're the best at what you do, there is always another company willing to pay you what you're worth. Therefore, you should always make it a habit to do some research into the salary range of your current job. What are other people in your field getting paid? How do these salaries compare to yours? Be sure to take into account the living expenses of the cities where these people live. For example, everything else being equal, someone in New York City will naturally be paid a higher salary than someone in Little Rock, Arkansas.

When speaking with people about their hierarchy of financial concerns, job security is always near the top of the list. This brings us to the concept of being a "10" employee. All employers or supervisors either consciously or subconsciously rate employees on a scale of 1 to 10, with 10 being a top employee.

The best way to create job security for yourself is to be a 10 employee. How do you do this? It starts with attitude and ends with job performance. There's a saying in the business world that "employers hire for skills and fire for attitude"—bad attitude, that is. There is also a saying that "success on the job is 85 percent attitude and 15 percent skills." Both of these sayings are true. So how do you become a 10? You should start with an honest self-appraisal. Complete the following personal assessment. Be sure to answer the questions honestly. One way to do this is to pretend you are your supervisor filling out the form. How would he or she rate you in each area? After you're finished, you should have a pretty good idea of where you are now and what you need to do to improve.

Personal Assessment

Name: _____   Date: _____

Scoring:

1–4	Unacceptable—Immediate Improvement Required
5–6	Fair—Improvement Needed
7–8	Good—Exceed Expectations in Some Areas
9–10	Excellent—Consistent Exceptional Performance

ATTITUDE. The Standard: I have a perfect attitude every day.

Score: _____ Comments: _____

Action to be taken: _____

APTITUDE. The Standard: I have the skills to consistently perform my job with excellence.

Score: _____ Comments: _____

Action to be taken: _____

ORGANIZATION. The Standard: I have excellent organizational skills.

Score: _____ Comments: _____

Action to be taken: _____

INITIATIVE. The Standard: I consistently and proactively find ways to improve my job performance and the performance of my company.

Score: _____ Comments: _____

Action to be taken: _____

TEAM PLAYER. The Standard: I work well with fellow employees and focus on *company* goals rather than my own personal agenda.

Score: _____ Comments: _____

Action to be taken: _____

DO WHATEVER IT TAKES. The Standard: I do whatever it takes to get the job done right, on time, and accurately.

Score: _____ Comments: _____

Action to be taken: _____

INTERACTION WITH CUSTOMERS, FELLOW EMPLOYEES, AND VENDORS. The Standard: I present a professional, friendly, and competent image.

Score: _____ Comments: _____

Action to be taken: _____

MY STRENGTHS: _____

MY AREAS OF IMPROVEMENT: _____

GENERAL COMMENTS: What can my company do to improve its
effectiveness?

_____

_____

_____

MY MAJOR OBJECTIVE(S) FOR QUARTER 200X: Here are three specific
things I can do to advance the company.

_____

_____

_____

After you've done your self-assessment, look around and see if you can identify someone who is excelling in your job. It may be someone in your company or at another
company. Although it's best if they have similar duties, it's not absolutely necessary.
Mainly what you're looking for is someone who is doing extremely well and who is
respected by others for the job they are doing. When you identify them, ask them to
meet with you and share their secrets of success. Again, you'll find that most people
want to help others who are trying to improve themselves.

One hint we can give you: begin thinking like an owner. You see, most employees
think like, well, employees. There is an "us versus them" mentality that is absolutely
counterproductive to becoming a 10. How do you adopt an owner mentality? Simply
take a step back in your thought- and decision-making process and ask the question, "If
this were my company, what would I do?" You will be surprised at how this will change
your perspective. Contrary to popular opinion, most employers do not view their employees as their personal slaves to be used and abused as they please. Great employers
want to create a team of talented people focused on achieving common goals.

After you've completed your self-assessment and have identified one or more people
who are excelling in their positions, and have received their insights, you're ready for
the hard part. Meet with your immediate supervisor and ask him or her to complete

the same assessment you have completed on yourself. This process should be approached with your supervisor as an informal discussion, because some supervisors may feel threatened or concerned about violating company policy if you approach it as a formal review.

Be prepared for an honest response, and if you receive scores that you think are lower than you deserve, accept them with humble appreciation. Remember, your supervisor's perception is his or her reality. The worst thing you could do is to try to defend yourself. Now that your supervisor has provided specific recommendations, it's your turn to make the suggested changes. You should agree to review your progress at an appropriate future date, which should be no longer than three to six months.

Four Ways to Automatically Build Wealth While Working for Others

Can you get to Wealth Stage 3 or 4 without starting your own company? Absolutely! We've met hundreds of people who've done it. If you want to build serious wealth, whether you work for yourself or someone else, the key is to live well within your means so you can save money systematically each month. At each pay period, a certain percentage of your income must go to your investment account, retirement plan, and savings account. It's even better if this takes place automatically at the time you get your paycheck.

Treasure Tip

Many of our clients have an investment net worth that exceeds $2 million. How did they do it? Did they sell a business? Did they inherit money? In some cases, yes. Many others accomplished this by systematically investing through their company retirement program.

If you're not doing this now, or if you haven't made the decision to do this, then stop right now and make the decision. Read this out loud: "I am a saver and a good steward of my money and financial future. I save a significant percentage of my income each month, which I invest for my future." If you don't make this a habit now, you may never reach Wealth Stage 3 or 4. It's only a decision; the rest is easy if you set it up to happen automatically.

Maximize Your Contributions to Your Retirement Plan

Most companies today offer a 401(k) or similar type of contributory retirement plan. You can elect to defer a percentage of your paycheck, and your employer often provides a matching contribution. You are then given a number of mutual fund investment options to choose from. Your contributions are not subject to income taxes, and the interest, dividends, and capital gains grow tax-deferred until you begin withdrawing your money during retirement. The combined effect of compound growth and tax deferral are powerful tools to help you achieve your target portfolio goal (TPG).

Treasure Tip

Visit with your human relations department or employer and maximize your 401(k) contributions. You not only get a tax deduction for the deposit, but you also get the benefit of tax-deferred growth.

It's important to note that if you take money out of any retirement plan before you reach age 59$\frac{1}{2}$, the government will charge you an early withdrawal penalty of 10 percent. You must also report your withdrawals as ordinary income on your tax return for the year in which the transaction occurred. The combination of the penalty and income taxes makes this an extraordinarily expensive proposition and should be avoided. All employer retirement plans allow you to roll over your account tax-free into an IRA after you retire or terminate your employment. This allows your money to continue growing tax-deferred until you're ready to begin withdrawals.

Investigate Additional Retirement Plans

In addition to employer-sponsored retirement plans, you may be eligible to contribute to a Traditional IRA account or a Roth IRA account. The Traditional IRA is similar to the 401(k) in that contributions are tax-deductible, earnings grow tax-deferred, withdrawals are taxable, and you must take required minimum distributions beginning at age 70$\frac{1}{2}$.

With a Roth IRA, you do not receive an income tax deduction for your contributions, but your money grows tax-deferred until retirement. Withdrawals after age 59$\frac{1}{2}$ are never subject to income taxes and there are no required minimum distributions. With either a Traditional IRA or a Roth IRA, you may contribute 100 percent of your earned income up to a maximum of $4,000 per year. If you're over age 50, you're allowed an additional "catch-up"

Treasure Tip

If you want to build wealth, you must consider investing in something that can produce a double-digit return. The most common investment with this potential is stock in a fast-growing company. There is risk, but your exposure can be reduced by spreading your investment among many different companies.

contribution of $1,000. Not everyone is eligible to contribute to a Traditional or Roth IRA. Check with your financial advisor to see if you qualify.

Start a Personal Investment Account

Your best first choice for investing is a qualified retirement plan such as your employer's 401(k), a Traditional IRA, or a Roth IRA. After you've done all you can do with retirement plans, it's time to start investing in your personal investment account.

You need a place to put that money you save. Where should it be invested? If you work for someone else and you want to get to Wealth Stage 3 or 4, your best option is to invest in stocks or stock mutual funds (also known as equities). This includes the money in your retirement plans and personal investment accounts. It may also include privately held stock of your own company or your employer's company. The stock market is one of the most powerful tools you can use to grow your investment net worth and beat inflation. Don't overlook ownership of your employer's stock as an investment alternative. Many fortunes have been built with stocks, both private and publicly traded.

In Chapter 9, we cover more on the benefits of owning equities of publicly traded companies. For now, take a look at the company you currently work for. Would you ever want to be a shareholder?

Buying Your Company's Stock

First, before you even consider owning your own company's stock, look back at the answers to the questions in the earlier section titled "What Are You Doing Now?" If you answered favorably and you plan on staying with this company for a long time, then buying their stock might be a good idea. You also need to consider your employer's earnings growth potential. Is your company making money? If the company's earnings aren't growing, you may want to avoid their stock.

Second, you have to consider the size of the company and the availability of the stock itself. If the company is small and owned by a few people (that is, if it's owned privately rather than traded on a stock exchange), then it may be difficult, if not impossible, to become a shareholder. You might have to convince the owners to let you buy shares or take shares instead of part of your salary or bonus. Your employer might say "no," but it won't hurt to ask. Many small, privately owned companies will use stock as a way to attract and retain key employees.

It's much easier to own your company's stock if you work for a company that has stock publicly traded on an exchange. Many publicly traded companies offer employees a stock purchase plan whereby the employees can systematically buy shares either at a discount or with little or no commission.

Whether your company is small or large, or has closely held or publicly traded stock, its stock might be available through an employee stock ownership plan or ESOP. The ESOP plan issues shares to its employees each month or year based on their salary or the profits of the company. ESOPs can also be part of a retirement plan, which means the gains and dividends can be tax-deferred until retirement. It's a great idea if you want to own your company's stock. If not, don't participate. One of the most successful ESOP plans ever was Wal-Mart's employee stock-purchasing plan. This plan made hundreds of their employees millionaires who might otherwise have retired with a small pension and Social Security check.

The Least You Need to Know

◆ Design your own job using your values, goals, and perfect day description.

◆ You can get your dream job if you have enough enthusiasm and a good enough job proposal.

◆ One single role model could save you years of experience, shorten your learning curve, and make your life much easier.

◆ Set up an automatic savings plan that requires little to no effort to maintain using a 401(k), IRA, and other retirement plans before investing in a personal investment account.

Part 2

Becoming an Investor— Wealth Stages 3 and 4

Your focus in Stages 1 and 2 was saving money. We now want to shift your focus to the twin issues of rate of return and risk management. In Wealth Stage 3, your portfolio is growing fast enough to cover your desired lifestyle and inflation. According to our research, only about 5 percent of the population ever achieves this stage of wealth by retirement age. We'll show you how. With some extra effort and some creative risk-taking, we'll also show you how to achieve Wealth Stage 4—that place where your cash flow significantly exceeds your lifestyle needs.

Chapter **8**

Gold Nuggets and Fool's Gold

In This Chapter

- ◆ What the basic concepts of investing are
- ◆ What brokers don't want you to know
- ◆ What is a Killer B fund?
- ◆ What the killers of wealth are
- ◆ When initial public offerings are bad
- ◆ What to do with a hot tip or rumor
- ◆ Why penny stocks, options, and futures ought to be avoided

This chapter could have been titled "It's what you don't know that will kill you." There are so many ways to make mistakes—even with the right investments! First we'll focus on some basic concepts of successful investing, then we'll point out a number of investments you should avoid.

It's vital to financial success that you begin your journey with an understanding of the basics of investing. First, there is so much information about investing that many people simply become overwhelmed. Making matters worse, much of this information is simply bad advice. By understanding a few basic concepts found in this chapter, you can establish guiding principles to use in your decision-making process.

Fixed Income vs. Equities

There are only two broad choices available for investing your money. You can buy fixed-income investments, or you can buy equity investments. With all fixed-income investments, you're a "lender," loaning your money, typically, to a financial institution. In return, the financial institution promises to pay you interest and typically promises to return your principal at a specific future date. Examples of fixed-income investments include money market accounts, savings accounts, certificates of deposit (CDs), bonds or bond mutual funds, and fixed annuities. For example, if you invest $10,000 in a 5-year CD, the bank agrees to pay you a stated interest rate, say 4 percent, and promises to return your principal at the end of 60 months. If you want your money sooner than the agreed upon 60 months, you'll typically have to pay a penalty.

Bond mutual funds are a bit different in that there's no fixed interest rate and no specific maturity date. This is because the bond fund manager is perpetually buying and selling bonds in the portfolio. Just the same, you're a lender, and as such your return possibilities will be limited.

If you invest in equities, you take an ownership position, and your return possibilities become unlimited. Examples of equity investments include stocks, real estate, and owning your own business. The potential for extraordinary returns is possible with equities. For example, if you'd invested $1,000 in Microsoft when it first went public in 1986, your shares today would be worth more than $350,000 (a 35,000 percent increase!). If your dream is to become rich, one of your best opportunities is through equity investments. Of course, along with these unlimited return possibilities go the added risks of owning equities. There is no guarantee of a return, and you may, in fact, lose part or all of your investment. We'll discuss how to control the risks of investing in equities in Chapters 9 and 10.

Priority Use of Money

Once you have money available that you plan to invest, it is important to understand how to prioritize your investment choices. Some choices will be better than others, and you want to make certain you make the best decision possible so that your money is invested in the most effective way. When discussing the priority use of money, the focus is on investment environments. The investment environment relates to whether you're investing in a retirement account, a tax-deferred account such as an annuity, or a personal investment account. If one environment offered far superior growth than another, you would want to invest your money in the best one, right? Well, retirement accounts offer superior wealth accumulation opportunities under most circumstances. This is because you receive an immediate income tax deduction for your contributions, and the taxes on interest, dividends, and gains are postponed until you begin drawing your money out at retirement. The following table illustrates the magnifying power of retirement plan investing over personal investing.

The table compares the benefits of investing $1,000 per month on a pre-tax basis in a retirement plan versus paying the income tax on $1,000 per month at a 28 percent marginal tax bracket and investing personally.

The Power of Retirement Plan Investing

Retirement	Personal
$1,000 per month	$720 per month
× 25 years	× 25 years
@12%	@10.5%
$1,897,635	$1,049,844

Note: retirement plan distributions will be subject to ordinary income taxes. (Federal maximum is 35% as of 2006.) Distributions from the personal investment program will likely be primarily subject to capital gains taxes. (Federal maximum is 15%.) If held until death, the personal account would receive a "stepped-up" cost basis and income taxes would be avoided. If the retirement plan were held until death, a beneficiary (under certain circumstances) could continue to defer a large portion of the gain.

This comparison suggests that you should exhaust all sources of retirement plan investments before investing any money in personal investments. In particular, if you're an employee, you should contribute enough to your company 401(k) plan to capture your employer's matching contribution.

The priority use of money specifically refers to investments in traditional securities such as stocks and bonds. If your preferred wealth-building strategy will be investing in real estate or your own business, then they might be considered an exception to this rule because of the power of leverage that they offer.

Investing for Capital Gains vs. Cash Flow

We have already discussed the importance of using equities as your primary wealth accumulation strategy, and we will reinforce this concept throughout this book. As you invest in equities, you should be clear about your primary objective. Are you investing primarily for capital appreciation, or are you investing primarily for cash flow? Although these are not mutually exclusive strategies, it's important that you know what your primary objective is. Let's look at a couple of examples.

We have one client who owns a number of real estate properties that he leases to a national retail chain on a triple net lease basis (the tenant pays all expenses including maintenance, insurance, and property taxes). This arrangement produces a steady, yet modest, cash flow for the owner. His primary goal is the cash flow rather than the appreciation of the property. In another case, a client purchased a pre-construction condo on the coast in hopes of selling the condo for a profit before the project is completed (called *flipping*). His goal is capital appreciation.

People often purchase apartment buildings for their cash flow, whereas raw land is typically purchased for capital gains potential. Either strategy can make you wealthy, but it's important to know which strategy you're operating under.

The Power of Leverage

In your quest for personal wealth, there are a number of tried-and-true paths you can take. Some you will find are more productive than others; some require you to accept more risk; and some will require that you do a lot of work whereas other strategies will require minimal effort on your part. What do all of these paths have in common? They each make use of leverage to some degree. Leverage is the key to accelerating your accumulation of wealth. Leverage, however, comes in various degrees, some much more powerful than others.

Level I Leverage: Stocks

Investing in stocks is your lowest level of leverage. Here you're leveraging your money by taking an ownership position in a company. The leverage comes from "piggy-backing" on company managers whose own interest is in seeing the value of the company grow. Stocks offer you a much higher potential return than typically available if you "lend" your money to a financial institution or corporation by investing in fixed-income securities. The downside is that you have no say over management decisions and the managers' own agenda may be different from yours.

Level II Leverage: Retirement Plans

As already noted, retirement plans offer greater growth potential than personal investment accounts. The leverage factor here is based on U.S. tax laws. Specifically, the tax deduction allows you to invest more money now and keep more of your money during the growth phase of your accumulation program. For example, let's assume that in January, you receive a $4,000 bonus that you plan to invest. If you invest the money in a non-tax-deferred account, you will have $2,800 to invest after taxes (assuming a 30 percent tax bracket); however, if you invest the bonus in your retirement account (IRA or 401[k]) the entire $4,000 is available to invest. In this example, you'll leverage your wealth accumulation program by 30 percent if you choose the retirement plan.

Level III Leverage: Real Estate

Buying real estate offers two different types of leverage: First, you're able to borrow money to make your purchase. Second, in many circumstances your cash flow is partially or fully sheltered from taxes. Suppose you purchase a rental property for $100,000 by putting down $20,000 and borrowing $80,000 from your bank (see Chapter 11 for dealing with bankers). If the property appreciates and later is worth $120,000 (a 20 percent increase), your return was 100 percent! Your original investment of $20,000 is now worth $40,000. Much of your rental income can be sheltered by depreciation and, when you sell your property, much of your profit will likely be taxed at favorable long-term capital gains tax rates (15 percent maximum for federal taxes). You might even be able to avoid all taxes on your gain through a like-kind exchange. As you might imagine, investing in real estate requires both hard work and expertise. The subject of investing in real estate will be covered thoroughly in Chapter 18.

Level IV Leverage: Own Your Own Business

Many of the self-made millionaires we know used business ownership as their primary path to riches. Owning your own business offers perhaps the highest level of leverage because you're able to take advantage of the greatest lever of all: other people. It's simply amazing what can be accomplished when a group of bright and talented people focuses on a common purpose. If you choose this path, you will face by far your greatest challenges and risks. Most start-up businesses fail, and if you want to avoid becoming yet another statistic, it requires extraordinary planning, time, and developed talent on your part. If you succeed, however, there is nothing in your financial life that will be more rewarding. Not only will you benefit from your success, but so will your employees, their families, and the customers you serve.

It's certainly possible to become rich without the use of leverage, but using one or a combination of these strategies will enable you to accelerate the accomplishment of your financial goals. As you start your journey, we can save you some time by outlining a number of investments you should avoid.

What You Should Avoid in Your Portfolio

The balance of this chapter outlines several investment tools that are mediocre at best. Avoiding them can save you money and frustration later in the life of your portfolio and, at the same time, improve your chances of making suitable, appropriate investment decisions. Don't be surprised if someone disagrees with the points we make here. Do your own homework and make your own decisions. That "someone" is most likely a person who makes his or her living selling the product that we're recommending you avoid!

This commentary is not designed to discredit these salespeople but rather to give you another point of view. If you're going to make investment decisions, you need to understand the pros and cons of every decision.

Proprietary Investment Products

Proprietary investment products are "packaged" securities that are sold by brokerage firms, usually in the form of unit investment trusts, limited partnerships, and mutual funds. They are underwritten or managed by the brokerage firm and are, in turn, then sold by their sales force. The problem arises out of the inherent conflicts of interest. Conflicts of interest often arise at banks, brokerage firms, and insurance companies.

We recently reviewed the portfolio of a prospective client whose money was invested with a local bank. Most of the mutual funds were the bank's own mutual funds. Upon analysis, with the exception of one fund, all performed in the bottom half of their peer group for 1-, 3-, and 5-year time periods. When challenged, the salesperson's response was to offer better-performing nonproprietary funds. With their proprietary mutual funds, the bank, along with the salesperson, was receiving a commission for selling the mutual fund as well as a portion of the fund's ongoing management fee. With the nonproprietary fund, they received only the commission. And the conflicts don't necessarily end there.

Sometimes the fund managers agree to execute their trades through a particular clearinghouse in which the bank or brokerage firm shares in the commission revenue. In other cases, the mutual fund manager might be purchasing securities directly from the brokerage firm where the brokerage firm "marks up" the securities and therefore benefits from a higher than normal spread. Your best defense is always to ask if the product being offered to you is a proprietary product and ask for a written disclosure of all fees and conflicts of interest.

Load Mutual Funds

A mutual fund is an investment company that raises money by offering shares of the company to investors. The money is then invested into a diversified portfolio of securities for the benefit of the shareholder. You can purchase shares directly from the mutual fund or through brokerage firms. The money from the purchase or redemption goes directly in or out of the portfolio. If a *full-service brokerage firm* offers a mutual fund to its clients, a load or commission is involved. It may be hard to find without a *prospectus* (the fund's disclosure document), but it's there. This commission, or load, pays the salesperson and brokerage firm offering the fund. You can always find the commission charges of a fund in the first few pages of the prospectus. Mutual funds can be categorized according to the commission they charge to purchase or own the fund:

> **Words of the Wealthy**
>
> A **full-service brokerage firm** offers its clients securities as well as advice. The firm is compensated by commissions that are paid at the time transactions are made. A discount brokerage firm offers the same selection of securities, but because they don't offer advice, their commissions are usually substantially lower than the full-service firm's rates.

> **Words of the Wealthy**
>
> All mutual funds have a **prospectus,** which is the fund's disclosure document. This multi-page document explains in great detail all the aspects of the mutual fund, such as fees, commission charges, fund manager restrictions, and the objective of the fund. Newly issued stocks and bonds also have prospectuses.

♦ Heavily loaded mutual funds—more than 6 percent commission

♦ Fully loaded funds—4 to 6 percent commission

♦ Low-load funds—2 to 4 percent commission

♦ No-load funds—0 percent commission

All mutual funds—both load and no-load—have a management fee that is charged by the company that runs the fund. However, not all funds have commission charges. Legally, a mutual fund can charge up to 8.5 percent in commissions at the date of purchase. If you paid an 8.5 percent commission on a $1,000 mutual fund purchase, the end result would be an investment worth $915 ($1,000 × .085 = $85). To break even with your original investment, you will first have to make a 9.29 percent return. We can't think of any investment worth that much commission. In researching this topic, we found a U.S. stock fund offered by a well-known brokerage firm whose front-end commission was 8.5 percent plus an annual expense ratio of 1.27 percent. Make sure you don't buy a fund like this.

Killer B Funds

The most misunderstood concept in the mutual fund industry is what we call "Killer B" funds. The problem with these funds is that the load or commission is almost invisible, which is not unusual in the investment world.

Often, the load or commission is hidden from the investor, and unless you carefully read the prospectus and understand it, you may never know how much you're really paying to own the fund each year. Killer B's come in two forms. The first is what is known as a 12(b)1 fee, which is a fee paid to the brokerage firm (and often the sales-person as well) for the purpose of "marketing expenses, distribution expenses, or sales expenses." You want to be certain that if you're paying a 12(b)1 fee on the mutual fund you're purchasing, it does not exceed 0.25 percent. Avoid funds that charge a higher amount. No-load funds may also charge a 12(b)1 fee, but it cannot exceed 0.25 percent. We don't like 12(b)1 fees, but if you're going to buy a fund that has them, make sure they don't exceed 0.25 percent.

CAUTION

Wealth Warning

Many fund managers have closed their funds to new investors yet still charge the 12(b)1 fees. Why does a fund charge a fee designated to promote itself if it doesn't allow new investors?

The second and more deadly form of Killer B is known as a "B-shares" mutual fund. With B-shares mutual funds, there is no up-front commission. Rather, when you buy a B-shares fund, you face what's called a declining surrender charge that typically lasts seven years. It might look something like this: you invest $10,000 in a B-shares stock mutual fund. Because there is no front-end commission, your whole $10,000 is invested. If you decide you want to take your money out for another purpose or change to another mutual fund company, you owe a surrender charge that might look something like this:

Year 1: 7 percent

Year 2: 6 percent

Year 3: 5 percent

Year 4: 4 percent

Year 5: 3 percent

Year 6: 2 percent

Year 7: 1 percent

Year 8: 0 percent

These back-end surrender charges tend to lock-in the investor because no one wants to pay a penalty.

Your best defense is to stay away from load mutual funds altogether. We'll show you how, with minimal effort, to build a properly diversified portfolio using no-load mutual funds in Chapter 10.

Unit Investment Trusts

Unit Investment Trusts, or UITs, include municipal (bond) investment trusts, equity (stock) investment trusts, and corporate (bond) investment trusts. They're sold in $1,000 units just like a bond. These investments are similar to traditional mutual funds in that money is raised initially by selling units to investors and is then invested according to the prospectus of the UIT for the benefit of the unit holder. What makes UITs different from traditional mutual funds is the method of investment management. UITs are nonmanaged, as opposed to traditional mutual funds, which are either passively or actively managed. By nonmanaged, we mean that after the securities are purchased, they're not traded or sold until the maturing or end date of the trust. At the time of the end date of the trusts, all the securities are sold and the proceeds are dispersed to the unit holders.

The main selling point of UITs is that the securities are professionally selected on the front end of the offering. But after that, there's no active management and minimal monitoring. Because they're nonmanaged, the portfolio remains static and cannot be maneuvered to take advantage of changing market trends. The fees are usually extensive and are not covered except in the prospectus. Normally, UITs have an up-front commission plus, oddly enough, ongoing administrative fees. Again, we would recommend that you avoid UITs and instead use no-load mutual funds.

Limited Partnerships

In the late '70s and early '80s, limited partnerships were all the rage with investors. This came to a screeching halt in the late '80s when Congress, under President Reagan, eliminated many tax loopholes that favored these types of investments.

The primary drawbacks of investing in limited partnerships are high fees and commissions, which often exceed 15 percent on the front end. In addition, the "sharing arrangement" both during the investment-holding period and upon sale of the real estate holdings ensures you a mediocre return at best. If you decide to sell your limited partnership early, you're likely to find there is no place to sell it and no one to sell it to. The only way you can sell is to accept the price a *scrap yard* will offer you.

Words of the Wealthy

A **scrap yard** is a company that researches limited partnerships around the country. They make their living by offering limited partners 20 to 50 cents on the dollar for their units. They're scavengers. They will buy the units and attempt to sell them at a higher price later or dismantle the whole partnership and sell off the partnership's individual securities, land, and so on.

Obviously there are some good deals out there, but determining which deals are good and which are not is too daunting a task for most investors.

Closed-End Funds

A closed-end investment company, also known as a closed-end mutual fund, initially buys a basket of securities. Once these initial securities are purchased, there is no active management of the securities and the company does not redeem shares for its investors. Instead, the closed-end fund shares trade on the secondary market with prices fluctuating based on supply and demand. In other words, investor activity establishes the price rather than the value of the underlying securities and, therefore, closed-end funds often trade at either a discount or a premium to the value of the underlying shares. Closed-end fund shares typically are thinly traded due to lack of investor interest. Obviously, you can make money investing in closed-end funds, but because of the complexities and lack of trading volume, we recommend that you steer clear of these investments.

Words of the Wealthy

A **secondary market** is any market where previously issued securities are traded. The NYSE is the best-known example. Investors can buy and sell stocks from each other through the designated traders on the floor of the exchange.

Options

Options are marketable securities that give their owners the right but not the obligation to buy or sell a stated number of shares of a particular security, at a fixed price, within a predetermined time period. Many different books published on this subject go into great detail. Fortunately for both of us, this is not one of them! The one thing you need to understand is that options are complicated, involve a lot of risk, and are not worth any attention. What kind of risk are we talking about? You can quickly lose 100 percent of your investment. We can tell you that we don't know anyone who made any significant money in the long run by buying options. We're sure such people exist, but they're the exception, not the rule.

The only possible exception is a strategy called selling covered calls. If you want to learn more, many other books available can teach you about this technique. It's a conservative way to add income to your portfolio.

Futures

A futures contract is a legal agreement in which a buyer promises to pay a seller some fixed price for a specified quantity of a particular good at some future date. The goods can be commodities or financial instruments such as Treasury bills or market indexes. These contracts are negotiable financial instruments that are bought and sold like stocks in a secondary market called commodity exchanges. Futures contracts are usually referred to as futures or contracts. They're similar to options, and the risk is not worth the reward. You can even lose more than 100 percent of your investment. Avoid futures like the plague.

Penny Stocks

Penny stocks are stocks that are initially offered to the public at a price of $1 or less and are traded primarily in the *over-the-counter markets* of Vancouver, Denver, and Salt Lake City. Some penny stocks trade for as much as $10 or more, but they are the exception and not the rule. Penny stocks are the black sheep of the investment industry. The brokerage houses that specialize in penny stocks are notorious for using fraudulent sales pitches. It's estimated that penny stock fraud costs U.S. investors $2 billion each year. We guess the salespeople are just too convincing for investors to "just say no." The Securities and Exchange Commission issued three primary warning signs of penny stock fraud:

1. Unsolicited phone calls from brokers offering penny stocks.

2. High-pressure sales tactics.

3. The inability to sell the penny stock and receive cash.

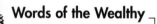

Words of the Wealthy

An **over-the-counter market** is a secondary market where securities are traded by phone and computer. The NASDAQ market is the largest and most popular over-the-counter market.

Rumors and Hot Tips

It seems like every investor in the world has fallen victim to a rumor or hot tip. Rumors and hot tips are normally intended to show others at parties and meetings the brilliance of the person sharing them. The person might mean well by sharing the information, hoping that others can profit, too. However, what people don't realize is that these rumors and hot tips usually result in exactly the opposite of what is intended. First, they can show the ignorance of the person sharing them. Second, if the information is garbage, the person receiving it may act on it and lose money. Avoid hot tips in your wealth-building program. Avoid listening to them and avoid starting them.

The Lottery

Need we say more? Amid the lottery craze across the United States, innocent people are being led to the financial slaughterhouse every day. We won't even discuss the statistical impossibility of winning the lottery. Sure, someone does win and when they do, it's so highly publicized that you get the impression "If they can win, why can't I?" You won't. It's a waste of money. If you need a visual aid for this, take out a dollar bill, drop it in the nearest toilet, and depress the lever. This applies to all forms of gambling as well, whether legal or illegal. The odds always favor the house, and eventually you *will* lose your money.

Life Insurance as an Investment

The purpose of life insurance is to provide income for dependants in the event of a premature death of a family breadwinner. In addition, insurance salespeople will often tout life insurance for its investment benefits. Because of high commissions and expenses, cash value life insurance will not be your best choice for your wealth-building plan.

In its most simple form, a cash value life insurance policy can be divided into two parts. First is the death benefit, known as the mortality charge. Based on historical statistics, the insurance company knows the life expectancy of any group of individuals and charges you a fee that is adequate to cover the costs of claims for a large group of policyholders. This is sometimes referred to as the term insurance charge. With a cash value policy, in addition to the mortality charge, you give the insurance company additional money that they invest on your behalf. The cash value grows without current taxation and avoids taxation altogether if you die while the policy is still in force. This sounds like an appealing idea on the surface, but there are a number of issues that make buying life insurance as an investment a bad decision:

- **High commissions.** Of all the financial products sold, none carry higher commissions than life insurance products. It's not unusual for the first-year commission to be 50 percent to 100 percent or more of the first year's premium. As a result, at the end of the first year of owning a policy, your cash value is typically zero. Because of the exorbitant commission, most policies take 10 years or more to break even, meaning they're worth what you've put into them.

- **Higher mortality charges.** The policy agreement allows the insurance company to adjust the mortality charges in your policy over time. Now they can't do this to you as an individual policyholder, but they can do it to you as part of a group of policyholders. Having reviewed policies over the past 30-plus years, we've found that many companies' mortality charges become uncompetitive over time as compared with a competitive level term insurance policy.

◆ **Surrender charges.** Most insurance companies impose a surrender charge if you cash in your policy within the first 10 to 15 years. It's hard to imagine voluntarily investing your money with a company knowing that if you change your mind during the first 15 years, you will owe a substantial penalty.

Cash value life insurance policies come in several varieties:

◆ **Whole life.** These type policies date back more than 100 years. With a whole life policy, your "investment" dollars are invested in the general assets of the insurance company including bonds, stocks, real estate, and so on. The insurance company pays a guaranteed fixed return of 3 percent to 4 percent and a dividend as declared by the board of directors.

◆ **Universal life.** Here the insurance company takes your investment dollars and invest in an array of fixed-income securities. Your return is directly tied to that basket of securities. Universal life policies were very popular in the '80s when interest rates were 9 percent or higher.

◆ **Variable life.** With a variable life policy, you get to choose how your money is invested among a number of preselected mutual funds including stock and bond funds, among others.

Avoid using cash value life insurance as part of your wealth accumulation strategy. If you need life insurance, level term life is a better choice and will be discussed in Chapter 20.

Annuities

Annuities are another insurance company product and are perhaps the most abusive product on the market today.

With a *fixed annuity*, the insurance company pays you a fixed rate of interest that will change every year or every few years. It's similar to buying a certificate of deposit from a bank except that your interest earnings are tax-deferred. You also don't receive FDIC insurance.

A *variable annuity* is similar to a fixed annuity except that, instead of a guaranteed fixed-income return, you get to choose from among a variety of mutual funds including stock funds, bond funds, and money market funds. Therefore, your return is based on how well your fund choices perform.

Annuity salespeople tout tax-deferred growth as one of their product's primary advantages. Investments in a nonqualified (nonretirement plan or personal annuity) annuity are not tax-deductible but the interest, dividends, and capital gains are not taxed until you begin withdrawing your money. There are a number of problems with annuities that make them a poor choice for your rags-to-riches game plan:

- **They convert what might have been long-term capital gains into ordinary income.** Remember, we've already suggested that equities are better than fixed-income securities for growing your wealth. Well, if you bought a stock mutual fund and held it until retirement and then began to sell shares to fund your retirement cash flow, your gains would be subject to long-term capital gains taxes, which, at the federal level, are taxed at a maximum of 15 percent. When you withdraw your gains from an annuity, they're taxed at ordinary income tax rates as high as 35 percent. Even worse, your withdrawals from an annuity are considered "last-in, first-out" so all of your withdrawals are taxed as ordinary income until you've depleted all of your gains. The remainder is then nontaxable. This makes tax planning very difficult.

- **Limited investment choices.** Variable annuities typically offer you a dozen or more investment choices. This may seem like a lot, but it isn't. There are more than 10,000 mutual fund managers and most are mediocre at best. If you invest personally through a discount broker such as Charles Schwab, Fidelity, or TD Waterhouse, you have access to literally thousands of choices.

- **Stiff surrender charges**. Most annuities charge you a penalty if you take your money out during the first several years. The surrender period can range from 5 to 10 years or longer and the surrender charges will typically be 5 percent to 7 percent or more. Usually, these surrender charges decline each year you own your policy.

- **High expenses.** The up-front and ongoing expenses of an annuity can be relatively high. It's estimated that the average annual expenses for an annuity equals 2.1 percent. Some companies offer annuities with much lower expenses (Vanguard and Charles Schwab are examples), but you will also find companies with much higher expenses. Remember that having higher expenses reduces the growth potential of your investments.

Let's look at an example of how taxation and high expenses associated with annuities limit their effectiveness. For our example, we'll assume that investor A invests $10,000 into a personal account using an S&P 500 index fund. Investor B invests $10,000 into an annuity also using an S&P 500 index fund.

Personal Investment vs. Variable Annuity

	Investor A	Investor B
	Without Variable Annuity	With Variable Annuity
Account Growth for 30 Years		
After-tax contribution	$10,000	$10,000
Growth factor based on 12 percent average annual return minus fund manager cost	× 22.65	× 16.98
Account value in 30 years	$226,500	$169,800
Tax Effect upon Sale in 30 Years		
Account value	$226,500	$169,800
Less capital gains tax*	–36,695	–0
Less ordinary income tax	–0	–59,430
Net to investor	$189,805	$110,370
Advantage to investor	**$79,435**	

For the index fund, reinvested dividends increase the cost basis.

So far we've been discussing annuities purchased with after-tax money. Many people make the mistake of buying an annuity in their retirement account such as their IRA. Big mistake! Buying an annuity in your IRA is a bit like taking a shower while wearing a raincoat. The raincoat is simply "in the way." The primary advantage of an annuity is *income tax deferral* on all dividends, interest, and capital appreciation. Because an IRA already has these features, buying an annuity rarely makes sense for an IRA or other retirement plans. What should you do if you already have an IRA annuity? First, check to see if the surrender charge period has expired. If so, you can simply roll over your IRA

Treasure Tip

Real wealth is built by owning equity in a company—if not your own, then someone else's.

annuity to a regular IRA. If you would incur surrender charges to roll over your IRA annuity, then your best bet may be to keep your annuity until the surrender period ends and then do the rollover. Understanding annuities can be tricky, so it's best to seek the help of a qualified financial advisor before making a final decision.

Hard Assets

In Holland in the mid-seventeenth century, there was wild investment speculation in, of all things, tulip bulbs. People were trading them as if they were the most precious commodities on earth. At the peak of the mania, a single tulip bulb sold for the equivalent of $150,000 to $1,500,000, depending on which historian you believe. We're sure you can imagine how this story ended. Thousands of people lost fortunes after the bubble burst.

Back in the seventeenth century, tulip bulbs were a form of hard assets; today, popular forms of hard assets include gold bullion, gold coins, numismatic (old) coins, silver bullion and coins, diamonds, stamps, coin collections, and artwork. Interest in holding hard assets is as old as, well, the hard assets themselves. After decades of working with wealthy clients from around the country, we have yet to find one who made his or her fortune by investing in hard assets. Some of these may make a nice hobby and others you may purchase for your own appreciation, but don't buy them as part of your wealth accumulation plan.

Avoiding Mistakes Is Critical to Your Success

Most people fail to become wealthy because they never really tried to succeed. These people have chosen their own fate, and it's difficult to garner a lot of sympathy for them. What is truly tragic is when people who are really trying to succeed fail due to investing in the wrong product or trusting the wrong person. There are plenty of things that can still go wrong even when you do invest in the right product and you have someone looking out for your best interests. One example is the generational bear market that occurred in 2000 to 2003, where the stock market dropped as much as 50 percent to 70 percent. You certainly don't want to handicap your success by investing in the products outlined in this chapter. To succeed, you will need to do your homework, particularly as it relates to whom you're dealing with. Make sure you understand exactly how they're being compensated in their dealings with you and be sure you understand the pros and cons of the products being recommended. One of the best ways to do this is to get a second opinion from a professional who does not sell products. For more information about the best way to do this, see Chapter 11.

The Least You Need to Know

- ◆ Learn the basics of successful investing, including the advantage of equities over fixed-income securities, the best environments to invest your money, and the power that leverage can have on your wealth accumulation strategy.

- ◆ Avoid complicated investments such as proprietary investment products, options, and futures contracts.

- ◆ Avoid investments that have little or no secondary markets such as limited partnerships, penny stocks, and proprietary products.

- ◆ Avoid the most expensive investments including load mutual funds, UITs, insurance products, and Killer B funds.

- ◆ Beware of the rumors and hot stock tips you hear at parties; they don't usually work out.

- ◆ Do your homework, don't be persuaded by a slick salesperson, and watch out for conflicts of interest.

9

Investments That Do Work

In This Chapter

- ◆ What you need to know before making an investment
- ◆ What the tricks of the trade are that most brokers aren't willing to share with you
- ◆ What to look for when selecting bonds and fixed-income funds
- ◆ What the power of stocks is in the wealth-building process
- ◆ How mutual funds can help the smallest and the biggest investors

Don't assume that the investment tools used to build wealth are too complicated to understand and use. They might seem complicated at first, but after you get the basics, it's relatively easy. However, you need the right tools. We've presented them in reverse order of importance and power. The first is the least important and least powerful tool, whereas the last is the most important and most powerful tool.

You can certainly buy illiquid securities, but as we said in Chapter 2, you'd better understand what you're getting into. This chapter deals with liquid securities—ones you can sell and convert to cash quickly.

Before You Invest

Before you buy any investment, you need to fully understand what you're buying. There are many hidden traps, and it's what you don't know that will hurt you. That's why you need to get answers to these five questions before you invest:

- **In one sentence, what exactly am I investing in?** Keep things simple. If you or the person selling you the investment can't explain in one sentence what you're investing in, then the investment might be too complicated. If so, don't buy it.

- **How does this investment fit into my plan?** Make sure the investment meets your own personal goals. If you want no risk of fluctuation, you'll focus on money market funds, short-term CDs, and Treasury bills. If you have a long-term horizon and can withstand higher levels of fluctuation, then stocks may be what you need. Make sure the investment accomplishes your mission and fits into your portfolio goals. Don't worry, you might not know the details of your portfolio goals now. The next several chapters will help you narrow them down.

- **What are the risks involved in owning this security?** Risk is always a confusing subject because there are so many different types of risk. There's inflation risk, fluctuation risk, and company risk. For now, just make sure you clearly understand the risks associated with the particular investment you're considering.

- **Is there a secondary market for this investment?** This question is important, and yet so few investors ask. A secondary market is simply a place where you can sell your investment whenever you want. When you purchase a security, you must have a secondary market that will allow you to sell the security later. If the security is a stock listed on the NYSE, then you know there's a real secondary market. If it's a packaged product, such as the ones mentioned in the previous chapter, then the secondary market is probably much smaller. If there's no established secondary market, the security is illiquid, and you should avoid it. Most investors don't appreciate the need for a secondary market until they need one.

  Without a secondary market for your investment, another problem is getting daily and monthly pricing data. If no one is making regular transactions, you don't have a source for current prices. If there's no way to get an accurate price each month, you'll rarely know what your investment is worth. Therefore, the price on your statement each month is an estimate.

◆ **What will this investment cost me?** Investment costs are easy to hide. If you buy a stock from a brokerage firm, you're charged a commission on top of the purchase price of the stock. What can be hidden from you is an additional commission, which is part of the spread. The spread is the difference between the price the brokerage firm paid for the security and the price at which it sold the security to you. Brokers are only able to make a commission on the spread with *over-the-counter (OTC)* stocks because the NYSE no longer allows this practice. Bonds are different in that the commission (called a dealer spread) is part of the price you pay for the bond. You may never know the commission. It's usually measured in percentage points. (One percent equals $1,000 commission.) Short-term bonds are easier to sell, and therefore, the commission can be a fraction of a point or a point. Long-term bonds can have as much as 5 percentage points in commission. Even if you ask the broker, "How many points did this bond pay you?" you might not get a straight answer. However, the broker may be amazed that you even knew to ask.

Words of the Wealthy

Unlike securities exchanges such as the New York Exchange or the American Exchange, the **over-the-counter (OTC) market** is a widespread group of dealers who make a market in securities not listed on the exchanges. Dealers negotiate through telephones and computers. While stocks traded through the OTC are generally considered more speculative than those listed on the exchanges, all government bonds and most corporate bonds are traded through the OTC.

You can also ask this question: "If I sell this investment tomorrow and the price of the security remains unchanged from today, what will it cost me?" This is a great question. If your proceeds are significantly lower than your original purchase price, don't buy the security. It's probably a commission trap.

We selected the tools in this chapter based on certain attributes that correspond to these questions. Almost all of the tools can be easily researched and understood. They all have certain types of risk that are somewhat measurable, and each has a secondary market that is easily accessible. These securities will cost you less than most other types of securities. However, these securities are still subject to hidden fees and commissions, so you will need to remain vigilant. If you're aware of this possible practice and you learn more about how to prevent it, you shouldn't encounter many hidden fees.

The Fixed-Income Tools

Fixed-income securities are basically IOUs issued by companies or the government that pay a certain amount of interest each year and the full principal amount at a certain known date in the future. By their very nature, fixed-income securities pay a fixed rate of interest that today, depending on maturity and quality, is barely above the inflation rate. Because your goal of building wealth involves beating the rate of inflation by a significant amount, fixed-income securities are not powerful tools. However, they can play an important role in your wealth accumulation and management plan under certain circumstances:

- **Emergency reserves.** You need to make sure that you have access to cash in case of a financial emergency. How much you should have in this reserve account depends on your personal circumstances; however, a reasonable rule of thumb would be to hold three months of your income. Any anticipated expenses that you're likely to incur within a five-year period should also be added to this reserve account. For example, if your monthly income is $5,000, then your basic reserve account should be $15,000. If you anticipate buying a car in three years for an estimated cost of $30,000, this amount should also be added to your reserve account. Generally the best choice for your emergency reserve account is a money market account, which we'll describe later in this chapter. One of the best ways to build your reserve account is to set up an automatic transfer of 2 percent of each paycheck into your reserve account.

- **Reduction of volatility.** We've already discussed the importance of primarily using equities in your wealth accumulation plan, and we've discussed how stocks, in particular, can be very volatile. Even the most conservative, diversified portfolio of stocks has a fair amount of volatility. If you want to reduce volatility further, you can do so by adding fixed-income securities to your investment mix.

- **Retirement cash flow.** After you're within 5 to 10 years of retirement, you will need to add a "stabilizing" element to your portfolio using fixed-income securities. The reason is that soon you will begin taking money out of your portfolio to replace a portion or all of the salary you had been earning. Having to constantly sell stocks to accomplish this will eventually present you with a very nasty surprise. The stock market might experience a significant correction and you might be forced to sell stocks when they're temporarily down. We call this "double-dipping" because you're having to dip into your portfolio at a time when it has taken a temporary, yet significant, dip in value. One of the best strategies to avoid double-dipping is to use a "bond ladder," as described later in this chapter. The value of each bond should equal your cash flow need for that particular year (not to exceed 5 percent of your total portfolio value). Typically, you would start with a bond ladder that covers five to seven years' worth of income. When you rebalance your stock portfolio each year, you should use this as an opportunity to rebuild your bond ladder by selling enough shares to extend your bond ladder one additional year. If the stock market is down, simply wait another year and then sell enough stocks to extend your bond ladder two years.

One prevalent conventional theory is important to understand. If you haven't heard it yet or read it somewhere, you will. Some advisors recommend that investors should have a percentage of their portfolio that is equal to their age invested in bonds. If the investor is 20 years old, then 20 percent of the portfolio should be in bonds. If the investor is 80, then 80 percent of the portfolio should be in bonds. If you fall for this outdated rule of thumb, you will find it very difficult to amass any significant wealth. Advances in the field of biotechnology suggest that the average life expectancy of 50-year-olds today could be as high as 120 years! If you live to age 100 or older, you will need an investment portfolio that continues to grow, and that means a substantial allocation to equities all the time. A portfolio's bond allocation should be based on an individual's risk tolerance and need for structured cash flow, not the age of the investor.

Money Market Funds

A money market fund is actually a mutual fund of short-term, fixed-income securities that all have maturities of less than one year. Most investment accounts are *automated*, which means that all deposits, dividends, interest, and proceeds from sales are automatically deposited into a money market account. These funds are primarily used as parking places for cash for emergency reserves or until you decide where you want to invest.

Words of the Wealthy

An **automated account** at a brokerage firm offers an automatic money sweep feature that transfers all deposits, interest payments, dividends, and proceeds of sales into a money market account. When purchases are made within the account, or when checks are written against the account, money is automatically withdrawn from the account. Some full-service brokerage firms charge a custodial fee, but almost all discount brokerage firms waive their fee.

Money market funds offer certain advantages that no other security can offer. The biggest advantage is the price, which is designed not to fluctuate. It's designed to stay constant at $1 per share, which means that there's little risk of loss. These funds have a next-day settlement, which means they can be sold one day and the proceeds will be available the next day. You can also write checks on most money market funds. The only real disadvantage is that they don't pay much interest.

Certificates of Deposit

Certificates of deposit, or CDs, are useful when you have short-term goals. If you have a sum of money that you know you'll need within three to five years, CDs might be a perfect solution. The advantages include them being insured by the FDIC (an agency of the federal government) for up to $100,000 and they often pay higher rates than money market funds.

The main disadvantage with CDs purchased directly from a bank is the penalty for early withdrawal. An alternative is to purchase marketable CDs from a brokerage firm. Many brokerage firms offer CDs from banks all over the United States. If you want to sell before maturity, the brokerage firm will offer you a price based on current interest rates. As with a bond, if interest rates go up, the CD's price will fall. If rates have fallen, then you might get a capital gain on your CD when you sell. However, if you plan to hold the CD until maturity, it really doesn't matter if the price fluctuates, because you're guaranteed to receive the face value of the CD at maturity.

Treasury Bills, Notes, and Bonds

The tool most often used when investors want fixed-income securities is bonds.

Treasury securities are IOUs offered by the U.S. The three most common types include:

- ◆ **Treasury bills.** You can buy treasury bills that mature in 1 month, 6 months, or 52 weeks. They are sold at a discount to the face value, which is $1,000 per bond. The difference between their face value and their discounted value is the interest you will receive at maturity. Until maturity, their price fluctuates daily according to short-term interest rates.

- ◆ **Treasury notes.** Treasury notes are issued with maturities of 1 to 10 years. They're issued at face value and pay fixed-interest payments every six months.

Their price fluctuates with interest rates, and the fluctuation is greater than that of Treasury bills.

♦ **Treasury bonds.** Treasuries are similar to notes, but their maturities are longer than 10 years. Their prices fluctuate the most because of the longer maturities.

The longer-maturing notes and bonds can be used strategically to take advantage of falling interest rates, but you should leave betting on the direction of interest rates to the professional money managers.

Words of the Wealthy

Bonds represent a form of debt of a company, or government body. If a company files for bankruptcy, bondholders are paid off before stockholders. The equity holder's claim to the company's assets is subordinated to the bondholder's claim.

Another type of Treasury bond you might hear about is a zero-coupon Treasury. A zero-coupon bond is one where the scheduled interest payments have been "stripped away" and is therefore sold at a discount from its face or maturity value. Your return is based on the difference between what you paid for the bond and its face value. They can be wildly volatile but tend to do extremely well when interest rates fall. Your "return" is taxed each year even though you're not receiving interest payments, so zero-coupon Treasury bonds are best held in your retirement account. Stockbrokers like to sell them because they pay high commissions. Unless you have a specific reason for buying a zero-coupon bond, these securities are best left to the experts.

Treasury Inflation Protected Securities (TIPS)

Treasury Inflation Protected Securities or TIPS, are the newest types of bonds issued by the federal government. They are intended to provide investors a bond that offers a hedge against inflation. If you believe inflation will be increasing in the coming months or years, then you might want to consider buying TIPS. As with regular Treasury bonds, TIPS pay interest semi-annually, but your interest payments and your redemption value at maturity are based on inflation (CPI-U). If inflation rises every year that you own your TIPS bond, your interest payments and your value at maturity will also rise. Because of this feature, the comparable interest rate paid on a TIPS bond is lower than a regular Treasury bond. In the unlikely event that there's deflation during your holding period, you're guaranteed that the redemption value at maturity will never be less than the original face value (par value) of the bond. However, your interest payments would decrease.

TIPS can be purchased in 5-, 10-, and 20-year maturities and may be purchased directly from the Treasury Department (www.treasurydirect.gov) or through a brokerage firm. TIPS owners pay federal income tax on interest payments in the year they're received and on growth in principle (called principal adjustments) in the year that it occurs. Note that the increases in value due to principal adjustments create what is called "phantom income." In other words, you owe taxes on money that you did not receive. Therefore, TIPS bonds may be most appropriate when held in your retirement account, particularly for 10- or 20-year bonds.

Municipal Bonds

Municipal bonds are IOUs issued by state and local municipalities, and the interest they pay is exempt from federal taxes as well as state taxes within the state that issues the bond. They are rated based on the issuer's estimated ability to pay the interest and principal payments on a timely basis. The two most prominent rating services are Moody's and Standard & Poor's (S&P), both of which have ratings that are similar:

Moody's	S&P
Aaa	AAA
Aa	AA
A	A
Baa	BBB
Ba	BB
B	B
C	CCC
	CC
	C
NR	NR

Below Baa and BBB is considered *non-investment grade*, which is sometimes referred to as *junk bonds* or *high-yield bonds*. The lower the rating, the higher the interest rate (and the risk). The more risk you're willing to take, the more the bond will pay.

Municipal bonds are only useful when they produce a tax equivalent yield that exceeds what you can get from a similar quality corporate or Treasury bond. To calculate the tax equivalent yield, simply divide the yield to maturity of the bond by the inverse of your tax rate:

(Yield to Maturity) ÷ 1 – (Your Tax Rate)
= Tax Equivalent Yield

For example, if you are considering purchasing a tax-free bond yielding 4 percent and you would like to know the tax equivalent yield based on your 35 percent income tax bracket, your calculation would be .04 ÷ .65 (1 – .35 = .65) = .0615 or 6.15 percent. If you can find a taxable bond of equal quality and maturity yielding higher than 6.15 percent, you should buy it rather than the tax-free bond.

Words of the Wealthy

A **junk bond** is any corporate or municipal bond rated below Standard & Poor's BBB rating or Moody's Baa rating. They're also known as **non-investment grade bonds** or **high-yield bonds**.

Most people buy municipal bonds only because they're tax-free. They focus on this first before they focus on the after-tax or "net" return, which is a big mistake. The net return should always be the first priority. If you're in the highest tax brackets, municipal bonds will often offer you a higher return as compared to a taxable bond of similar quality and maturity. However, if you're not in the higher tax brackets, you'll likely be better off buying a taxable bond. This tax-free feature is their strongest benefit. The disadvantage is that currently they pay relatively low interest rates.

Corporate Bonds

Corporate bonds typically offer higher yields than Treasury bonds, but they involve more risk. They're also rated according to the issuing company's estimated ability to pay the interest and principal payments on a timely basis. High-quality corporate bonds are designed to give portfolios stability. They're not designed to produce double-digit total returns.

More aggressive investors might consider junk bonds. If you consider buying these bonds individually, you're asking for trouble. A better choice is to purchase a mutual fund whose manager specializes in buying and selling junk bonds.

Hybrid Fixed-Income Securities

Convertible bonds and preferred stocks are sometimes are called hybrid fixed-income securities. These securities act like both a stock and a bond. Convertible bonds are bonds that can be converted into stocks. Because of this conversion feature, the interest rate on convertible bonds is lower than similar bonds that are not convertible and thus reduces the issuing corporations' costs of raising money. Investors are attracted to these securities because they can benefit if the stock appreciates in value substantially and will receive interest income while they wait. The convertible bondholder has the right to convert to a given number of shares of stock at any time. If the value of the shares is greater than the bond, the investor is said to be "in the money," meaning a conversion to stock would yield a profit over continuing to hold the bond.

A convertible preferred stock is a preferred stock with a convertible feature. Preferred stocks are normally issued without voting rights, but with higher dividends. Often these stocks move with the dividends rather than earnings, which limits their upside potential. Therefore, some companies issue these preferred stocks with a conversion feature that allows the shareholder to convert the preferred stock into so many shares of common stock. This gives the shareholder the opportunity to take advantage of the common stock price appreciation if something spectacular takes place later at the company.

Like a bond, hybrid securities do well when interest rates go down, and like a stock, they go up when the underlying company's earnings grow substantially. When you need to stabilize the value of your portfolio, these types of securities can help. They pay higher income than traditional stocks but don't fluctuate as much in price. These hybrids are great for the more conservative part of your portfolio.

Bond Mutual Funds: Secrets You Need to Know

A mutual fund company, also known as an investment company, is a corporation, trust, or partnership into which investors combine their money to benefit primarily from professional management, diversification, and liquidity. Each fund has a manager or management team responsible for making the investment decisions for the fund and for purchasing securities with the money invested by the shareholders. The securities can include stocks, bonds, options, CDs, and real estate, depending on the fund's stated objective. For now, let's focus on the advantages and disadvantages of bond mutual funds. We'll talk more about mutual funds in general, and stock mutual funds in particular, later in this chapter.

Bond funds provide the shareholder diversification with many different individual bond issues, which is a great benefit. However, if you're going to build a portfolio and you need to allocate money to bonds, you should first consider buying individual bonds. The only exception might be if you want to buy junk bonds or international bonds, or if your portfolio is too small to diversify your money into at least 5 to 10 investment-grade bonds.

The problem with a bond fund is twofold. First, in a relatively low interest rate environment, the fund company management fees eat away too much of your return. Typical bond fund management fees are around 0.60 percent but can exceed 1 percent per year. Compare this to buying a 10-year individual bond where your annual carrying costs is 0 percent. Second, with bond funds there is no maturity date because bonds are constantly being bought and sold. This means your bond fund is constantly fluctuating in value based on changing interest rates, making it a poor choice for planning purposes under many circumstances.

If you want to take the guesswork out of buying bonds in the face of ever-changing interest rates, consider a Bond Ladder Strategy. Laddering is a strategy where you buy an equal number of bonds that mature each year for a period of years:

Year 1	$1,000 bond matures
Year 2	$1,000 bond matures
Year 3	$1,000 bond matures
Year 4	$1,000 bond matures
Year 5	$1,000 bond matures

This strategy is used to reduce the risk of interest rate fluctuation. If rates are going up, you can use a bond that is maturing to reinvest at the higher rates. If interest rates are going down, you have existing bonds that are paying higher rates.

The Equity Tools

You can invest your money in a conventional savings account or in CDs, but your net return after inflation and taxes will not be strong enough (at least at today's rates) to grow your wealth at a sufficient pace. Equities, however, should provide sufficient growth over time. The equity tools include stocks and stock mutual funds, exchange traded funds, investment real estate, and owning your own business. Each of these tools have advantages and disadvantages, which we will explore to help you determine which choice or choices are best for you. For this chapter, we'll focus on stocks, stock mutual funds, and exchange traded funds. Investment real estate and owning your own business will be covered, in detail, later in this book.

Stocks

Whether they're publicly traded or privately held, stocks offer the opportunity to build wealth much faster than fixed-income securities because they represent equity ownership in a company and their value will grow relative to the growth in net earnings. If a company is expected to have a continued earnings growth of 30 percent or more, its stock price may have the same growth potential. Few opportunities in the investment world offer this much growth potential. Investing in stocks is the single biggest and most popular wealth builder in the world, but ironically, most people don't take the time to understand the concept or its power.

The market value of a stock is based on what people perceive the value to be. This perception of value is normally based on the amount of net cash the company produces (or is perceived to produce) on a per-share level after expenses. This cash is referred to as earnings or earnings per share. The majority of these earnings are usually retained by the company and are used to finance additional growth with the remainder distributed as dividends to shareholders. Small or fast-growing companies usually don't distribute any earnings as dividends because they need all the money to continue their fast-paced growth. On the other hand, larger, more mature companies often distribute a great deal of their earnings as dividends. Companies that reinvest their earnings in their own growth offer the investor a greater opportunity for growth but are riskier and more volatile than their blue-chip, dividend-paying counterparts.

Historically, stocks, as a whole, have been a much better hedge against inflation than bonds and other fixed-income investments. Their only real disadvantage is the performance risk that stocks carry. If the underlying company goes bankrupt, the stock could become worthless.

Words of the Wealthy

The **P/E ratio** is a stock's price per share divided by its earnings per share. It's used to estimate the true value of a stock and is often used in comparison with other stocks. If Wal-Mart's market price closed at $25 per share today and its current quarterly earnings equaled $.25 (or $1 on an annualized basis), its P/E ratio is 25.

The relative comparison of a company's stock price to its earnings is commonly referred to as the price/earnings ratio (or *P/E ratio*).

Value investors look for stocks that have P/E ratios below their industry average. Growth investors, by contrast, are looking for companies with above-average expected increases in revenues and earnings. These growth companies typically carry relatively high P/E ratios and their share price often fluctuates widely as well. With more than 7,000 stocks traded on the various U.S. exchanges, identifying the real winners is quite a challenge. You should not attempt to buy individual stocks unless it's your passion and you're prepared to invest a lot of time in research. If you do decide to pursue a strategy of buying individual stocks, keep a few basic rules in mind. First, you should own a minimum of 20 different stocks to eliminate what is called single-company risk. Single-company risk relates to the classical error of putting all your eggs in one basket. Thousands of people learned this lesson the hard way when Enron went broke. Second, you should not own more than 50 stocks. Typically 20 to 40 stocks is enough to get adequate diversification and eliminate single-company risk. Owning more than 50 stocks becomes too unwieldy and difficult to manage and is unnecessary. Third, you want your stocks to represent companies across several different industries. We divide the United States into nine different industries:

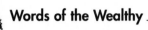

Words of the Wealthy

A **value investor** is someone who looks for good value in the market. A stock selling at an unusually low P/E ratio is a great example. Occasionally, stocks drop in price well below what they should. Value investors search for opportunities such as this and try to take advantage of the stock's price returning to more normal (higher) levels.

Consumer discretionary	Consumer staples	Energy
Financials	Health care	Industrials
Materials	Technology	Utilities

A good rule of thumb is to make sure you own stocks across at least five of these nine industries. Sage advice from legendary investor Warren Buffett is to choose your stocks as if you had a punch card with only 20 spots. After you've used your 20 spots, you can buy no more stocks. This forces you to choose your stocks very carefully indeed!

If you have limited time or expertise, or investing in stocks is not your passion, your best bet is to invest using mutual funds.

Stock Mutual Funds

Stock mutual funds operate just like the bond mutual funds except the fund manager(s) picks and manages a basket of individual stocks. The objective of the fund, which is stated in the prospectus, outlines the intentions of the manager, including the type of investments he or she will use as well as the different philosophies or strategies he or she will employ. The objective is the most important item in the prospectus to understand. The second most important item to look for is the list of restrictions. These guidelines are set up to keep the fund manager focused.

Stock mutual funds are normally segmented by their investment objective. Here are a few different types:

Aggressive growth funds	Equity income funds
Growth funds	Balanced funds
International	Flexible portfolio funds
Global equity funds	Index funds
Growth and income funds	Specialized industry funds

Stock mutual funds (and bond funds) are either actively managed or passively managed (sometimes referred to as index funds). With an actively managed mutual fund, the fund manager or managers determine which securities to buy or sell. Passively managed funds use a computer to buy and sell securities that are held in a particular index such as the *S&P 500 Index*. These indexes are used to track certain segments of the market.

Words of the Wealthy

The **S&P 500 Index** is made up of 500 of the largest publicly traded companies in the United States and is often used as a benchmark for how the U.S. stock market is doing.

There is an ongoing debate as to whether investors are better served buying actively managed mutual funds or passively managed mutual funds. Historically, more than 80 percent of actively managed mutual funds underperform their benchmark so, understandably, many investors suggest you would be better off to simply "buy the benchmark" by using a passively managed fund. One of the major benefits of buying passively managed mutual funds is that their management fees are typically much lower then their actively managed counterparts.

Our own experience is that if you do your homework, you can find active managers who do outperform their benchmarks and are worth the additional management fees. However, if you're unwilling to do the research necessary to identify these top managers, you would be better off using passively managed mutual funds. If you prefer to use index mutual funds, one of the top mutual fund companies that specialize in index funds is Vanguard. Visit their website at www.vanguard.com or call them at 1-877-662-7447.

Mutual funds have become so popular over the past three decades that they're worthy of further discussion at this point. Professional management and diversification are two of the most important reasons to buy a mutual fund. But there are numerous additional benefits as well:

- Because you're able to virtually hire several money managers at one time, you benefit from combining all their unique investment styles into your portfolio.

- Services such as automated checking account debit purchasing make it easier to invest on a monthly basis.

- Mutual funds offer individual investors access to some of the world's best money managers for a relatively small fee.

- Mutual funds provide a cost-efficient method of investing all over the world, considering the high cost of foreign security commissions that are charged to individuals.

- You have the ability to diversify among hundreds of securities all over the world—which is almost impossible for an individual investor to do with a small amount of money and a limited amount of time to do research.

- Mutual funds offer a high degree of liquidity, allowing you to sell shares in your fund very efficiently.

- Investing in mutual funds gives you peace of mind that someone is watching the portfolio.

Mutual funds are not perfect. They do have their limitations and disadvantages. Here is a list of possible disadvantages:

- High portfolio turnover can result in higher management fees.

- Some people think mutual funds are too limited because they can only invest in listed securities.

- Investors may experience a loss of control over when taxable gains are taken.

- Mutual funds can see poor performance during bear markets.

- Legal limitations of the fund manager could affect performance.

All mutual funds require their shareholders to pay a management fee. This fee can range from .10 percent to 3 percent per year. This fee goes directly to the fund manager and fund company for operating expenses.

However, some funds also charge a load or commission, which is an additional charge levied at the time of purchase, at the time of redemption, or each year the fund is held. This commission is paid to the salesperson or broker who sold the fund and the brokerage firm that hired the salesperson.

That Reminds Us ...

We have all heard the saying, "If something sounds too good to be true, it probably is," and this is the reaction most investors have when they first hear about no-load mutual funds. The first question that pops into their minds is, "What's the catch? How can these mutual funds make money when they don't charge anything?"

Salespeople will often tell you that the management fee on a no-load fund is higher than that of a load fund to compensate for the absence of commission. This is not necessarily true. Many load funds have higher management fees than no-load funds. Buying no-load funds is like buying directly from the manufacturer. This secret can save an investor up to 9.29 percent on every net invested dollar. If you're willing to do a little bit of homework, no-load mutual funds will be your best choice.

So why do people still buy load mutual funds? The two most common reasons are that the investor is unaware of what a no-load fund can offer or the investor does not know how to find a no-load alternative to the load fund he or she has selected. We assure you that an alternative is available—you just need to look for it. Popular magazines that run extensive stories on no-load mutual funds include *Money*, *Kiplinger's Personal Finance*, *Fortune*, and *Forbes*.

There are two ways to buy a no-load mutual fund: directly from the company or through a discount brokerage firm. If you want to buy direct, *Morningstar* can provide you with each fund company's phone number (www.morningstar.com). You should call the company and request a prospectus and new account application. If you decide to buy the fund, fill out the application and send it back with a check made out to the name of the mutual fund company.

If you want to buy mutual funds from different companies, your best bet is to consolidate everything into one account at a discount brokerage firm. These discount brokerage firms allow investors to purchase no-load mutual funds within the same account with either a small or no transaction fee. Top discount brokerage firms worth considering are …

- Charles Schwab & Co.   1-800-435-4000   www.schwab.com
- Fidelity   1-800-544-6666   www.fidelity.com
- TD Waterhouse   1-800-934-4448   www.tdwaterhouse.com

Exchange Traded Funds

The newest mutual fund–style investment available to investors is called an Exchange Traded Fund or ETF. ETFs offer a number of advantages over both managed mutual funds and index mutual funds. Like index mutual funds, an ETF represents a specific index such as the S&P 500 (U.S. large companies), the Wilshire 5000 (the entire U.S. stock market), or the Russell 2000 (U.S. small companies). By buying the ETF version of the S&P 500 Index, with one security purchase you own shares in 500 companies. Like index mutual funds, fund expenses are very low. Where Vanguard S&P 500 fund charges 0.18 percent annually, the ETF version charges a meager 0.09 percent annually. Compare this to the typical managed mutual fund, which averages 1 percent or more annually.

Another advantage of ETFs over mutual funds is they're more tax efficient. By law, mutual funds are required to distribute at least 95 percent of all net realized capital gains each year to their investors as of a certain date, called the "record date." Although this has been less of a problem with index mutual funds, it's been a significant problem with many managed mutual funds. Because of this law, it's possible to actually have losses for the year, yet get hit with taxable gains on fund distributions. ETFs minimize this problem and gains are typically only recognized when you sell an ETF in which you have a profit. Another advantage of ETFs over mutual funds is that you can trade ETFs on an intra-day basis, whereas mutual funds settle at the close of the day's prices. Under the new paradigm in which we find ourselves today, where dramatic market changes can happen in the course of a single day, this can be an important benefit.

Finally, many mutual funds, even no-load funds, charge a redemption fee when you sell your fund within a certain period of time from purchase (typically 90 days). ETFs do not have such restrictions, which allow the investor to remain mobile and responsive to rapidly changing events. Although we believe in having a long-term investment strategy, it's also important you maintain the flexibility to make changes should extraordinary circumstances arise. ETFs give you that option.

There are now over 200 different types of ETFs, which makes it possible for you to be very strategic in your investing while still maintaining significant security diversification. We use ETFs extensively in managing our clients' portfolios and have found them to be a better choice than mutual funds in many circumstances. For more information about ETFs, go to the Resource Center at www.welchgroup.com.

The Optimal Investment Strategy for Getting Rich

If your route to riches includes the tools outlined in this chapter—fixed-income and equity investments—here are some broad guidelines for making sure that your money works as hard as it should:

♦ Your portfolio should be dominated by equity investments to maximize your opportunity for growth.

♦ Because of the interconnectivity of the world's economies, your portfolio should include international stocks. This can be accomplished using international stock mutual funds or ETFs, individual foreign stocks, or domestic stocks that have large international operations.

♦ Use fixed-income securities primarily to fund emergency reserves and expected spending needs over the next three to five years (buying a car, and so on). Also use them to establish a bond ladder for cash flow during your retirement.

♦ Make sure each investment is highly liquid so that if there's a good reason to sell it, you're not prevented from doing so because of penalties or surrender charges. Note: for retirement plans, we're referring to the investments within the plan. We're not suggesting that you not invest using retirement plans. In fact, retirement plans are one of your best choices.

♦ Keep the costs associated with your portfolio low. Make sure you know all the costs of owning and managing your investments.

By reading Chapters 8 and 9, you now have the basics of what to invest in and what to avoid. It's now time to put your newfound knowledge into practice. In Chapter 10, we'll help you set up your winning portfolio.

The Least You Need to Know

- Whatever the investment, make sure you ask the right questions and keep everything simple.

- Bonds and other fixed-income tools have a place in your portfolio under specific circumstances.

- If your goal is to maximize the growth of your portfolio, you have to use stocks or stock mutual funds.

- The best portfolio is one that is custom designed to your particular circumstances.

Chapter 10

Jumping into the Market

In This Chapter

- ◆ What should your first investment look like?
- ◆ How much money will you need to start?
- ◆ What are some fund ideas that will get you started?
- ◆ How do you invest automatically?
- ◆ Where should you hold your first investment?

Where exactly do you start? Just how do you get started with the first investment? In Wealth Stage 1, when you make your first investment decision, you might feel somewhat overwhelmed. This chapter will help you narrow your focus considerably and get you started on the right track. The first mistake most investors make when they begin investing is procrastination. Most investors fear their first investment decision so much that they procrastinate, sometimes for years. They think they have to buy a stock or something complicated that requires days of study and research. If you follow the five questions in the first pages of Chapter 9, you'll instantly narrow your choices. Therefore, the first investment decision should actually be the easiest, and this chapter gives you a nudge in the right direction.

Most first-time investors are also so afraid of making a mistake that they actually become frozen in fear. Don't let this happen to you. Remember from Chapter 3 that the most important element initially is the amount of money you save, not total return. Your first investment decision is important, but the amount of money you save is much more important. Mistakes early in your journey can often be completely covered by one or two savings deposits down the line.

Don't Swallow That Hook!

There are so many ways you can make mistakes. The one most people hate the most is when someone takes advantage of them. Your best defense is knowledge. Now is the most important time to learn—when you make your first investment. However, it's also the best time to make mistakes. Why? Because it's best to learn from them early on instead of later when the mistakes are usually more expensive.

The first investment for most people can still be expensive. Why? The first-time investor usually knows the least, which means he or she falls pray to commission traps sold by brokers, insurance agents, and other salespeople. The typical first-time investor buys a load mutual fund or an insurance policy as an investment.

Some load mutual fund investments are sold as contracts that require monthly deposits, usually in the form of automatic checking account debits. The debit concept is great. Automatically, without any effort on the part of the investor, money is withdrawn from the investor's checking account and invested for him or her. However, if you're buying a load fund, the commission usually bites heavily into the deposit before any money actually gets invested.

If you're a novice investor, it's difficult to prevent a smooth salesperson from selling you an investment product with heavy commissions. They're trained to sell, and they're wonderful at it. Refer back to Chapters 8 and 9 to remind you of good and bad basic alternatives.

For your first investment, pass on anything that seems to have a high commission attached. Also, trust your gut and pass if the salesperson is using heavy handed tactics or is trying to rush your decision. Before you buy any investment product, don't forget to ask how the advisor is being paid. There are a lot of well-intentioned salespeople who truly have your best interests in mind. There are also a lot who are focused on the commissions they'll earn, and then there are those who are simply incompetent. It's your responsibility to figure out who is who.

A Portrait of Your First Investment

If you understand the necessary characteristics of a properly diversified portfolio, you'll find that the list of investments is quite short. Because the list is small, you might not need an advisor to help you. If you're uncomfortable with making a decision after reading this chapter, then you might want to get some help from a fee-only investment advisor, using the questions in Chapter 11 to help select one with whom you're comfortable.

Near the end of Chapter 9, we gave you a list of optimal wealth-building portfolio characteristics. Here's a reminder of the most important elements:

- The portfolio is built primarily of stocks or stock mutual funds.

- The stocks are diversified among many different countries and industries to help maximize return while reducing risk.

- The portfolio's expenses are low and the portfolio can be adjusted with minimal additional expense.

 Treasure Tip

If you had to pick one investment idea that covers all the necessary characteristics of an optimal wealth-building portfolio, the single best investment idea is a diversified no-load stock mutual fund.

One stock can't meet all these characteristics. However, if you think the preceding characteristics are boring, and if you have your heart set on buying a stock or another investment idea, go ahead and try it. Make your mistakes now while they don't hurt so much. Go with your gut, and with a little luck, you might do well.

The only way you can possibly design a portfolio of less than $100,000 using the portfolio characteristics listed here is with no-load mutual funds. Therefore, before you make your next investment decision, let's take a closer look at mutual funds.

How Much Will You Need to Start?

All mutual funds have a minimum investment amount you must meet to initially buy shares in the fund. Therefore, you have to pay attention to minimums when you design your portfolio. If you have only $1,000 and you want to get started with a mutual fund, you might have difficulty finding a fund. Many funds have a minimum initial investment of $3,000. Some have much higher minimums. The minimum is always listed in the prospectus, or you can find it online at www.morningstar.com.

You might want to go directly to the fund company to make your first investment, especially if you're starting with less than $5,000. If you go to a discount brokerage firm, they may charge you transaction fees as well as a custodian fee. Your account isn't profitable for them at this size, so they don't encourage you to start there.

Risk and Return

Risk and return work hand-in-hand. Return is the reward you get for the risk you take. Risk is something that should be managed, not avoided. You may have heard of the term *risk/reward ratio*. This measures the relationship between risk and reward, which is not an easy calculation.

Stock market risk is normally associated with portfolio or market fluctuation. The stock market lost almost 80 percent of its value in the crash of 1929. The market did come back, but it took a few years to do it. A less severe crash occurred on October 19, 1987, when the market dropped 20 percent over a one-day period. The market recovered from this before the year ended. Another significant bear market occurred from 1973 to 1974, when the stock market dropped 48 percent. It took $7^1/_2$ years to fully recover. Most recently, in the second worst bear market in history, stocks dropped more than 50 percent between March of 2000 and March of 2003. Analysts call these last two bear markets "generational" bear markets and only expect to see them once every 25 years or so. What you should expect is that you'll incur losses in your portfolio once every three to five years. More specifically, the stock market tends to go through market cycles that last three to seven years—let's say five years on average. One year you're going to lose money; one year you'll make more than you expected or deserved; and the remaining three years' returns will be dotted around your expected return, say 9 percent to 10 percent. The point is that periodic losses are part of the game. This is also logical because if you never lost money in stocks, why would anyone ever buy bonds or other fixed-income investments? To earn the higher returns on your money needed to reach your financial goals, you must be willing to accept periodic losses.

> ### Words of the Wealthy
>
> The **risk/reward ratio** is a term used to describe a security's return relative to its risk. If a security has the potential for a 10 percent return on the upside, you should only be willing to accept an equal or lesser degree of risk on the downside. For example, why risk a 20 percent loss for a possible 10 percent return?

To Thine Own Self Be True

Most investors overestimate the level of risk they can actually handle. Unfortunately, it usually takes a big drop in the market to find a person's actual risk tolerance. What you want to avoid is this scenario taking place after you've reached Wealth Stages 3, 4, and 5. That's when it might be too late to make any adjustments. We consider Wealth Stages 1 and 2 training stages. Get to know your risk tolerance early in the game so you can reduce surprises later in life. As you learn more and your portfolio grows, you might want to change your risk tolerance either way. Keep in mind during the rough times that you're investing for the long run.

Treasure Tip

The worst thing you can possibly do during a stock market correction is sell. A correction is simply an absence of buyers amidst a flood of investors wanting to sell. If you join them, you'll completely miss the market rebound when there's an absence of sellers and a flood of buyers. Stay off the bandwagon.

What Kind of Return Do You Expect?

During the late 1990s, the market made some unprecedented gains. If you use these as benchmarks, you'll make a huge mistake. Be reasonable with your expectations.

Historically the stock market has returned 9 percent to 11 percent. You may be able to do better with a particular market strategy, but if you need to make a much higher return to meet your financial goals, you'll need to consider investing in investment real estate or starting your own company. To put these returns in perspective, your money will double every 7.2 years at 10 percent. Not bad if you are consistently investing each month and every year. Given enough time, these returns will allow you to achieve financial independence.

Don't try to hit home runs, no matter how much risk you think you can tolerate. Investing is like baseball. It's won with base hits, not home runs. The more home runs you attempt, the more you'll strike out. However, if you're bored with base hits, go for the fence now, early in your career when the mistakes don't hurt as much.

Learn from Your Mistakes

When you do make a mistake, learn from it. Spend some time learning why you failed. Ask yourself the following questions:

♦ What could I have done to prevent this loss?

♦ If I had to do it all again, what would I do differently?

♦ What will I do next time to improve my results?

Take some time to learn from the loss, but don't let it discourage you. So many people take their mistakes personally. They say to themselves, "I guess that's just the kind of investor I am." Or we hear them say, "If you want something to go down, just let me buy it." This is a horrible attitude to have, and ironically, it's self-fulfilling. If you think this way, you'd better believe you'll lose money. But if you take the time to learn from your losses, you'll become a great investor.

Don't Let the Market Control Your Life

If you're focusing on achieving Wealth Stage 2, now is not the time to look at your investments every day. In fact, we don't ever recommend this practice unless you're a professional. We know so many people who let the stock market dictate their daily mood. They are happy when it's up and depressed when it's down. They lose sight of the long-term strategy behind their investment decisions.

> **Treasure Tip**
>
> If your yearly savings deposit exceeds 10 or 20 percent of your total portfolio, then don't concern yourself with any possible stock market correction until after you've reached the first stage of Wealth Stage 2.

There are two things that are more important to focus on. When you're in Stages 1 and 2, your savings amount and investment knowledge should be of key importance. At these stages, you actually want the market to fall and keep falling. Why? Because you're investing money each month. Don't you want to buy low and sell high? If so, you want the market to be down when you buy and up when you need your money at a later date.

The Tortoise and the Hare

Most beginning investors worry too much about picking the fastest-growing investment. They're into the action and excitement of the market. This is fun and you feel mighty smart when the market is rising but mighty discouraged when it's falling. This is not what successful investing is all about. Your goal is to build solid wealth over your working life; wealth that will sustain you during your retirement years. In the early years, what is critical to your success is the consistency and adequacy of your

contributions. It's much later that your investment returns become a vital concern. It's the
classic tortoise and hare story. While the hare
runs around frantically trying to buy the best-
performing stocks each month, the tortoise
wins the race because he saved as much as he
could each year. His returns might not be all
that incredible, but his account value sure is. Try
to be the tortoise, not the hare.

Treasure Tip

One way to assure finan-
cial success is to save automatically by letting a
mutual fund debit your
checking account each
month.

Invest Automatically

Most mutual funds offer an automatic debit service from your checking account. This
is a no-brainer, yet so few people take advantage of it. We've found that many people
are afraid of automatic debit accounts. The reasons are varied but here are a few of
the most prevalent:

- Fear of the mutual fund company taking advantage of them
- Fear of an invasion of privacy
- Fear of losing control
- Fear of forgetting to record the deposit in the check register

First, the mutual fund can't take advantage of you. Why would they jeopardize their
registration with the SEC just to get a few more dollars out of your account? Second,
the mutual fund can only debit a certain amount, not check your balance. Third, this
service is a way to gain control over spending, not lose control. Fourth, post a big
note to yourself where you pay your bills to record the debit each month.

The debit service is too easy and powerful not to take advantage of it.

Where to Put the First Investment

As mentioned earlier in this book, your best first investment is in your company
401(k) plan, especially if your employer provides a matching contribution. You won't
have as many investment options as we would like, but you can still use the portfolio
design strategies outlined in Chapter 9 and this chapter. In fact, because 401(k) plans
don't have any minimum investment requirements, consider using the asset allocation
recommended for a portfolio size of $100,000 to $500,000 under the section titled

"The Perfect Portfolio for Where You Are Right Now," which follows. After you've funded your 401(k) plan, then fund any individual retirement plans you're eligible for such as the Traditional or Roth IRA. You can open an IRA account at any mutual fund company, bank, brokerage firm, or life insurance company. When you've invested in all the retirement plans that you're eligible to invest in, you should start your personal investment program by opening an account with a mutual fund company or discount brokerage firm.

Treasure Tip

The best place to start your investment program is in a retirement account such as a 401(k) plan, Traditional IRA, or Roth IRA because they allow your money to grow tax-deferred over time. After you've completely funded all retirement plans, you're ready to begin investing in a personal account.

The Perfect Portfolio for Where You Are Right Now

In the early stages of building your investment program, you want to focus on simplicity, low expenses, and automating your investment contributions. Vanguard is a mutual fund company that has built a reputation for being the low-cost producer of mutual funds. They're now the second largest mutual fund company in America. This is where we want to start your investment program. You can contact a Vanguard representative at 1-800-662-7447 or www.vanguard.com.

What follows are asset allocation recommendations for the equity portion of your portfolio strategy based on how much money you have to invest:

- ◆ **$1,000 to $10,000.** Begin by setting up an auto-transfer monthly from your checking account to a money market account until you have the required $3,000 minimum investment ($1,000 for IRA accounts). Then contact Vanguard and ask for an application for the Vanguard Total Stock Market Index Fund, symbol VTSMX. Continue your automatic investment into this fund ($100 per month minimum) until your account value exceeds $10,000.

- ◆ **$10,000 to $25,000.** You're now ready to begin diversifying your investments a bit. Transfer the greater of $3,000 or 25 percent of your funds to Vanguard Total International Stock Index Fund (VGTSX). Continue your automatic investment program targeting a 25 percent allocation to the Total International Stock Index Fund with 75 percent continuing to go to the Total Market Index.

◆ **$25,000 to $100,000.** As your account value continues to grow, you want to continue adding diversification to your portfolio. At this point, keep focusing on simplicity and low costs. Continue your 25 percent allocation to the Total International Stock Index Fund but now add a 10 percent allocation to Vanguard Small-Cap Index Fund (NAESX) and a 10 percent allocation to Vanguard REIT Index Fund (VGSIX). The REIT Index Fund invests in a broad array of U.S. real estate. The remaining 55 percent will continue to be invested in Vanguard's Total Stock Market Index.

◆ **$100,000 to $500,000.** You're now beginning to accumulate some serious money and can afford to begin adding active fund managers to your portfolio if you desire. Your goal is to find active managers who have consistently outperformed their particular benchmark over three to five years or more. Be sure to look at year-by-year comparable returns because you're looking for consistency of returns. Otherwise, you might fall into a trap of buying a fund where the manager got lucky on one particular year but otherwise produced mediocre returns. Also, you should further diversify by taking 10 percent of your international stock allocation and buying an emerging markets fund such as Vanguard Emerging Stock Index (VEIEX) or seek an actively managed emerging markets fund.

An excellent research source of actively managed funds is Morningstar Fund Selector. This monthly publication provides a wealth of information about the best-run mutual funds (both load and no-load). It even has model portfolios based on varying degrees of risk tolerance. For information on this publication, call toll-free 1-866-608-9570 or visit *Morningstar* online at www. morningstar.com.

◆ **$500,000 or more.** Having a portfolio of this size is akin to owning and running a small business, and you're ready to seek some professional help. With this much money, owning individual stocks and ETFs makes sense as well. Owning individual stocks will allow you to further reduce the costs of owning securities because you're eliminating the ongoing fund management fees.

As discussed earlier in this book, you should approach your personal finances as if you were running a business, and now it's time to put together a team of professional advisors who can help accelerate your progress. Finding the right team members is both critical and challenging and will be discussed in the next chapter.

To recap, the following table summarizes the investment strategies we recommend.

Recommended Investment Strategies

Investment Amount	Investment Strategy
$1,000 to $10,000	100% Broad Stock Market Index (Vanguard Total Stock Market Index)
$10,000 to $25,000	75% Broad U.S. Stock Market (Vanguard Total Stock Market Index)
	25% International Stock (Vanguard Total International Stock Index)
$25,000 to $100,000	55% Broad U.S. Stock Market (Vanguard Total Stock Market Index)
	10% U.S. Small Caps (Vanguard Small-Cap Index)
	10% Real Estate (Vanguard REIT Index)
	25% International Stock (Vanguard Total International Stock Index)
$100,000 to $500,000	55% Broad U.S. Stock Market
	10% U.S. Small Caps
	10% Real Estate
	15% International Stock
	10% Emerging Markets Stock
$500,000 or more	Customized portfolio using individual stocks and ETFs

The Least You Need to Know

◆ The first thing you invest in should be a no-load mutual fund that invests primarily in stocks.

◆ Avoid being sold by a smooth-talking salesperson who wants to take advantage of you by selling you an expensive investment product.

◆ Make your mistakes early when you're working with smaller amounts of money; you can learn a lot from them and they won't be as expensive as they will be later.

◆ Don't monitor your investment every day; you'll drive yourself and everyone else crazy.

◆ Focus on learning more about the market and maximizing your savings amount.

Chapter 11

Building Your Own Brain Trust

In This Chapter

- How to find the advisor who is ideal for you
- What you should expect from an advisor
- What you need to watch out for before hiring an advisor
- How to interview a potential advisor

Through the first 10 chapters of this book you've acquired the necessary knowledge to establish your financial goals and to begin building your wealth. Don't forget that you're managing your personal finances as you would a small business. It's not too early to start identifying top professionals to help you with your quest. You should find people with expertise in areas such as financial planning, accounting, law, insurance, and investments. By putting together a team of top experts in various fields, you create a brain trust—a force that can help you tackle the toughest problems.

We all need help, especially if we're going to accomplish big goals. However, bad "expert" advice can torpedo your success plan faster than just about anything. If you have good advisors, it's just as important that they work together in a coordinated fashion to help you accomplish your goals. This cooperative alliance is what will turn a group of good advisors into a team of great advisors. This chapter is devoted to helping you choose the right advisors to manage your growing wealth.

Four Keys to Selecting a Great Advisor

Identifying great advisors requires that you do your homework in four main areas: experience, competence, compensation, and chemistry. Let's look more closely at each of these areas.

Experience

Experience is the foundation of all competence. Each advisor you choose should have a minimum of 10 years' experience in their field. We strongly believe that *no* professional advisor should have unsupervised client responsibility until they have "apprenticed" under an experienced advisor for a minimum of five years. We know that we're going to make a lot of advisors who are new to their field unhappy because we're recommending that you avoid using them for now. They're caught in the dilemma of "If no one will hire me, how will I ever get the experience I need?" The answer is that someone will hire them, we're just suggesting that you not be the one. It might cost you more to have someone with this much experience, but we believe that it is worth it. And don't forget: We're expecting you to grow financially very fast, so you want an advisor who you won't outgrow.

Competence

Look for advisors who have earned advanced designations in their field. Although having an advanced designation is no guarantee of competence, it is an indication of a commitment to staying on the leading edge in one's field.

Compensation

When choosing your advisors, it's vital that you understand how they're being paid. Of all the areas where people have a problem with advisors, misunderstandings about compensation happen most often. At first, the topic of fees might make you both uncomfortable. Often the advisor is not used to being asked this line of questioning—it may even seem like you're questioning his or her integrity. You're not; so ask your questions and keep asking until you fully understand exactly how the advisor is being paid for working with you.

Chemistry

When you choose a professional advisor, make the decision as if you plan to work with this person for the rest of your life. Most professional advisors will meet with you initially without charge. Use this first meeting not only to determine the scope of the work to be performed but also to determine if the advisor is someone you feel you would be happy working with long-term.

Building Your Executive Advisory Team

Eventually, you'll end up working with numerous advisors with expertise in a variety of fields. It's important that you have a basic understanding of what to expect from each advisor and how to get the most benefit for the least cost.

Remember our original success paradigm: think of your personal finances as if you're running a small business. Under this paradigm, your advisors are your executive officers, or what we call your Executive Advisory Team. To get the most from them, they need to work together as a team while staying focused on your goals and objectives. You should seek out people who are the best in their chosen field. What we've found from experience is that those professionals who are truly committed to being tops in their field have invariably gone the extra mile by acquiring advanced designations related to their work.

The Ideal Financial Planner

A financial planner may be best qualified to head your Executive Advisory Team because she's trained to help you develop, implement, and monitor an overall financial game plan. Most financial planners also have expertise regarding investments.

The ideal financial planner is a fee-only *Certified Financial Planner™ (CFP®)* practitioner with a

Words of the Wealthy

A **Certified Financial Planner™ (CFP®)** certificant is someone who's been licensed by the CFP® Board of Standards by virtue of having passed a comprehensive national exam, agreed to abide by a strict code of ethics, and receives continuing education of 30 hours every two years.

minimum of 10 years' experience. To become a CFP® practitioner, one must meet education requirements, pass a rigorous national exam, complete 30 hours of continuing education every two years, agree to abide by a strict code of ethics, and have three years of experience in the financial planning field. The CFP® certification is the gold standard in the financial planning business. Ideally, your CFP® practitioner is "fee-only," which means that he or she is compensated based solely on fees paid by you. Fee-only CFP® practitioners' compensation is typically derived from one of four sources:

♦ **Hourly fees.** Hourly rates vary widely but typically range from $75 to $400 per hour.

♦ **Initial fee and annual retainer.** Under this arrangement, you pay an initial fee, typically based on case complexity. After the initial analysis is completed, you pay a monthly, quarterly, or annual retainer that is based on an estimate of the time the CFP® will spend working on your case.

♦ **Fee based on a percentage of assets under management.** Under this arrangement, the CFP® practitioner actively manages your money. You're charged a quarterly fee based on the total amount of assets that are being managed. The amount of this fee varies widely, but a good baseline is 1 percent. For example, if your advisor is managing $1 million for you, he or she would charge you $10,000 per year or $2,500 per quarter. Note that as your investment account varies due to market fluctuations, so will the fee you pay your advisor. This helps to align your advisor's interests with your own. For example, if your account grows in value to $1,500,000, your fee goes up to $15,000 (based on 1 percent). If your account drops to $800,000, your advisor's fee income also drops ($8,000).

♦ **Flat fee.** Here the advisor charges a flat fee (computed annually, but paid quarterly or monthly). The fee is typically determined based on expected time involved in your case and an initial estimate of your net worth. Going forward, your fee will typically be automatically adjusted based on some variation of the CPI (inflation). The fee, in this case, is always quoted in advance of you hiring the advisor.

The majority of CFP® practitioners are not fee-only but rather receive part or all their compensation in the form of commissions from the sale of products such as life insurance, load mutual funds, and stocks and bonds. There are plenty of highly talented, client-centered CFP® practitioners in this category. The main thing you need to be concerned with is the potential conflict of interest associated with buying products from your advisor. Is this person recommending the very best, most competitive life insurance policy for you or is the practitioner offering the policy that pays the highest commission? To resolve this conflict, you either have to fully trust your advisor or get additional quotes from other advisors to make certain you're getting the best deal.

One problem in the field of financial planning is that virtually anyone can say she's a financial planner. There are no educational requirements and no licensing requirements. People who hold themselves out as financial planners to the public are required to be registered (Registered Investment Advisor or RIA) with either their State Securities Commission or the Securities & Exchange Commission (SEC). But being an RIA with one of these agencies is no assurance that the financial planner is qualified to give advice.

You should ask whether the planner is registered with the State Securities Commission or the SEC. If their answer is "no" on both counts, ask why he or she is exempt. There are virtually no exemptions from registration, so a "no" answer should serve as a red flag. If the planner is registered with the state, this means that he or she has less than $25 million of assets under management and is an indication that the planner is relatively new in the business; he or she is not working with many clients; or he or she is only working with lower net worth clients. Again, this may be a red flag.

Treasure Tip

To locate a CFP® practitioner near you, go to www.fpanet.org. The listings at this website include CFP® practitioners who are fee-only as well as CFP® practitioners who receive commissions. The National Association of Personal Financial Advisors (NAPFA) is a financial planning association made up of fee-only financial advisors, not all of whom are CFP® certificants. Through their website you can search for a fee-only advisor in your area (www.napfa.org).

To get the most benefit from hiring a CFP® practitioner, you should work with her firm to develop a comprehensive written financial plan. Think of her as your CEO/CFO, the top member of your Executive Advisory Team. Your job, as Chairman of the Board, is to create the vision of what you want to accomplish. Your CFP® practitioner can help you fine-tune this vision and memorialize it in the form of a written goals statement. Together you will develop a written action strategy (financial plan) that consists of the steps needed to accomplish your goals. Your CFP® practitioner's job is to then accept responsibility for implementation of your plan, monitor results, and periodically report back to you on your progress. You can be as involved in the process as you want to be.

Questions you should ask include …

♦ *Do you have minimum fee requirements for new clients?* Fee-only CFP® practitioners, particularly, often have minimum fee requirements.

♦ *Can you describe your approach to financial planning and investment management?* The advisor should be able to explain how they work with clients and manage the clients' money in a way that is clear to you.

The Ideal Accountant

Having an accountant on your team will ultimately be vital to your success. A good accountant can help you with both tax and business planning. Many have expertise in financial planning as well.

The ideal accountant is someone who is a Certified Public Accountant (CPA). All CPAs must pass a series of national exams that test competency. CPAs must also complete 40 hours of continuing education each year. They must also agree to abide by a Code of Ethics. Most are compensated based on hourly rates. Hourly fees vary widely but typically range from $100 to $400 per hour.

A small percentage of CPAs now sell products and receive commissions. Often this is done through a separate company owned by the CPA or the CPA's firm. We have the same caution here as we did for financial planners and strongly prefer our CPA not receive commission income either directly or indirectly. To determine this you'll need to ask, "Do you, your firm, or any affiliated company(s) receive any compensation in the form of commissions?"

In addition to asking about how the CPA is compensated, here are several other questions you will want to ask:

♦ *Who will be my day-to-day contact person? May I meet him or her now?* You want to make sure you can get along well with that person, not just the partner who is courting you.

♦ *Outside of the traditional tax and accounting services, what does your firm offer?* You may need other services that you don't even know about now.

♦ *What fields of expertise does your firm have?* Learn what their specializations are. They might be just what you're looking for, but you won't know until you ask.

♦ *Do you have other clients in my industry? If so, can you provide me with names?* If your business is in a specialized industry, this could be vital.

The Ideal Investment Advisor

Of all the financial areas that you might need assistance with, managing investments may be the most important. This is because your money is the glue that holds your financial picture together. The perfect investment advisor is someone who is fee-only, meaning the only compensation the advisor gets comes directly from you. He or she does not receive commissions from the sale of products, and therefore the potential for conflicts of interest is minimized. Notice we did not say eliminated, for potential conflicts of interest are always present to some extent.

To determine if an investment advisor is fee-only, you will need to ask some very specific questions. Some investment advisors claim to be fee-only when they're not. First, start by stating, "I am looking for a fee-only advisor." If the person tells you that he or she is a fee-only advisor, ask this follow-up question: "Do you or your firm under any circumstances, from any clients, receive commissions?" If the answer is "yes," then you need to keep looking.

It is particularly important that your investment advisor have at least 10 years' experience managing money for clients, because it will generally take this long to experience all the market and economic cycles: bull market, bear market, inflationary cycle, recession, deflationary cycle, and so on. Each cycle provides a learning experience for the investment advisor—experience that will help the advisor do a better job advising you about your investments.

Most investment advisors fall into one of two groups. They are either a Registered Investment Advisor or a Full Service Investment Broker. Since it is important to distinguish between the two, let's look at both in more detail.

Registered Investment Advisors (RIAs) are typically independent business owners, choosing to run their own business free of the influence associated with brokerage firms. RIAs are paid in one of three ways: fee-only (percentage rate based on assets managed or hourly based on time), commission (based on the sale of products), or a combination of fees and commissions. As with your financial planner, we prefer that your investment advisor be compensated solely by fees rather than commissions.

RIAs, by law, have a *fiduciary* responsibility to their clients regarding investment management. This means that the RIA must place the client's interests ahead of his or her own interests. This will become an important distinction in a moment. Questions to ask include ...

> **Words of the Wealthy**
>
> An investment advisor who is a **fiduciary**, by law, must place the interests of the client ahead of his or her own.

- *Do you require a minimum size investment account or a minimum fee to work with you?* Many investment advisors, particularly fee-only investment advisors, have minimum account sizes.

- *How many clients do you have and what is the average size account that you handle?* Many advisors take on way too many clients. If the advisor is responsible for more than 100 clients, individual client service is likely to suffer. Some advisors are able to effectively expand this number by teaming up with a talented junior associate. By asking about their average account size, you'll get a sense of whether your account is significantly smaller or larger than the advisor's average. If your account is much smaller than average, you may be considered a "small fish" and not receive the attention you deserve. If your account is much larger, this is typically less problematic but it could mean the advisor has little experience with cases as large as yours.

> **Treasure Tip**
>
> If you divide the amount of money under management by the number of clients, you'll find the advisor's average account size.

- *What is your investment philosophy?* The advisor should be able to articulate how he or she manages money in a way that you understand.

- *What will be the various fees and costs associated with managing my account?* Fee-only investment advisors typically charge an annual fee of between .7 percent and 1.2 percent. There are typically fees associated with money management other than the advisor's fee, such as trading costs. Make sure you understand all the fees you will be paying.

- *Will my account be managed on a discretionary basis or a nondiscretionary basis?* An advisor who has discretionary authority over your account is not required to get your permission to buy or sell securities. This is a typical arrangement with a fee-only investment advisor. Because the fee-only advisor does not benefit from the trades in the account (no commissions), there is no conflict of interest. Investment advisors who use discretionary authority typically also develop, with the client, an *Investment Policy Statement (IPS)* that outlines the parameters of how the investment account will be managed. The IPS includes such limitations as the allocation between stocks, bonds, and cash; the suballocations of large versus small company stocks, domestic versus international stocks, short-term versus medium- and long-term bonds, and value versus growth stocks; and the

> **Words of the Wealthy**
>
> An **Investment Policy Statement (IPS)** is a written document between the investment advisor and the client, which outlines how the investment account will be managed.

amount and frequency of cash distributions. If the investment advisor only has non-discretionary authority, he or she must get your permission before making any trade in your account. This is a typical arrangement of an investment advisor who receives commissions for selling investment products.

◆ *What type of reporting can I expect and how often?* Most investment advisors provide quarterly reporting that includes rate of return on your investment account.

◆ *How accessible are you when I have questions?* Open communication is the key to a good working relationship. Make sure your investment advisor is accessible. In addition to ongoing communications, your investment advisor should meet with you at least annually to review your account.

◆ *Will I be working directly with you, and if not, who? Can I meet her?* Make sure you meet the person(s) responsible for handling your account. As stated previously, good chemistry between you and your investment management contact is very important.

◆ *Where will my assets be held?* If you're considering an independent investment advisor, an independent third-party custodian should hold your assets for you. Normally the fee-only RIA will set up *discretionary authority* for your account at this custodian so he or she can place trades on your behalf. This custodian should be a brokerage firm that sends you statements every month. The money manager should have a limited power of attorney agreement with the brokerage firm that allows him or her to buy and sell securities for you, deduct his or her fee quarterly, and get a copy of your monthly statement and daily account information. Having this independent firm separates your money manager from your account and reduces the possibility of fraud. When you open an account with an independent advisor, make your check out to the brokerage firm where your account is being held, not to your advisor. After your account is opened, call the brokerage firm and check your account number and balance. You should also receive a confirmation of the account being opened in the mail. Be sure to compare the statements you receive from the advisor with those of the brokerage firm.

Words of the Wealthy

An advisor with **discretionary authority** is authorized to buy and sell securities on behalf of the client, without the client's express permission. This authorization is given in the form of a limited power of attorney signed by the client.

Full Service Investment Brokers (broker) typically work for a brokerage firm such as Merrill Lynch, Morgan Stanley, and so on. Other titles used to describe a broker include registered representative, financial consultant, investment banker, and even vice president (usually awarded after certain levels of income are achieved).

A broker typically receives part or all his or her income in the form of commissions from the sale of products. This is not necessarily a bad thing, but it does require you to be alert for conflicts of interests. Commission products can also cause a misalignment of your objectives when compared to your broker's. One of the most common areas we see this occur in is when a broker sells mutual funds. For example, if you give your broker $50,000 to buy mutual funds, a typical commission might be $2,875. Not a bad day's work. Going forward your broker will only receive a small amount of commission, if any. This arrangement does not tend to encourage the broker to "manage" your account, and often we find that there have been no recommendations from the broker even years after the account was established.

There are many brokers out there who will take good care of you, but finding one may be a challenge. Brokers seldom have fiduciary responsibility for client's accounts, so the clients must be contacted prior to and must agree to any investment transactions. More and more brokers are moving away from the commission model of doing business and working on a fee-only basis. This is a good thing and will make it easier for you to find a client-centered investment advisor.

In addition to all the questions we suggest for the RIA, you should ask any full-service broker the following questions:

- *What are your recommendations for managing my investments?* If the recommendations include a lot of high commission products, you should look for another advisor for all the reasons we listed in Chapter 8.

- *How often will you review my portfolio?* This should be done at least once per quarter.

- *Will you be acting as a fiduciary as related to my account?* Acting as a fiduciary indicates the broker's commitment to put your interests ahead of his or her own. If the broker's answer is "no," ask what his or her responsibility to you is.

Wealth Warning

The terms *fee-only* and *fee-based* are not the same. An advisor who is fee-only never receives compensation in the form of commissions. Fee-based advisors will use commission income to offset part or all the fees paid to them by their clients.

As far as advanced designations go, ideally your investment advisor will either be a CFP® practitioner or a Chartered Financial Analyst (CFA). As we've already discussed, CFP® practitioners typically provide financial planning as well as investment management services. If your investment advisor does not also do financial planning, then ideally he or she would hold the CFA designation. This designation is specific to securities analysis and requires successful completion of three very difficult, globally administered exams as well as three years of experience in the field of investment management.

The Ideal Attorney

If for no other reason, you will need an attorney to help you develop your estate plan (wills, power of attorney, advance health-care directive, and so on). The ideal attorney for estate planning is one who is a member (called a Fellow) of the American College of Trust and Estate Counsel (ACTEC). Fellows are accepted based on their professional reputation, contributions to the field of estate planning, and recommendation by another Fellow. To find an ACTEC member near you, go to www.actec.org.

An alternative is to work with an attorney who is an Estate Planning Law Specialist (EPLS). Attorneys with the EPLS designation have passed a comprehensive exam, have a minimum of 5 years' experience, and do estate planning as a substantial part of their practice. You can find one near you by going to www.naepc.org.

ACTEC members and Estate Planning Law Specialists practice estate planning as a significant part of their practice. There are many other attorneys who are also highly qualified to do estate planning but are not included in these two groups.

You may also find yourself in need of an attorney for purposes other than estate planning, especially if you decide to start your own business. Your best bet here is to ask your CFP® practitioner or CPA for a referral. You can also search for attorneys by their area of practice by going to www.abanet.org.

Most attorneys are compensated on an hourly basis. Fees vary widely and may be as low as $75 per hour to more than $1,000 per hour. A few attorneys also sell products and receive commission income. Most don't, but you'll need to ask to be sure.

Questions you should ask include …

- *What are your areas of expertise?* You want to make certain that your attorney has a lot of experience in the area in which you need assistance.

- *How do you bill for your services?* You do not want surprises here. Be sure to ask for a fee estimate based on the work that you are asking to be performed.

The Ideal Life Insurance Representative

If you have dependants, there's a good chance that you need life insurance. We'll cover how much and what kind of life insurance you need in Chapter 20. For now let's focus on the basic qualifications to look for in your life insurance representative.

The ideal life insurance representative is one who is a Chartered Life Underwriter (CLU). To achieve this designation, one must complete a series of nationally administered exams, have a minimum of three years of business experience, agree to abide by a code of ethics, and complete 15 hours of continuing education each year. Most life insurance representatives also sell other products including disability income insurance and long-term care insurance. The CLU is the gold standard in the life insurance business. Questions you will want to ask:

♦ *How many different companies do you represent?* Ideally, the answer will be several companies. Many agents are "captive" agents, meaning they cannot sell products offered by other companies. Invariably, no one company has the best deals on all the products.

♦ *Who is your primary company?* Often agents represent primarily one company and may even have a career contract with that company. They use other companies mostly under special circumstances. In many cases the agent will receive more compensation for selling products of his primary company. In some cases this additional compensation will be in the form of retirement benefits or sales award vacations. If the majority of his income comes from one company, you will need to be more cautious about the agent's recommendations.

♦ *When recommending products, will you shop different companies to find the best deal for me?* To find the best deals, the agent must shop around. Hopefully the agent will offer you products from several different companies to choose from.

The Ideal Property and Casualty Representative

If you own your own home, rent your living quarters, or own or lease a car, you will need to have a qualified property and casualty representative on your team.

The ideal property and casualty representative is someone who is also a Certified Insurance Counselor (CIC). To become a CIC, one must pass a series of five nationally administered exams. The person you're looking for will be very service-oriented; good at balancing risks versus premium costs; and provide annual reviews as part of his service model. Representatives receive commissions for selling insurance products so there's an inherent conflict whereby the higher your premium, the higher the commission received by the representative. To find a CIC representative near you, go to www.scic.com.

Questions you should ask include …

♦ *How many companies do you represent?* As with the life insurance agent, the ideal answer is several.

♦ *How often will you review my coverage to make certain it is up-to-date and competitively priced?* Once every 12 to 24 months is appropriate.

How to Control Costs and Fees

Great advisors deserve to be paid well. At the same time, you do not want to overpay for their services, be surprised by a fee that is much larger than you expected, or end up paying commissions that you didn't know about. A little preparation on your part will ensure that you get what you pay for.

Advisors Who Are Paid Hourly

If your advisor is paid hourly for working with you, you should request an estimate of the amount of time he or she expects to have in your case based on a defined scope of the work you've requested. Typical advisors in this group include accountants, attorneys, and some financial planners. Ask the advisor to contact you if at any point he or she needs more time than estimated. You will also want to receive a bill at predetermined intervals (monthly or at the completion of various phases of the work) that details date, time, and subject of the work performed.

Advisors Who Are Paid Based on Fees

If your advisor is paid a fee for his work, be sure to ask what the fee will be in advance of hiring the advisor. Whether it's an initial fee for a financial plan or an ongoing fee for money management, you want to know what it will be. Fee-only financial planners and investment advisors often charge fees for their work, as do some accountants and attorneys.

Advisors Who Are Paid Based on Commissions

If you work with an advisor who receives commissions from the sale of financial products, you should insist on full disclosure of the source and dollar amount of all commissions and fees being paid. Any reputable advisor will be happy to accommodate this request. You might want to compare the products offered to similar products offered by other companies. For example, it's relatively easy to compare your auto insurance by going to www.geico.com. Or you could get a quote from more than one agent.

Where to Find Great Advisors

Perhaps the best way to find a top advisor is to ask a professional advisor that you respect. All top professionals are plugged into the professional community and can refer you to a top professional in any field. For example, if you're looking for a CFP® practitioner but know a respected CPA, call him or her and ask for a referral to a CFP® practitioner. Be sure to detail the qualities that you're looking for (fee-only, 10 years of experience, and so on).

CAUTION

Wealth Warning _____

Before hiring any type of professional advisor, you might want to see whether any complaints have been filed against them. The following organizations provide this information:

- Certified Financial Planner™ (CFP®): Certified Financial Planner Board of Standards; www.cfp.net; 888-237-6275
- Certified Public Accountant (CPA): American Institute of Certified Public Accountants; www.aipca.org; 888-777-7077
- Chartered Financial Analyst (CFA): CFA Institute; www.cfainstitute.org; 1-800-247-8132
- Broker: National Association of Securities Dealers; www.nasd.com; 301-590-6500
- Attorney: American Bar Association; www.abanet.org; 1-800-285-2221
- Insurance Representative (life, property, and casualty): The National Association of Insurance Commissioners; www.naic.org; 816-842-3600

You will find that all professional advisors will be happy to help you find another top professional. All you have to do is ask. Simply give them a call, tell them you respect them as a professional and would like their recommendation to a top professional in the field of your choice. Your next best choice is a referral from friends who are using an adviser they're happy with. After you identify a prospective advisor, simply take that person through the screening process outlined in this chapter.

Treasure Tip

If you're starting from scratch, you should interview at least three advisors before making a decision.

Creating the Ultimate Executive Advisory Team

As your net worth grows to the point that you seek advice from multiple professional advisors, it is vital that a communication link be established. You've done the hard work of screening and choosing a group of top advisors. To turn a talented group of individuals into a dynamic "brain trust" who are united in their desire to help you achieve your goals, you must bring them together and share your goals. The ideal way to do this is for you to schedule a breakfast or lunch meeting (you'll pick up the tab). Breakfast or lunch are typically the easiest times for professional advisors to meet.

Here's a sample agenda:

◆ Open the meeting with a few brief comments about the overall purpose. Your purpose is to have your chosen advisors meet each other and for you to share your goals.

◆ Have each advisor introduce himself and give a brief overview of his practice. You go first.

◆ Outline your financial goals and provide your advisors with a copy of your financial statement.

◆ Ask for input from your advisors. They may immediately provide insights based on their experiences that will be valuable to you.

◆ Close the meeting by thanking them for their time and tentatively scheduling a follow-up meeting to report on progress. Ask them how often they feel the group should meet.

Be sure you make it clear to them that they're both free and encouraged to share information and ideas with each other on your behalf. The results of this "group-think" process may just amaze you!

The Least You Need to Know

- ◆ Like any great athlete, you need to surround yourself with great coaches. Consider hiring a team of great advisors, but do your homework during your search.

- ◆ The right credentials indicate an advisor who is committed to his field of practice.

- ◆ To get the most out of your advisors, make sure they work together as a team.

- ◆ Control advisor fees and avoid surprises by asking the right questions.

Chapter 12

Advanced Investment Strategies

In This Chapter

- Having a real-life asset allocation strategy
- Choosing the ideal investment strategy for you
- Having zero-based thinking and knowing when to sell
- Dealing with the next bear market

There are many different investment management strategies that will produce successful results. This chapter takes you to the next step in portfolio management—building the perfect portfolio based on your management style. Okay, so there's no such thing as a perfect portfolio. However, there is a perfect portfolio for you. This portfolio should be custom designed for you with your risk tolerance and goals in mind. Just like the concept of wealth, the perfect portfolio is a journey, not a destination. In this constantly changing investment market, you must be flexible enough to make changes when necessary. You must also be cognizant of how your own life changes. These changes will force you to keep an eye on your portfolio— or at least hire someone else to do it for you.

As you review each of these strategies, think about how each fits your own natural style. Are you looking for a strategy that requires minimal effort? Do you enjoy doing investment research and following the markets and economic news? We believe that after you read through this chapter, you'll find yourself naturally gravitating toward a particular strategy.

The Perfect Strategy Doesn't Exist

Before we get started, it's vital that you understand the most important law in the investment universe: There is no perfect investment strategy. In fact, every investment strategy will appear broken about one third of the time. "One third of the time!" you scream. To which we respond, "Yes, one third of the time." Think about it logically. If we found a strategy that worked perfectly 100 percent of the time, everyone would use it. If everyone used it, it *couldn't* work! The markets depend on both buyers and sellers.

So here is what you should expect with your chosen strategy. About one third of the time you will earn a higher return than you expected or deserved. Approximately one third of the time you will earn a return about what you expected to earn. Finally, about one third of the time your strategy will look like a complete failure. This is a critical concept for you to learn, because not understanding this will be the downfall of most investors. Here's why. You choose a particular investment strategy and it's working well for a while. Then, all of a sudden, you start losing money. You're at a cocktail party bemoaning your dismal investment performance and someone begins to brag about how much money he or she is making based on a completely different strategy. You explore their strategy in greater detail and determine that it's a sound strategy so you decide to throw in the towel on your strategy and adopt hers. Have you guessed what's about to happen? You're jumping on someone else's strategy just about the time it's about to look broken! This jumping from one investment strategy to another will do very little to help you grow your wealth.

The Beginning: Your Asset Allocation Decisions

Effective portfolio management requires that you go through a never-ending cycle of decisions, reviews, and monitoring. The first step in the portfolio management cycle is the broad asset allocation decision between stocks, bonds, and cash.

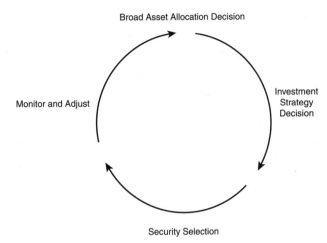

Broad Asset Allocation Decision

Monitor and Adjust

Investment Strategy Decision

Security Selection

The Portfolio Management Cycle.

Your Cash Allocation

You will need to keep some money in a money market account for unexpected emergencies (such as the air conditioner breaking); nonmonthly expenses (such as semi-annual auto insurance premiums); and planned purchases (saving to buy a new washer-dryer or auto). For the emergency portion of this account, we recommend a minimum of three months of take-home pay. You might want to extend this depending on your sense of job security. If you were to lose your job, how long would it take you to find another one? If you thought it might take six months or a year, prudence would suggest that your cash account match the number of months of potentially lost income. This money should be invested in a high-yielding money market fund. To find the highest yielding money market accounts, go to the Resource Center at www.welchgroup.com.

Your Bond Allocation

The historical return for intermediate term (3 to 7 years) bonds is 5.4 percent, about half the historical return for stocks. Consider using bonds in your portfolio for one of two reasons: to reduce volatility and/or to provide cash flow during retirement.

Reduce Volatility

Even the most conservative of stock portfolios is very volatile, especially over shorter periods of time (36 months or less). If you want to reduce the volatility of your stock portfolio even further, you can do so by adding bonds or bond mutual funds to your asset allocation mix.

One traditional rule of thumb is based on the principle that an investor's bond allocation should be based on his or her age. If you're 25, then 25 percent of your portfolio should be in bonds and 75 percent should be in stocks. If you're 80, then 80 percent of your portfolio should be in bonds and 20 percent in stocks. In the old days, when life expectancy was age 72, this might have made sense. It doesn't make sense today when life expectancy continues to be extended through continuing advances in medical science. Instead, your allocation in any type of investment should be based on your risk tolerance and how you feel about that investment, as well as the risk you're willing to assume to meet the goals you want to achieve.

Because managing risks (volatility) in your portfolio is an important concept, we're going to get technical for a moment. A simple measure of security volatility is called *standard deviation*. The standard deviation of a security (stock, bond, mutual fund, and so on) describes the expected variation of returns around the historical return for that particular security. For example, we know that the historical return for the U.S. stock market is approximately 10 percent. We also know that when we invest in stocks,

Words of the Wealthy

Standard deviation is a statistical measure of varying distributions around historical returns of a specific security or group of securities.

we're not going to earn 10 percent each year. Some years we'll earn more than 10 percent and some years we'll earn less than 10 percent. It's the range of variation of returns that defines the standard deviation. Knowing the standard deviation of a security you own or are considering buying will give you insight as to how risky that security is. You can also use standard deviation to compare the relative risks of various securities.

Standard deviation can also be helpful in managing risks of your overall portfolio. For example, we've already stated that the historical return for the U.S. stock market is 10 percent. The standard deviation of the U.S. stock market is 20 percent. This means that the expected range of returns is –10 percent to +30 percent. Now compare this to the U.S. bond market. Although the historical return for intermediate bonds is 5.4 percent, the standard deviation is only 5.7 percent. This means that your expected range of returns is –0.30 percent to +11.1 percent. Now you can see that as you add bonds to your stock portfolio, you reduce what we term negative volatility, or downside risks in your portfolio. Obviously, you also reduce potential returns. And while we're being technical, let us clarify standard deviation a bit further. If you study historical returns for the stock and bond markets, you'll inevitably discover that on occasion the actual returns fall outside the standard deviations we have discussed thus far. This is because in the investment community, the standard deviation used is

1 standard deviation. This means that the returns cited are based on what occurs approximately two thirds of the time. There are other actual returns that fall outside of the 1 standard deviation, but they don't happen very often.

So if you're going to use bonds or bond mutual funds to reduce volatility in your portfolio, what percent allocation should you use? Our recommendation is that if you're 10 years or more away from retirement, your allocation to bonds should not exceed 20 percent.

Provide Cash Flow During Retirement

If you're a retiree or a pre-retiree (someone who is within 5 to 10 years of retirement), you should have bonds in your portfolio as a way of securing your retirement cash flow needs.

The traditional way of handling this is to use bond interest as your primary source of income from your portfolio. Suppose you have $1,000,000; you need $40,000 per year to pay your lifestyle expenses; and bonds are yielding 5 percent. You would allocate $800,000 to bonds and $200,000 to stocks for growth. The main problem with this strategy is that it does not provide enough opportunity for growth in your portfolio over time.

Although this strategy should reduce portfolio volatility, it also significantly reduces the long-term growth potential of your holdings. We believe this "old age" way of approaching investing is out of touch with the world we now find ourselves living in. Advances in medicine and biotechnology have allowed scientists to better understand the aging process and develop methods for enhancing longevity. Some scientists now believe the average 50-year-old will live to well over 100. Talk about a need for growth in your portfolio!

A Growth Strategy with a Safety Net

One of the greatest fears retirees have is that they might outlive their financial resources and become dependant on their children (or the government) for their financial support. To address the need for a portfolio that could provide significant long-term growth *and* income for retirees, co-author Stewart Welch developed the Growth Strategy with a Safety Net, which today represents one of the best solutions for the possibility of "living too long." The goals of the Growth Strategy with a Safety Net are to …

♦ Protect your retirement income from market fluctuations.

♦ Maximize your retirement income.

♦ Produce an ever-increasing income stream that will more than offset the ravages of inflation.

♦ Provide for significant portfolio growth, ultimately providing a legacy for your heirs or favorite charitable organizations.

Sound impossible? Well read on!

First, determine how much annual income you need and multiply that number by the number of years that you want to "protect" your income. Use this scale:

Conservative: 6 to 8 years

Moderate: 4 to 5 years

Aggressive: 2 to 3 years

Your Safety Net

As in our previous example, we'll assume you have $1 million and need $40,000 to cover your annual expenses. We'll also assume that you've chosen to protect seven years worth of income. Using a laddered bond strategy, your initial portfolio will look something like this:

$40,000 money market for current year's cash flow

$40,000 bond maturing in 12 months

$40,000 bond maturing in 24 months

$40,000 bond maturing in 36 months

$40,000 bond maturing in 48 months

$40,000 bond maturing in 60 months

$40,000 bond maturing in 72 months
_____

$280,000

This, along with your cash reserves, represents your safety net.

Your Growth Strategy

The balance of your money will be invested in a diversified portfolio of stocks or stock mutual funds and will represent your growth strategy. As you "spend" your bonds, periodically you will sell stocks and use the proceeds to "replenish" your bond ladder. In a year when stocks do poorly, you postpone sales and wait for the market to recover. Historically, one to three years is sufficient time for this to occur.

Under a more traditional approach to retirement planning, your allocation was 80 percent bonds and 20 percent stocks. While producing the same initial cash flow, the Growth Strategy with a Safety Net allocates only 28 percent to bonds and a whopping 72 percent to stocks. This strategy meets all of its objectives. Your portfolio is protected from market fluctuations because you have seven years of guaranteed cash flow before you would have to consider selling any stocks. You're maximizing your cash flow because you're receiving as much money as you would have under the traditional strategy where, in our example, you had $800,000 in bonds producing $40,000 per year of income. Your annual cash flow will increase as your overall portfolio grows in value. And finally, with a 72 percent allocation to stocks or stock mutual funds, your portfolio has ample opportunity to grow in value.

We should add that this strategy is very tax-efficient for taxable accounts because a relatively small portion of your portfolio is producing taxable income in the form of interest (your safety net) and distributions from a relatively high portion of your portfolio are subject to the lower long-term capital gains tax (the growth portion).

Your Stock Allocation

Whew! You got through the boring stuff. Now to the fun stuff! If you're looking for excitement, stocks and stock mutual funds are the place to be. Because you've already made the decisions for your allocations to cash and bonds, by the process of elimination, your remaining investments will be allocated to stocks or stock mutual funds. When you invest in stocks, you should be aware that you are accepting a certain level of volatility no matter how conservative your stock investments are. What becomes important now is for you to choose an investment strategy that has the opportunity to meet your financial goals and one that is acceptable to you from a risk tolerance point of view.

Choosing Your Investment Strategy

Let's look at the tried-and-true investment strategies that you can count on to work, plus a couple that you should be very cautious of. Don't forget that each strategy has its strengths and weaknesses and all will appear to not be working for extended periods of time. Some will require more time and effort on your part. It's important that you understand the strategy you choose, that you recognize its weaknesses, and that you have patience to stay the course when things aren't working out as you expected.

Modern Portfolio Theory Strategy

In 1990, Harry Markowitz and William Sharpe shared the Nobel Prize for their development of Modern Portfolio Theory (MPT). MPT uses historical return data for various asset classes (U.S. large and small company stocks; international stocks and bonds; U.S. long-, intermediate-, and short-term bonds; and so on) to determine something called the correlation effect between the various classes. The goal is to put together a group of asset classes that have a low correlation of returns. Sound confusing? Let us help simplify this concept.

If two assets are perfectly correlated, it would mean that when one rose, say 10 percent, the other would also rise 10 percent. If one of the assets then dropped 4 percent, the other asset would also drop 4 percent. On the other hand, if two assets were perfectly negatively correlated, when one rose 10 percent, the other would drop 10 percent.

Now let's be a little more specific by using a hypothetical example. Let's assume that, based on your study of historical market returns, you discovered that international stocks and U.S. small company stocks both earned average annual returns of 12 percent over time with a standard deviation of 20 percent. You also discovered that their returns had a low correlation to each other, say 20 percent. This means that over the long term, a portfolio of 50 percent U.S. small company stocks and 50 percent international stocks could be expected to earn 12 percent, but your portfolio will experience much less volatility than owning 100 percent of either asset class because their actual returns differ from year to year. In other words, when one is zigging, the other is likely to be zagging. To maximize this result, a whole cottage industry has sprung up whereby you can use a computer to identify the most efficient mix of asset classes to produce the highest return on your portfolio for a given level of risk you're willing to take (called the efficient frontier).

Institutional investors (foundations, college endowments, and pension funds) have a strong preference for MPT because of its focus on reduction of volatility and its disciplined approach to investing. For individual investors, this strategy is best implemented using mutual funds because of the ease of identifying multiple asset classes and then creating immediate multiple stock diversification by buying a mutual fund. Here is an example of what your portfolio might look like under an MPT strategy:

2% Cash

10% U.S. bonds (investment grade)

3% U.S. bonds (noninvestment grade—junk bonds)

5% International bonds

45% U.S. large company stocks

10% U.S. small company stocks

10% real estate investment trusts (REITs)

12% International stocks

3% Emerging markets stocks
_____

100%

What should be obvious here is that you've taken your money and spread it among multiple asset classes whose returns have varying degrees of correlation. For example, U.S. large company stocks and U.S. small company stocks have a relatively high correlation of returns. When one rises or falls, the other tends to do so as well but not to the same degree. On the other hand, U.S. stocks have a low correlation of returns with international bonds. These differences tend to create a stabilizing effect on your portfolio.

In terms of ongoing monitoring of your portfolio, you will need to set up guidelines for rebalancing because as soon as you invest, your actual allocations to each asset class will begin to move away from your target allocation as your investment values change. One way to do this is simply to rebalance once every 12 months. Twelve months is a good time frame because any sales that yield a profit will be taxed at long-term capital gains rates (maximum 15 percent federal). A second strategy is to rebalance anytime an asset class position gets beyond its target by 10 percent to 12 percent. This works best if you're systematically adding money to your portfolio, because you can simply apply the new cash to the asset class that needs more money.

Here is a summary of the focus of this strategy, as well as its strengths and weaknesses:

- **The focus of MPT.** This strategy focuses primarily on diversifying your investments across a wide variety of asset classes to reduce risks.

- **Strengths of MPT.** This is perhaps the easiest of all strategies to implement and manage because it can easily be done using no-load mutual funds and does not require that you constantly monitor or make changes to your investments. You can actively manage mutual funds, index funds, and Exchange Traded Funds (ETFs) using this strategy.

- **Weaknesses of MPT.** Because you're broadly diversified at all times, your portfolio returns will always lag behind whatever sector or asset class is leading the market. For example, in 1998 and 1999, the return for the U.S. large company stock market significantly outperformed all the other market segments (24 percent and 19 percent respectively). Because in our example you only had 50 percent in U.S. large company stocks, your portfolio would have significantly underperformed by comparison. This can lead to feelings of "MPT no longer works" and you might be inclined to change to a new strategy. But when the 2000 to 2002 bear market came along, MPT held up quite well.

Wealth Warning

A lot of MPT enthusiasts use a computer model to help determine the ideal asset allocation. All of these computer programs are very sensitive to even small changes in your assumptions so you should use them as a very general guide only; not as if you've discovered the Holy Grail.

Buy and Hold Strategy

This is what we sometimes refer to as the Warren Buffett strategy. Buffett, who is regarded as one of the smartest investors of our time, is famous for carefully choosing a few stocks across a number of different industries and then holding on to those companies for the long haul. The long haul for Buffett is typically indefinitely. The analogy he likes to use is to act like you have a card with only 20 spots on it. Each time you pick a stock, you "punch" a hole in one of your spots. After you've punched 20 spots, you're done for life! When you adopt this mindset, you tend to be much more thorough in your research.

Buffett likes to look for companies that are what he calls "fortresses with moats and drawbridges." In other words, companies that are so dominant that it would be difficult, if not impossible, for another company to take their place. A good example is Coca-Cola (ticker symbol KO). Coca-Cola has such a strong brand and such world-wide market penetration that it's hard to imagine it not doing well over a 10-, 20-, or 30-year period of time. Another example might be Microsoft (ticker symbol MSFT). With their operating system installed in the majority of personal computers, no debt, and holding billions in cash, who do you think has the ability to knock Microsoft off its lofty pedestal? If a company comes up with a great new technology, Microsoft will simply buy them!

Here is a summary of the focus of this strategy as well as its strengths and weaknesses:

- **The focus of Buy and Hold.** If you're picking individual stocks, your focus with this strategy is *fundamental analysis* of corporations. Fundamental analysis attempts to determine the true value of a company. Your goal is to make certain that you do not overpay for a company and hopefully, you are able to buy a company for less than its true value. You're attempting to identify companies with very strong fundamentals (healthy balance sheet, earnings growth, sales growth, and accelerating market share). If you're using mutual funds, your focus is on broadly diversified funds.

> **Words of the Wealthy**
>
> **Fundamental analysis** is the study of the basic facts that determine a security's true value. A fundamental analysis of a mutual fund includes the study of the securities within the fund, the manager, the philosophy, the expenses, and the average P/E ratio.

- **Strengths of Buy and Hold.** Keeping portfolio expenses low is one key to successful management, and the Buy and Hold strategy minimizes trading costs. This strategy also reduces your ongoing monitoring responsibilities, but it does not eliminate them. You must always monitor your holdings for changes in fundamentals. Remember the lesson from railroad stocks. In the early days of the twentieth century, railroad stocks were considered the bluest of the blue chip stocks because the railroad was the primary means for transporting passengers and goods. That fundamental changed with the mass production of the automobile. Railroad stocks lost their lofty position forever.

- **Weaknesses of Buy and Hold.** One of the biggest weaknesses of a buy and hold strategy is that when a stock does well it can easily grow to the point where you're accepting a lot of single company risks. It's the proverbial "all your eggs in one basket" approach that destroyed so many lives when Enron, Worldcom, and Global Crossing went bankrupt. You can overcome this weakness by buying mutual funds instead of individual stocks. This is particularly true if you use a broad market based index mutual fund such as Vanguard's Total Market Index fund, which covers most of the publicly traded stocks in the United States.

Core and Tactical Strategy

The Core and Tactical investment strategy combines some of the elements of MPT and Buy and Hold but then adds a bit of excitement to the mix—an element of active management on your part. For the core of your portfolio, you can use either MPT or Buy and Hold or our Rising Dividend Strategy discussed later in this chapter. This core should represent a minimum of 60 percent of your allocation. Because you're more likely to make mistakes in the beginning, you might want to consider starting out using 80 percent to 90 percent for your core. With the remaining, say 20 percent, invest tactically by taking advantage of current market conditions or what we some-times refer to as investing in "fat pitches." A fat pitch is a baseball term that refers to the situation when a pitcher throws a pitch and the batter sees the ball coming very clearly. To the batter, the ball appears to move in slow motion and is the size of a grapefruit. Fat pitches don't come very often, but when they do, the batter has an opportunity to hit a home run. The same thing is true in the investment world. If you pay attention to what is going on, periodically, you will find an investment opportu-nity that looks like an odds-on favorite to deliver superior returns. This will give you, in essence, an opportunity to use two strategies at once. You can rely on your core strategy to work for you with a minimum of attention and monitoring while actively seeking higher returns with your tactical strategy. Visually, your portfolio might look something like this:

Core and Tactical

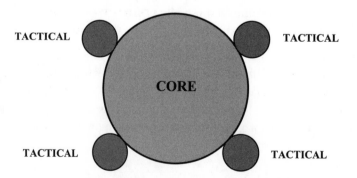

Although your tactical positions are going to be strategic fat pitches, you want to make sure that you're adequately diversified by the number of securities. The best way to ensure this is to use either ETFs or no-load mutual funds. One big advantage of ETFs is that they're highly liquid and can be bought and sold quickly and inexpensively. Mutual funds, even no-load mutual funds, often impose a fee if you sell your fund within a certain time frame from the time you purchase it (called an early redemption fee). This time frame can be as short as 90 days or as long as one year or more.

To put the tactical component of this strategy into perspective, let's take a lesson from one of the world's greatest athletes. It's said that Wayne Gretzky, one of the best and most popular hockey players in the world, was asked by a reporter one day, "Wayne, I don't get it. Why are you so much better than your teammates and opponents? You're not the fastest skater on the ice. You're not the best puck handler. And you're certainly not the meanest hockey player. What is it that makes you one of the best players of all time?"

Wayne thought for a moment and said, "Well, most of the players skate to where the hockey puck is. I skate to where I think the hockey puck is going to be." If we applied this concept to investing, we'd find that most investors don't even invest where the market is. They invest where the market has been, right? Your goal for the tactical portion of your portfolio should be to invest where the market is going and not where it's been. You must be willing to invest your money based on what you think is going to happen. To do that, you have to understand trends by using what you learned to spot trends (fat pitches).

Here is a summary of the focus of this strategy as well as its strengths and weaknesses:

♦ **The focus of Core and Tactical.** Your focus for the core portion will be the same as either MPT or Buy and Hold. For the tactical portion of your portfolio, you will focus on identifying market trends.

♦ **Strengths of Core and Tactical.** If you have a talent for identifying fat pitches, you have an opportunity to enhance performance of your portfolio, learn a lot about the markets, and have some fun along the way.

♦ **Weaknesses of Core and Tactical.** For most people, it takes time to develop investing skills for the tactical portion of your portfolio. Your attempts may hurt portfolio returns.

Market Timing Strategy

In its most basic form, market timing is simply the strategy of being in the market when it's going up and out of the market when it's going down. This is quite a seductive strategy, but it's difficult to accomplish consistently over time. This is because you have to make, not one, but two perfect decisions. When you're "in" the market, you have to decide when is the right time to sell. And after you're "out" of the market, you have to accurately determine when you should buy back in.

By far the biggest problem with this strategy is that the typical investor is using his or her gut to drive the decision process. Both decisions are counterintuitive, meaning that you're deciding to sell when the market is doing very well, then you must buy when the market is doing very poorly. Many professional investors and most financial writers say market timing is impossible. What they fail to acknowledge is that every time you make *any* decision to buy or sell securities in your portfolio, you're making a market-timing decision. We agree that using your gut instincts to make your buy and sell decisions is a market-timing strategy that is doomed to fail.

To improve your chances, you will need to adopt some technical trading rules. There are any number of successful technical trading strategies. One of the more popular approaches is to track the momentum of the market using moving averages. Short-term market trends are often followed by tracking the 50-day moving average while longer-term trends are often tracked using the 200-day moving average. You can experiment with this strategy by going to the Charting section of www.investor.com.

Here is a summary of the focus of this strategy, as well as its strengths and weaknesses:

- ◆ **The focus of Market Timing.** With this strategy, you'll need to focus your attention on the *technical analysis* of the markets. By using a technical trading strategy, you'll take your emotions out of the decision-making process and thereby improve your chances of success.

- ◆ **Strengths of Market Timing.** This is a compelling concept, and if implemented effectively, can be used to enhance returns and reduce volatility.

- ◆ **Weaknesses of Market Timing.** Those who say that timing the market is impossible are not correct. It would be correct to say that it's very, very difficult, and we recommend that if you're

Words of the Wealthy

Using charts to read the price history and other statistical patterns of stocks or mutual funds is known as **technical analysis.** Many investors and professionals use charts to help make investment decisions.

attracted to this strategy, you use it for only a portion of your portfolio, particularly until you gain confidence in your skills.

Variations of Investment Strategies

So far we've covered four main investment strategies, but we have far from covered all the investment strategies being used. You will find, however, that most strategies are a result of some variation of the four strategies discussed. The following sections detail a couple more you should be aware of.

Rising Dividend Strategy

The Rising Dividend Strategy is a variation of the Buy and Hold Strategy whereby you buy quality blue chip companies that pay a solid dividend (2 percent to 4 percent) and have a history of raising their dividend over time.

During President George W. Bush's first term of office, he signed tax reform legislation that reduced the taxation of corporate dividends from your highest marginal tax rate to a maximum of 15 percent. This was certainly a big boon for investors who were receiving dividend income because their net earnings got a big boost. It also directed a lot of attention to quality companies that had a history of not only paying dividends but also raising dividend payouts over time. For retirees and pre-retirees, the rising dividend strategy is ideal, and we will often use it for the core portion of a client's portfolio. Our key stock selection factors include the following:

- Start with the 1,000 largest companies in the United States. Most companies started out small and did a lot of things right over a lot of years to finally become one of the largest companies in the country. In other words, they paid their dues.

- Screen for companies with strong financial statements.

- Identify companies that consistently make money year after year. Consistent cash flow is critical because you're counting on it to fund the dividend payout each quarter.

- Make certain there is consistency of rising dividend payout for a minimum of 10 years. These companies did not have to raise their dividend each year over the past 10 years, but they should have risen it for a minimum of 5 years.

Zero-Based Thinking

As we mentioned earlier in the book, all sell decisions should start with this question: "If your portfolio were all in cash today, would you buy what you own?" If the answer is no, make the changes necessary to get to where you want to be. If the answer is yes, do nothing. Your decision should be based on your continued research of world markets and trends. You can use this strategy with your entire portfolio or each individual investment. It makes every investment decision so much easier.

Bear Market Strategy

Historically, you will experience a market correction or *bear market* once every 3 to 5 years and it will last an average of 14 months. Because you know it's coming but you don't know when, you need to decide now what changes, if any, you will make to your portfolio when the inevitable happens. For purposes of definition, we'll define a bear market as a market decline of at least 20 percent. We'll define a market correction as a decline of at least 10 percent.

Words of the Wealthy

A **bear market** is simply a time when few (if any) people are buying. Therefore, it's the worst time to sell. History shows that periodically, the market will pull back and correct itself. This is normal but often difficult to accept.

Most of the conventional wisdom says that if you are years away from retirement, you should not concern yourself with bear markets and market corrections. If you are retired or a pre-retiree, consider using the Growth Strategy with a Safety Net, described earlier in this chapter. The bond ladder will provide a buffer so that you'll not have to consider selling stocks for several years; enough time for the stock market to recover. Also note that several of the strategies discussed, including the Core and Tactical and Market Timing strategies, should provide some natural defenses against negative market volatility.

If you're on a systematic (monthly) investment program, your attitude toward a market decline should actually be one of excitement because you're buying stocks at lower and lower prices. When the market finally recovers, you will own more shares.

Investment Policy Statement

No matter what investment strategy you decide to pursue, you should document it in a written Investment Policy Statement (IPS). The IPS details your strategy, your target allocations to various asset classes, your rebalancing procedures, and how you will react to market corrections and bear markets. The importance of having an IPS cannot be overstated, for it is your IPS that will help you stay the course during trying times. When you feel like bolting from your chosen strategy, reviewing your IPS will remind you why you chose that particular strategy. A sample IPS can be found in Appendix C.

Maintenance and Review

Obviously, after you've implemented your investment strategy, you will need to monitor your investments and make adjustments as appropriate. How often will depend on the strategy you have chosen. Decide on your monitoring procedure and add it to your IPS, then make sure you follow through. If you find that, for whatever reason, you are not monitoring on an appropriate time table, you have likely chosen the wrong strategy and should reconsider your choices.

Treasure Tip

Figuring the actual rate of return can be difficult unless you're using special software. Check out Appendix A for resources to aid you.

Part of the monitoring process involves measuring your results as compared to your goals (remember the target portfolio goal from Chapter 5) and expectations.

The Least You Need to Know

♦ Begin by making the broad asset allocation decisions between stocks, bonds, and cash.

♦ Choose an investment strategy that fits your investment style, temperament, and desired time commitment to investment management.

♦ Always ask yourself, "If my portfolio were all in cash today, would I buy what I own?" If the answer is no, make the necessary changes.

♦ You must make monitoring your portfolio's progress part of your investment strategy using your Investment Policy Statement (IPS) as a guide.

Part  3

Building Wealth with Your Own Business

Wealth Stages 3 and 4 are achievable using the strategies you've learned so far. However, if you want to increase your chances of achieving Wealth Stage 4 and even Wealth Stage 5, you should explore starting your own business. It might not be a requirement for achieving Wealth Stage 4, but it's almost impossible to reach Wealth Stage 5 without your own business.

We'll begin by helping you select a business that you will enjoy, and explain what you can expect by working for yourself. You'll learn how to use the skills of your CPA and banker to effectively monitor your business as well as make certain that you have access to the capital you need. We'll identify common mistakes that many business owners make and how you can avoid them. You'll also learn how to hire and keep talented employees. Finally, we'll show you the keys to building a profitable business and how to prepare your business to be sold for its highest value.

13

Start with Your Hobby

In This Chapter

◆ What you should focus on before you start your own business

◆ Why you should use your hobby to start a business

◆ How to write a successful business plan

◆ What the new business checklist is that can save your life

Harry Brock was a natural-born salesman and spent the early part of his career in various sales jobs before joining a local bank. But Harry's dream was to run his own bank, one that would be like none other in his home state of Alabama. In 1964, desire met opportunity when he, along with six businessmen, raised $1 million and founded what today is Compass Bancshares, Inc. (www.compassweb.com). He built the bank based on a sales culture rather than the stodgy white tower culture of the banks of that era (same as today!). All of the board members had sales goals and contests and all enthusiastically pursued new customers for the bank. They managed to ruffle a lot of feathers in the state's banking community with programs such as all-day banking and Saturday banking. The bank was new, full of fresh ideas, truly customer focused, and began to grow rapidly under Harry's aggressive leadership.

Banking laws did not allow banks to have branches outside of their home county, which clearly limited growth. Undeterred, Harry orchestrated the takeover of the third largest bank in the state—the only bank in the state not bound by county boundary rules due to its special charter. What was extraordinary was that the 76-year-old acquired bank was two and a half times the size of the 4-year-old Compass Bank. This was the first round in a David versus Goliath battle that pitted Harry against virtually all the other major banks in the state. He won the war and, in so doing, changed the landscape of banking forever in the state of Alabama. Today, Compass Bank is one of the largest regional banks in the country with more than 375 branches in 6 states and $28 billion in assets. Not only did Harry Brock become a multimillionaire, he became a legend in banking history in the state of Alabama. You see, a lifetime of accomplishment often starts with a simple dream.

Ideally, you choose to start a business based on something you love. If you love to cook for other people, it might be a restaurant. If you love mountain climbing, it might be an outdoor store specializing in mountain climbing gear where you both sell goods and act as an instructor for beginners.

Can you imagine starting your own business with one of your favorite hobbies? It's a dream that only a few people realize. Why? First of all, most people don't even think it's possible. They think you have to be extremely talented, rich, or famous to start a business. Second, they think that making money should be hard. That's simply not true. If you're doing what you love doing, it will seem more like play than work. Others may look at you and say, "She's a workaholic." But you won't see it that way. You see, other people look at what you do and think it's work because it's not something that excites them. You, however, are having a blast (at least most of the time).

Three Reasons for Failure

Fear of failure prevents most people from starting their own businesses. Yet, the reason people make so much money in their own businesses is because they chose to accept the risk of failing.

Another reason why most people don't start their own businesses is also a big reason why most businesses fail: they are more concerned about making money than doing something they are passionate about. When most people start considering their own businesses, they focus on what they think will be successful or make the most money. The focus is primarily on making money, which might sound smart at first, but it can be a mistake. Many initially successful businesses fail because the owner gets burned out or loses the drive after they find out that making money is not as easy as they thought it would be. They lose interest because they were only in it for the money.

The third reason most people don't start a business doing what they enjoy is because they haven't taken the time to figure out what they enjoy doing, much less make a plan to implement it. This chapter begins to explore how your own business can be part of a plan to achieve the wealth level you want to achieve using a hobby or career that you enjoy.

Wealth Warning

Not only is it okay to have fun at work, but if you don't enjoy your work, you're in the wrong job and you need to make a change!

If your target is Wealth Stage 4, you'll have to accumulate enough assets to produce a total return sufficient enough to substantially increase your desired lifestyle and keep up with inflation. That charge may seem overwhelming at first, but you *can* do this. We both did it, and it is one of the best ways to build a multi-million dollar net worth. Think about it. Everything that you love to do, someone is making a living at doing. Not only that, almost certainly someone has built a multi-million dollar net worth doing it. If you want to achieve Wealth Stage 5, starting your own business is almost a requirement.

Why Start Your Own Business?

Here is a list of the most common reasons why people want to start their own businesses:

- To control their own destiny
- To achieve financial independence
- To pursue their dream jobs doing what they enjoy
- To escape corporate bureaucracy
- To achieve creative independence
- To achieve a more flexible schedule
- To build wealth
- To enjoy life more

Treasure Tip

The primary key to success in your own business is to be passionate about what you're doing. Passion creates tenacity, and if you're tenacious enough to give it everything you've got, the money will follow.

Do any of these reasons apply to you? Have you ever asked yourself why you want to start your own business? Now is a good time to do it. Ask yourself these questions. If the answers are positive, you should definitely explore business opportunities:

- ◆ Why do you want to start your own business?

- ◆ What would starting your own business accomplish for you?

- ◆ Would you enjoy working for yourself? Why?

What Business Will You Start?

Deciding what business to start can be one of the hardest questions for some people to answer. Unless you've had a burning desire to start a particular type of business, you might get stuck here. We're going to coach you through this process and make it easier for you.

The first step is to review your answers to the five questions in the Chapter 5 section "Follow Your Passion."

Wealth Warning

Most people think that to start a business, they need some incredible new invention or product that will change the world. It would certainly help if you did have such a product, but it is in no way a requirement to start a business. All you need is a passion for producing a product or service and customers who will buy it from you.

Do not read any further until you have completed this exercise. The answers to these questions should give you a clear picture of your goals and values in life. Basically, you list your passions and dreams. Use them to find and design the business of your dreams.

If a business idea doesn't come to you right away, you might want to take some time and use the answers to at least design the parameters of the business you're going to start. For example, if you enjoy spending time at home, you might declare this as one of your business parameters. If you know and enjoy working with computers, this might be a key parameter also. If you continue listing your desired parameters, it will be much easier to select the perfect business for you.

After you have a list of parameters, your next step is to screen every business idea you have. The perfect business might not meet every parameter for you, but it should satisfy at least your top three. Therefore, it is necessary to prioritize your parameters. Which one is the most important to you? Which is second? Third?

> ### That Reminds Us ...
>
> After having spent a number of years in sales, I knew that what I truly wanted to do was make a real difference in the financial lives of other people. To accomplish this I knew I had to leave my job and build a fee-only financial advisory business. The company I built enabled me to "drill down" into the deepest crevices of our clients' financial lives and help them accomplish their goals and dreams.
>
> —Co-author Stewart Welch

If you're still having trouble finding the perfect business, here are some extra questions that might help you:

- What do you enjoy doing in your free time?

- What do you like to read in your free time?

- What do you excel in? What are you good at?

- What do others say you are good at?

- What do you want more of in your life?

- What do you want less of in your life?

Whatever you decide to do, make sure your business enables you to achieve at least your top three priorities. Your goal should be to get more life out of your business. If not, you might not be able to maintain the necessary passion you'll need to be successful. If this is the case, redesign the business concept to meet your goals.

We believe that no matter what kind of hobby or passion you have, you can build a business around it.

One of our favorite examples is Gordon Rathbun, whose passion is competitive waterskiing. Most people agree that there's no way you can make money waterskiing. Well, don't let Gordon hear you say that. As a teenager, he skied every morning and waited tables in the afternoons. Later on, he sold cable television services, but still skied every morning. In 1984 at the age of 34, he was ranked tenth in the world as a slalom skier! Gordon lived and worked to ski. Skiing is Gordon's passion.

After taking some friends to Acapulco to ski one winter, Gordon had an idea. At the age of 38, he started Ski Paradise—year-round ski schools in Acapulco, Mexico, and Lake Tahoe, Nevada. Gordon is now living his dream. A six-time national champion,

Gordon spends his winters in warm Acapulco and his summers in beautiful Lake Tahoe teaching people from all over the world how to ski like champions. Gordon says, "If you become an expert at your field of passion, you will become a natural sponge for knowledge, you will work harder than most other people, and you will be in demand for your service." Gordon would be the first person to tell you that if he could do it, you can, too.

After you've decided on the business ideas that fit your parameters, you need to focus your market (potential customers). Who will buy your product or service? Do some research to find a market willing to buy from you. Here are some questions to ask yourself about your market:

◆ Will your business fill a need (for your customer)?

◆ Who is your competition?

◆ What is your strategic advantage over your competition?

◆ What makes your product or service better?

◆ How can you create a demand for your product or service?

Writing a Winning Business Plan

Before you get started building your wealth further with your business, make sure to take time out to design and plan exactly what you're going to do. Don't worry if it's crude and embarrassingly simple at first. Its purpose should be to focus your thoughts. Something truly magical happens when you take pen in hand and articulate your thoughts, hopes, and dreams as well as your strategies for obtaining them.

To write a good business plan, you'll have to do some research. The following is co-author Larry Waschka's business plan outline. This business plan was not only used to help plan and develop his business; it was also used to secure a $100,000 loan from a local bank. Larry was 31 years old at the time and had very little collateral. He convinced the bank gave him the money primarily because of the organization of the plan.

Use this outline to help you organize your plan. Record the outline on paper or in your computer, and fill in the blanks, adding in the supporting documents where needed. You'll notice the term

Words of the Wealthy

Pro-forma financial **statements** are used to project the estimated financial results of a new company. They consist of an income statement, balance sheet, and cash flow statement.

"pro-forma" with several of the financial statements that are needed in the plan. *Pro-forma* refers to the projected financial statements of a company.

Part I: The Proposal.

What Is Waschka Capital Investments or WCI?

Loan Request and Purpose (Estimated Start-Up Costs).

Method and Terms of Repayment.

Part II: History of WCI and the Investment Advisory Business.

History of WCI and Larry Waschka.

Mission Statement and Investment Philosophy.

Ownership and Corporate Structure.

Description of Services.

The Investment Industry.

What Makes WCI Different from the Competition?

Part III: Marketing Plan—How We Build Our Business.

Who Is Our Market?

Marketing and Advertising Strategy.

Pricing Strategy.

The Competition.

Economic Overview.

Part IV: Management.

Principals and Key Associates.

Organizational Chart.

Research and Development.

Part V: Financials. (This is a view of the beginning.)

Balance Sheets (pro-forma).

Income Statements (Profit and Loss Statements) (pro-forma).

Statements of Cash Flow (pro-forma).

Ratio Analysis *(if you are an existing business)*.

Part VI: Financial Projections—Short Range (First Year).

Assumptions.

Projected Income Statements (Profit and Loss Statements).

Projected Cash Flow Statements.

Projected Balance Sheets.

Projected Ratio Analysis.

Part VII: Financial Projections—Long Range (Three Years).

Assumptions.

Projected Income Statements (Profit and Loss Statements).

Projected Cash Flow Statements.

Projected Balance Sheets.

Projected Ratio Analysis.

Part VIII: Supporting Documents.

Gross Income Projections on a Worst-Case Scenario.

Related Estimates for Expenses, Payroll, and Net Income.

Graphs and Data.

Gross Income Projections on a Best-Case Scenario.

Related Estimates for Expenses, Payroll, and Net Income.

Graphs and Data.

Gross Income Projections on an Outrageous-Case Scenario.

Related Estimates for Expenses, Payroll, and Net Income.

Graphs and Data.

Part IX: Appendix.

> Principals' Resumés.
>
> Job Descriptions for All Associates.
>
> Business Advisors and References.
>
> Client References.
>
> New Office Lease.
>
> New Office Improvement List.
>
> Automobile, Equipment, and Furniture List.
>
> Results of Recent Client Survey.
>
> Larry Waschka's Personal Financial Statement.
>
> Personal Budget.
>
> Copy of Life Insurance Policy on Larry Waschka.

Every business plan is different, so some of the titles in this plan may not apply to you. This is just an example of a plan that worked. Where necessary, we've inserted optional items that you might consider. The bottom-line question is "Will your company make money?"

If the task of writing your business plan and doing your financial statements seems overwhelming, buy one of the many business plan software packages on the market. One source we can recommend is Bplans.com (www.bplans.com). This site has scores of helpful articles as well as sample business plans for a large variety of businesses. It also has sample marketing and web-based plans. You can even buy software to help you produce your own professional-quality business plan; ready to present to your banker.

Buy a Franchise

One way to increase your opportunity for success is to buy a franchise. Franchises are thriving not only in America but all over the world, and with good reason. A franchise takes most of the guesswork out of starting and running a business, because the franchisor has made all of the mistakes; learned from them; succeeded in the business; and developed detailed processes that can be successfully repeated. Whatever your passion, whatever your dream business is, there is likely a franchise for it.

Jay Weston was an elementary school assistant principal. One afternoon in July of 2002, he and his wife, Angie, were working in the yard when the lawnmower stalled because a wire tangled around the blade. Jay disconnected the cable to the spark plug before turning the mower over to remove the obstacle. Tragically, however, the mower restarted and cut off his arm in the process. Not uncommon to amputee victims, Jay experiences what is called phantom limb pain. In Jay's case the severity of the pain becomes debilitating in the afternoons, making it impossible to perform his responsibilities as assistant principal. He had to work but he knew he couldn't work at a "regular" job. Jay and Angie decided the best solution was to own their own business and that buying a franchise was the way to go. He and Angie were thorough in their due diligence. Their decision-making process was so well done that we asked Jay and Angie if they would share their step-by-step approach with you. Here is what they had to say:

Jay and Angie Weston:

- ◆ We first decided whether we wanted to work for others or ourselves. After researching the backgrounds and occupations of most wealthy working Americans, the common theme is that they work for themselves rather than working for someone else. Besides that fact, my limitations with the PLP allow me to work about four or so "quality" hours per day. Any time spent beyond that is relatively useless, and it's really hard to find many high-paying jobs that allow you to only work four hours per day.

- ◆ Then we had to decide on a franchise or an independent business. This was the easiest decision to make, as the mortality rate for new start-up businesses is about 80 percent versus only 20 percent for the average franchise. Therefore, franchising puts the "odds" in your favor.

"The following decision points were the hardest and most important," says Jay:

- ◆ We had to decide which franchise to choose. We used *Entrepreneur Magazine's* Franchise Issue and website (www.entrepreneur.com) to help us narrow the search. We wanted a franchise that would allow us to work a few hours per day "working *on* the business rather than *in* the business." The information provided by *Entrepreneur* was great, as it allowed us to easily compare which franchises would allow this. We made a list from the top 500 franchises listed by *Entrepreneur* that met this criteria, then began to scratch off franchises as we narrowed our search. The information available through *Entrepreneur* was so thorough, we didn't feel the need to use a lot of other external research. They do the legwork for you.

◆ From our list (which was very long), we looked at the net worth and investment requirements. We didn't want to put all of our eggs in one basket, so we decided to cull those franchises which would have required too high of an investment compared to our net worth.

◆ We next looked at where the franchisor was looking to add locations. Again we culled those franchises which were only offering franchises in places where we didn't want to live.

◆ Next, we looked at the different types of industries, and culled out those that we could not feel passionate about. For example, we couldn't feel passionate about selling high-fat, greasy hamburgers, but we could feel passionate about helping people look and feel better about themselves.

◆ By this time our list was down to probably 20 or so franchises, so we looked at the growth or decline of each industry. We learned that franchise salon operations only accounted for about 20 percent of total hair care at the present time, with independents accounting for 80 percent. But this is expected to reverse during the next 20 years, whereby franchise salon operations will account for 80 percent and independents will account for only 20 percent. Therefore, we felt that this would be similar to getting in on the ground floor of McDonalds in the '50s.

◆ By this time, we were "sold" on the hair care industry, but which franchise? Our list was down to about six at this time. So we dissected each company, looking for levels of support with issues such as real estate, training, and so on. Sport Clips, Great Clips, and Supercuts were our top three.

◆ We spoke with current franchisees of all three as well as company representatives of all three, and we looked for negative publicity about all three. Everyone we spoke with and everything we read about Sport Clips was very positive.

◆ We also looked for potential growth for all three. Most salons cater to the whole family, and originally we thought this would favor Great Clips and Supercuts, as Sport Clips was *only* going after half of the market. But after consulting with a business coach, he convinced us that specialization was the wave of the future, and that often providing a service to a niche in the marketplace (especially a niche as large as half of the population) would probably be best.

◆ Finally, we went to Austin, Texas, for what Sport Clips calls Discovery Day, whereby potential franchisees get to meet with top management and get a feel for the company, as well as the company getting a feel for the franchisee to see if they will prosper in the system.

- After all the elimination process had been completed, there was only one franchise left (from the original list of 500 from *Entrepreneur*), and that was Sport Clips.

- The last question, therefore, was "Are we ready?" We felt we were, and as they say, "the rest is history in the making." We currently have two Sport Clips open in Mobile, Alabama, and plan to open a third operation in Foley, Alabama, this summer. We are committed to opening a minimum of six operations over the next 3 to 5 years.

Unusual circumstances caused Jay and Angie to dream of owning their own business. They turned adversity to their advantage by developing and then following a logical process that led to making that dream become their reality. You may have a completely different business idea in mind, but the methodology they used could easily serve as a model for finding your own dream business.

The Pro-Forma Financial Statements

If you plan to achieve Wealth Stages 4 or 5 using your own business, you have to understand financial statements. They are key tools for measuring efficiency and profitability. The first critical element in your financial statements is your return on your investment in the business. Before you start a business, you need to make sure your business passes the *Return on Equity* (*ROE*) test. Many business owners don't understand this test. They jump into a business without even considering (or knowing) what their ROE target should be. To pass the ROE test, you must prove to yourself that your return on equity can exceed the historical returns of the stock market (approximately 10 percent per year). You can calculate your ROE by dividing your net income (after all business expenses including business taxes but before income taxes) by the amount of capital you've invested in your company. The obvious goal of your business should be to maximize the ROE, and you can do this by reducing your expenses or increasing your gross income.

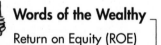

Words of the Wealthy

Return on Equity (ROE) is a measure of the stockholder's (or business owner's) percentage return on his investment based on the net income of the business.

Why is the ROE so important? If you can't beat the stock market's return, why start a business when you can invest your money in the stock market? Why work so hard in your own business when you can invest money in the stock market from the comforts of your own home without any employees? And in most cases, investing in the stock market is less risky than starting your own business.

How do you know what your ROE will be? You need to prepare pro-forma financial statements using accurate or best judgment data. Pro-forma statements are simply estimated financial statements based on several assumptions. They enable you to answer questions such as, "Given a certain amount of estimated sales and expenses, how much profit can be produced by your business?" The easiest way to complete these statements is with software or a good CPA. Take some time to learn the basics of how these statements work and how to read them. You might hate accounting, but we promise you'll hate failure and bankruptcy more.

That Reminds Us ...

A 61-year-old business owner told me one day that he wasn't in business to make money. He was trying to say that his focus was more on the welfare of his employees and customers. I couldn't believe his statement. This guy was either full of garbage or had his priorities completely backward. I quickly responded, "The best thing you can do for your employees and customers is make money. If you don't, there will be no business, no salary for your employees, and no service for your customers."

—Co-author Larry Waschka

A critical element of your pro-forma statements is cash flow management, which is measured using a statement of cash flow (also called a cash flow statement). This statement measures the actual beginning and ending balance of cash within a company. If you've never owned your own company, you might not realize how important cash flow can be. We've seen businesses that grew more than 100 percent per year in sales, but they went bankrupt because of poor cash flow management. Because their clients didn't have to pay for the goods for 90 days, the business found itself with great sales growth but no cash to continue operating.

The key is to plan in advance with estimated monthly cash flow statements and to know exactly how big your line of credit at the bank should be. We discuss bankers and how to get an adequate line of credit in Chapter 14. You and your banker will want to know where your breakeven point will be. If you want to ensure success in business the first few years, take the time to learn all you can about cash flow management. Buy a book or take a class if you have to. Many tricks of the trade can help you when you get into a crunch. Prepare detailed projected pro-forma financial statements, including cash flow statements, for a minimum of three years. These will serve as budget guidelines for your business. Each month, as soon as the prior month has ended, compare your actual results with your estimates and determine where the variances occurred and why they occurred. Use this information to help manage your business. Make any needed adjustments to your projected statements going forward. This is critical to the management process.

Taking on a Partner

One solution people often consider when starting a business is taking on one or more partners. Having like-minded people join you on your venture makes the whole thing less frightening and intimidating. However, our experience is that partnerships rarely work. Partnerships fail for a number of reasons, but we believe that the two primary reasons are diverging interests and control issues. Think of a partnership as a perfect circle. In the beginning, both partners fit very nicely in the circle, with each partner having harmonious goals. If this were not the case, the partnership would not be formed because the would-be partners would recognize that each had different objectives. However, after the business gets underway, almost immediately the partners will begin to grow in different directions; they begin stepping outside the circle. In the early going, these changes may be almost imperceptible but over time they will become more pronounced. Ultimately there will be conflicting opinions regarding critical decisions, and here is where control becomes an issue. If you and I are equal partners, it means we have an equal say. If we cannot reach a compromise agreement, then we must ultimately go our separate ways. This is what happens much of the time.

> **Treasure Tip**
>
> A great way to test compatibility with a future partner is to take a short vacation together. Don't bring the entire family. Only the two (or three) of you should go. You'll know in three days whether you can work together.

Yet another common partnership problem is that one partner perceives that he or she is doing more of the work, yet has to split the profits equally. If you want to achieve Wealth Stages 4 or 5, don't take on a partner unless you have to.

The potential problems are extensive, but not insurmountable. One possible solution to this issue is to make sure that you maintain a controlling interest in the partnership (at least 51 percent). Another possible solution is to set up the partnership agreement so that you are the managing partner and as such, you have the controlling vote over all matters.

> **Words of the Wealthy**
>
> **Outsource** simply means to pay someone outside your company to do a job for you. It's an alternative to putting someone directly on your payroll.

Instead of forming a partnership, try your best to hire or *outsource* everything you need to start your business. Only if you can't hire or outsource what you need should you consider a partner. If it's money you lack and someone's offering you money for a partnership or equity interest in your business, try every other angle first before you accept it. If at all possible, don't trade control for money. You should always maintain control over your business. A partnership may take away from that control.

Not all partnerships are bad. Before considering one, get to know the person well. Ask yourself whether you can work together in good times and bad.

A Last-Minute Checklist

The following is a list of other items you might want to think about:

- ◆ Where will your business be located?

- ◆ What will be your legal structure? (See a CPA or attorney.)

- ◆ What insurance coverage will you need?

- ◆ How will you compensate yourself? What is the minimum amount of salary you need each month?

- ◆ Will this business help you do more than make a decent living?

- ◆ Can you do this without a partner?

- ◆ Can you sell this business later?

> **Treasure Tip**
>
> I spent more than three months setting up my company before I left my employer. After giving my final notice, I walked into my own office ready to do business on the first day.
>
> —Co-author Larry Waschka

Don't Get Too Anxious

If you want to achieve Wealth Stage 4 using your own business, don't quit your existing job until you know that your venture can eventually produce an equal or higher income for you. Make sure you have adequate capital or income for the first year of living expenses. Be sure to finish your business plan, and then test your theory on a small scale before you jump out on your own. Don't get caught up in too much planning. Do a small-scale test of your business. Test-market your product, and test your production idea. Then learn from those tests. Don't go into a full-scale business until you know your idea will work. This can save you hours of time and thousands of dollars later.

How to Tell Whether You've Arrived

You know you've arrived when you reach the point where you can afford to spend a week every quarter on vacation somewhere in Europe or the Caribbean, but you don't because you're having too much fun at work. When you reach this mindset, achieving Wealth Stage 4 is easy.

You also know you've made it when someone calls you on the phone and asks whether you might be interested in selling your business. In Chapter 17, we'll show you how to build a business that others will want to buy, but next we'll show you how to put your new business on the fast track to profits beyond your wildest dreams!

The Least You Need to Know

- Don't start a business just to achieve a certain wealth stage; start a business that will give you an opportunity to focus on your passion and make money at the same time.

- All you need to start a business and achieve Wealth Stage 4 (and maybe 5) is a passion for your work, a market for your product or service, and a potentially sellable business.

- Planning is the most important part of starting a successful business, and a good business plan is the key to that planning process.

- Be patient and start your business slowly while maintaining your current job; get it off the ground before you jump out of your job.

Chapter 14

Avoiding the #1 Reason Most Businesses Fail

In This Chapter

◆ Determining the amount of capital you will need

◆ Identifying the best source of capital

◆ Working with a banker to get what you want

◆ Creating a loan proposal that will get you to a "Yes"

If you're successful in starting and running your own business, you could become a millionaire many times over. Remember, Bill Gates of Microsoft dropped out of college and started his company in the basement of his parents' home. Today he is one of the richest people in the world. You might not be the next Bill Gates, but you can become a multimillionaire.

After spending countless hours studying wealthy people, we've come to one definite conclusion: the key to great wealth is passionate ownership of something unique and attractive that either produces income and capital gains or has the potential to do so in the future. A successful business can do this for you faster than any other strategy because of the potential for extraordinary growth.

Unfortunately, a passion, a great idea, and hard work are no guarantee of success in the business world. Of all new small businesses started, 90 percent fail during the first year. Of those that survive, 90 percent will fail during the next four years of operation. The overwhelming number-one reason businesses fail is they lack adequate capital to see them through to the point where they become profitable. Most people approach starting a new business based on the least amount of capital they believe they will need. And they are almost always wrong in their estimates.

Capitalizing Your Business

An excellent way to test the waters and determine the validity of your business venture is to start your business as an extension of a hobby and cover your expenses out of earnings from your regular job. At some point, though, you will likely need to raise capital to continue to expand your business.

When the time comes, follow these guidelines for raising enough capital to succeed.

Prepare Pro-forma Financial Statements

You need to start your business with a very good handle on what it's going to cost to run it until it's consistently making money. To do this you will need to prepare the following pro-forma financial statements:

Balance Sheet

A balance sheet provides a snapshot of your company's assets and liabilities at a particular point in time. When starting a business, you need to prepare one as of the date of starting your company as well as a projected balance sheet for every 12 months for the next 3 to 5 years.

Income Statement

The income statement will show you the expected flow of sales (money coming in) and expenses (money going out) and the expected profit or loss for the period reviewed. For the first 12 months, prepare very detailed income statement projections on a monthly basis. As you complete each month of operation and study your results (actual sales, expenses, and profit or loss versus your projected sales, expenses, and profit or loss), you should use what you learn to extend your projection for an additional month so that you always have a projected income statement for 12 months available. For the next 24 months, prepare quarterly income statements.

Statement of Cash Flow

The statement of cash flow, in essence, integrates the balance sheet and income statement by showing the effect sales and expenses have on your balance sheet. Let's use a very simple example to explain. Assume you personally put up $100,000 of savings to start your business (your company balance sheet shows $100,000 in owner's equity). During the year, you have sales of $400,000 and expenses of $450,000, resulting in a loss of $50,000 (this is your income statement). Your balance sheet would now show your business is worth $50,000. Your statement of cash flow would show the flow of capital from your balance sheet at the beginning of the year through your income statement during the year and result in a change to your balance sheet at the end of the year. The results show the source of your cash flow. Is your cash flow coming from profits, paid-in capital, or from financing?

In many cases, charting your balance sheet, income statement, and statement of cash flow will reveal that you are expected to lose money during the first few years of operation. This is not unusual, and it is exactly the reason you need to be prepared to raise capital to cover your losses until your company becomes profitable. If your balance sheets reveal a loss for the first couple of years, it's time for you to put together a loan proposal for your banker.

> **Wealth Warning**
>
> People invariably underestimate how much money they will need to start and operate a business until it becomes profitable. Whatever your best estimate is, we recommend doubling it.

Choosing Your Funding Sources

You've gone to the time and effort to complete pro-forma financial statements, which should give you a very good sense of what to expect, financially speaking, during your first few years of operation. What we've found is that most people who complete this exercise do so from a very conservative perspective. In other words, they use lower numbers for sales than they actually expect and higher numbers for expenses than they actually expect, "just to be safe." In reality, even this seemingly conservative approach to estimating income and expenses is often not nearly conservative enough. Based on our experience, whatever amount of capital you estimate needing, you should double that number.

After you determine that you're going to need additional capital for your business, your next decision is finding where to get the money. There are a number of options available to you and each has its good points and bad.

Use Your Savings

Some people will save money for a number of years in anticipation of starting their own business. This is a great strategy, and if you've chosen this route, we applaud you.

> ### That Reminds Us ...
>
> When I started my Wealth Management firm, I knew that my savings were enough to cover living expenses for three years. Based on my pro-forma financial statements, I believed that this would be more than enough time for my new business to become profitable. In my first year, I broke even and was happy with that result but was determined to accelerate my progress. In my second year, I made a good profit.
>
> —Co-author Stewart Welch

If you're using your own money to fund your business, you want to be certain that you have enough to fund operations and a healthy reserve for nonbusiness emergencies.

Borrow Against Your Home Equity

We often find that people don't have a lot of cash savings but do have equity in their home they can tap using a Home Equity Line of Credit (HELOC). A bank will typically lend up to 80 percent of your home's value less your first mortgage balance using a HELOC. Closing costs are minimal, if any, and your interest rate is typically tied to the prime lending rate (prime), which means your interest rate changes when prime changes. The obvious danger in using your home equity to fund your business is that if the business fails, you may lose your home in addition to your business.

If you decide to go this route, ask for your loan to be interest only, meaning that the bank will send a bill for interest on the outstanding balance but will not require principal pay-down each month. This gives you the most flexibility and you can make principal pay-downs as your cash flow permits. Also, shop around before deciding which institution to do the loan with. You should be able to get your loan interest rate at prime, but we have seen many cases where loans are prime minus $1/2$ percent.

Tap Your 401(k)

You could get a loan from your 401(k) plan at work. Although federal law allows you to take a loan from your 401(k) plan, some companies do not, so you will need to ask someone in your human resource department. If your plan does allow loans, the most you can borrow is the lesser of 50 percent of your vested balance or $50,000. You will be required to repay your loan over a five-year period; however, the interest rate is typically very favorable to you. One critical thing to know is that if you terminate employment with a loan against your 401(k), you must repay the loan prior to termination or it will be treated as a taxable distribution. If you are under age $59^{1}/_{2}$, you will likely also owe a 10 percent federal penalty for early withdrawal.

Borrowing money from your 401(k) to start your business is our least favorite option and we would highly recommend you choose another course of action.

Borrow from Friends and Family Members

This is an obvious choice for many people. After all, these are the people who know you best and who are anxious to see you succeed. The obvious downside risk to this approach is that if your business fails, you risk damaging important relationships. If you go this route, be sure to heed our warning about raising enough capital to see you through to the point where your company will become profitable.

A nasty little footnote to loans of this type is that if the business fails, the loan may be considered a gift for gift tax purposes and the lender (your family member) may owe gift taxes in addition to losing his or her money.

Borrow from a Bank

By now you know there are many different sources of capital for your business venture. There are banks, venture capital firms, investment bankers, pension funds, insurance companies, and private placement firms. However, some of these sources are more expensive than others. The least expensive institutional source of money is a bank loan. Banks don't usually ask for equity positions (ownership) in your company. All they want is interest paid on the loan and the principal paid back on a timely basis. Therefore, a bank loan is the most efficient and cost-effective source of capital.

After all, banks are in the business of lending money. Banks are also careful about who they lend money to. If your banker does not believe that you are likely to succeed, he or she will not loan you the money and this should serve as a red flag for your game plan. It is true that if the banker believes in your idea but you have no collateral, he or she is likely to still turn you down. This is because the bank wants you to have a stake in the deal or at least assets backing a portion of it.

Good Credit Is Essential

Establishing good credit is vital to the wealth-building process. How do you do it? Borrow money and pay it back on time. It's as simple as that! The first thing a lender will want to know is how well you've done in the past regarding your ability to pay back loans on time. He determines this by requesting a credit report. This report will tell you (and your lender) about most of the loans you've had, as well as any late payments on bills or loans. Considering how important this report is, we suggest you get copies before your banker does.

Current law requires each of the three major credit reporting agencies (Experian, Equifax, and TransUnion) provide you with a free report once every 12 months. Be sure you take advantage of this, because erroneous errors are common.

Treasure Tip

Without a good credit record, you can't borrow money to buy a car, home, or anything without paying exorbitant interest rates. A bad credit rating left unattended will kill your chances of building wealth. To get a free credit report, go to www.annualcreditreport.com or call 1-877-322-8228.

When your credit report arrives, review it carefully and look for anything that might be detrimental to your credit. If you see any discrepancies that might disturb your banker, write an explanation of your side of the story and submit it to the credit agency. Include all the facts, names, and dates. By law, you can insert up to 100 words into your file at the credit agency. Also include a copy for your banker in the Bank Book, which we will describe later in this chapter. When your banker sees the discrepancy, he'll also see the explanation, which may help to ease his concerns.

Working with a Banker

Two things never seem to change in the business world:

- Businesses need to borrow money to survive and be profitable.
- Banks need to lend money to survive and be profitable.

If it's that simple, why are so many people turned down for loans? They don't understand how to borrow money from a bank. Bankers look for specific documentation before they can lend money. If you have the qualifications and know the documentation you need and how to present it, you should be able to borrow all the money you need.

A good relationship with a banker who understands your company and your needs is key to your wealth-building success. A banker will be assessing your financial strength as well as your financial character. Your personal financial statement is a reflection of your financial character. For example, if your financial statement shows a lot of debt, fancy cars, boats, jewelry, and homes but few investments, this weakens your perceived financial character. If you are 50 years old and have no significant assets, this too shows a lack of financial character.

Another part of the character equation is trust. Always be completely honest with your banker on all matters. If he or she calls you, return the call right away. If you agree to do something, do it in a timely manner. Stay in close communication with him or her, even when you don't need anything. Provide your banker with updated financial statements every 12 months. Don't wait for your banker to ask for them. If you have a problem, don't hide it. Rather, consider your banker a vital part of your Advisory Team—someone who can help you in good times and bad.

> **Wealth Warning**
>
> Most large banks don't like smaller businesses. They focus on medium- and larger-size companies. Smaller loans are usually delegated to the junior lending officers, where both inexperience and turnover can be problems.

The right banker can help you reach Wealth Stages 4 and 5. Notice we said *banker* and not *bank*. We prefer working with someone who can make a lending decision, so it's important that you determine early on what the loan approval limits are for the banker you are considering. If his limits are below the loan amount you will be requesting, you have two choices. Look for another banker who can decide on a loan your size or at least make sure you understand the loan approval process. For some banks, loans above certain limits must *all* go before a loan committee.

One thing you will want to determine early in your selection process is if the bank has experience with your type of business. For example, if you plan to start a restaurant but the bank has no experience with the restaurant industry, they will not be a good fit for you. You won't learn anything from them because they will have no expertise and they are likely to overscrutinize your business due to their lack of experience.

Treasure Tip _____

Ask your CPA for the names of three bankers he or she knows and recommends.

The best way to find a good banker is to get recommendations from other successful small businesses in your area. Find at least three bankers. Stop by and introduce yourself. Tell them you are looking for a banker and that you will have a proposal soon to present to them. Get to know a little about them personally. Do they seem easy to talk to? Are they interested in you and your company?

The Bank Book: Getting Your Banker to Say "Yes"

You need money to start and maintain your business so you can expand and achieve Wealth Stages 4 and 5. Your banker needs to lend money, and all he or she wants is a client who will borrow money and pay it back in a timely fashion. The best way to prove you can satisfy your banker is by preparing a Bank Book. A Bank Book is essentially a detailed proposal requesting a loan along with specific loan terms. It will provide your banker with all the information he or she needs to make a decision on your request. It should have a professional appearance and include a table of contents, numbered pages or section dividers, and a front and back cover. Here are what you will need to include:

- **Cover Letter.** Your cover letter should be clear and precise and include a brief summary of your business; why you need a loan; how much you need to borrow; how you will use the loan proceeds; and how the loan will be repaid. You also want to outline the terms you are requesting, including the interest rate charges, term of the loan, payments (fully amortizing, partially amortizing with a balloon payment, interest only, and so on).

- **Personal Biography.** The banker is loaning money to *you*. This is where you want to let him or her know who you are. Include your business background, job experience, civic activities, credentials you have earned, and any other accomplishments you feel show you in a good light. You should also include the biographies of any key employees.

- **Description of Your Business.** You've covered this briefly in your Summary Letter, but now is the time to provide a detailed history of your business. When did you start the business, what are the products and services that you offer, who are your customers, and what are the prospects for future growth? Much of this information will also be in your Business Plan, but don't use the same descriptions. Here you are selling your business as one with great prospects.

- **Personal Net Worth Statement.** You developed your personal net worth statement in Chapter 3. Make sure it is up-to-date and insert it here. Your banker will be looking here for potential *collateral* to secure the loan. To a banker, collateral is anything of value that they can legally assign to the bank as security for your loan. It should be noted that under federal law, retirement plans (IRAs, 401[k]s, and so on) cannot be used as security for loans under any circumstances.

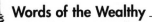

Words of the Wealthy

Collateral is something of value that is pledged against a loan in case of default. When you list collateral, such as furniture, equipment, property, or accounts receivable, you should also include documents that will verify the value of these items.

- **Personal Cash Management Report.** Okay, this sounds better than your personal budget, but it's the same thing. This report should reflect your personal spending for the past 12 months and projected spending for the next 12 months.

- **Schedule of Life Insurance.** If the bank loans you money and you die, how are they going to pay their money back? In most cases, the bank will require that you assign to the bank enough life insurance to pay off your loan if you die. You should anticipate this and purchase enough life insurance to cover your loan and what you need to protect your family (see Chapter 20).

- **Schedule of Disability Income Insurance.** What if you don't die, but become disabled and can't run the business? Often bankers will overlook this potential problem, but you shouldn't. You will need to get the maximum disability income insurance that you qualify for. See Chapter 20 for more details.

- **Personal Credit Report.** You should've already pulled one and reviewed it in detail. Your banker is likely to order one anyway, but by including one here, it may speed up the approval process.

- **Business Financial Statements.** Now you know you didn't do all that hard work for nothing! The banker will definitely want to study these, and you should be prepared to respond to detailed questioning in this area. Your financial statements will include the following:

  - **Balance sheet.** Current and projected in one year.

- ◆ **Income statement.** Detailed month-by-month for 12 months and at least quarterly for 2 to 4 additional years.

- ◆ **Statement of cash flow.** Month-by-month for the first 12 months, then at least annually for 2 to 4 additional years.

- ◆ **Three years of tax returns.** Include three years of personal tax returns (signed copies).

- ◆ **Copy of your business plan.** Much of the information contained in your business plan is already included in your Bank Book, but including a full copy here will help your banker understand how you organize your thoughts and your business.

That Reminds Us ...

When a bank takes care of you, don't forget them. It makes money from deposits as well as loans. Be sure to maintain a significant amount of your company's deposits in an interest-bearing checking account with that bank. You could use a brokerage firm money market account for a higher rate, but the marginal interest rate you'll make isn't worth spoiling your relationship with your banker. You might need to borrow more money later.

Gathering these documents is a lot of work, but it will increase your chances of getting the loan you want under the terms you ask for. The less information a lender must ask for, the more credibility you'll earn. If you skimp on information, the banker might think you're trying to hide a negative aspect of your business or personal history. Bankers are more likely to make loans on a marginal transaction if the lender believes in the customer.

Make certain your proposal is completely free of spelling errors and grammatical mistakes. The newest word processors are great, but they are no substitute for getting another person to look over the document for errors, especially if he or she is a good editor. The errors just might kill your chances of getting a loan. Hire an English teacher if you have to.

Presenting Your Loan Proposal

We don't know whether bankers do this consciously, but most banker meetings are somewhat intimidating. You arrive at the reception desk on time, but you have to wait. Then some assistant "delivers" you to the banker's office. Once seated across the desk from the banker, it feels like your chair is about 4 inches shorter than his or hers, making you seem small compared to the huge desk and lofty leather chair. Do they do this on purpose to gain a negotiating advantage and make you feel you are lucky to get any loan? We don't know the answer, but we do know that it is your job to take control. After all, your objective is to find a bank and banker to serve your needs. You are the one who is going to be successful and pay them a lot of interest.

You should arrive on time dressed in professional attire and fully armed with your Bank Book. Know your numbers inside-out and be prepared to discuss what you will do for the bank—average deposits and balances, transfer of personal and business accounts, and collateral you are prepared to give them. Don't forget that this is a two-way interview. You should be prepared to ask questions to make sure this is the right bank and banker for your needs. Your loan will not be approved at this meeting so ask when you can expect to hear from him or her and be sure he or she has your best contact information in case additional information is needed. It should give you a lot of confidence knowing that the banker will have only rarely encountered someone as organized as you. We promise you, your banker will be impressed!

What to Do When the Bank Approves Your Loan

When your loan is approved, your banker will set up a meeting to go over all the terms and paperwork that you will be signing. Often this review and the signing of the various loan agreements and collateral agreements will happen in one meeting. We would encourage you to have the banker review all the terms and paperwork and then request a couple of days to review these documents in greater detail. This will give you time to really understand the deal that is being offered and perhaps even further negotiate some of the terms.

One of our client couples were purchasing land adjacent to their home. The bank offered a reasonable interest rate but requested our clients put up the land, their home, an investment account worth more than $1 million, and their personal guarantee as collateral for the loan! We felt this was overkill and unreasonable and countered with the land as security plus their personal signature as guarantee for the loan. The bank accepted.

CAUTION

Wealth Warning

If you are married, most banks will ask your spouse to also sign the bank loan agreements, even if he or she has nothing to do with the business. We prefer not to do this for a number of reasons (divorce, etc.) and recommend that you avoid this if at all possible.

> **Wealth Warning** _____
>
> When borrowing money from a bank, the banker will attempt to require that you use virtually everything possible as collateral for your loan because the more collateral, the safer the loan from the bank's perspective. You need to decide what you are willing to put up as collateral before you request a loan.

What to Do if Your Loan Is Rejected

If your best efforts fail, do not get discouraged. There are a lot of other banks that may be happy to work with you. It is important, however, that you ask the banker why your loan was turned down. Do not accept vague answers here, because you are trying to learn what needs to change to get approval next time. This "exit" interview should be handled with the same degree of professionalism as in your prior meetings. Your goal is to learn specifically what you need to do to get approved on your next loan request. Take what you learn, update your presentation, and go to another bank.

If you cannot find a bank to loan you money after all this effort, find a family member or friend (with good credit) to co-sign the loan for you. This will enable you to establish a strong credit history. After you've paid off that loan without missing a payment, the bank will be more inclined to loan you money again—without a required co-signer. Our two warnings about borrowing money from family and friends also apply to having them co-sign a loan. If the business fails, the co-signer will have to pay off your bank loan and the co-signer may be subject to gift taxes.

The Least You Need to Know

◆ Without adequate capital, the odds of a business surviving are low.

◆ Learn to use financial statements to help manage your business.

◆ Having a good credit history will be important to your success.

◆ Your banker can be a great ally if you know how to work with her.

◆ Creating a Bank Book is the best way to present your loan proposal and get your banker to say "yes."

Chapter **15**

Avoiding the #2 Reason Most Businesses Fail

In This Chapter

- Building an outrageously good service system
- Setting up a marketing system to keep a constant flow of new customers
- Creating a procedures manual to systematize your business
- Working effectively with your CPA
- Understanding other common mistakes business owners make

You've raised enough money to fund your business, thereby eliminating the first reason most businesses fail: inadequate capital. Now it's time to tackle the second reason most businesses fail: poor management.

Creating Excellence in Business Management

So, in the broadest sense, what does it take to ensure business success?

Co-author Stewart Welch interviewed dozens of self-made multimillionaire businesspeople, including such well-known businessmen as Steve Forbes, president and editor-in-chief of *Forbes Magazine*. One person he interviewed, Lee Styslinger, Chairman of ALTEC Industries, Inc. (www.altec.com), gave the most precise summary of the key to business success we have ever heard. In 1952, he stepped in to run the family business due to the untimely death of his father. At that time there were 12 employees and sales of approximately $100,000 per year. Mr. Styslinger was age 19.

Mr. Styslinger says that being successful in business requires you to do three things: stay close to your numbers; stay close to your associates (employees); and stay close to your customers. He went on to say that staying close to your numbers meant that you need to use your cash flow statement, income statement, and balance sheet as tools to help you manage your business. Without a complete understanding of these tools, it would be like driving a car on the freeway while blindfolded … life-threatening! He said your associates are your best assets and you need to consider them vital team members and treat them with the respect every team member deserves. Not family members, because family membership implies you will stick with them no matter what. As team members, you give them the opportunity to be a valued member of the team. But if they can't produce, ultimately you have to help them find a place they can excel. And finally, you need to always be sensitive to the needs of your customers. For if you can keep them happy, they will be repeat customers and they will be your best ambassadors for more customers. Mr. Styslinger built a company that today has over 2,300 associates and worldwide sales approaching $1 billion per year.

Three Rules for Creating a Wildly Successful Business

Making money in business is not all that difficult. You can do a little home-grown research by visiting some of your favorite stores and other businesses that really stand out. Pay close attention to what they are doing that is most appealing to you. Now go visit a store in the same business that you are less impressed with. What is it about them that disappoints you? Typically what you will find is that one store is more customer-focused, and pleasing the customer is the biggest key to massive sales.

Here are the keys to creating a wildly successful business:

◆ Be careful what you promise. You see, most people overpromise what they or their product will do for you. Then, when put to the test, the service or product fails to meet expectations. Overpromising and underperforming is a killer when it comes to repeat sales and customer referrals.

The key here is to be really careful about the promises you make. That goes for not only customers, but employees and vendors as well.

◆ Do all that you promise. When you make a promise, you have to keep it no matter what it takes. If you bid on a job and it turns out you miscalculated and will lose money, complete the job anyway. Not only that, do the work with a positive attitude.

By following the preceding two rules, you will solve the sales side of your business and should have no trouble generating adequate revenue. But if you want to succeed beyond your wildest dreams, you need to take one additional step:

◆ Then do something *extra*. The possibilities are endless. What's important here is that this extra something should either be something the customer does not expect (the unexpected) or something that you become well known for (the expected). For example, the Hatcher Agency, a health insurance sales agency based in Little Rock, Arkansas, always gives customers and potential customers gourmet chocolate chip or macadamia nut cookies. Whether the salespeople are making a sales call, service call, or someone drops by the office, customers are going to receive a bag of fresh cookies. A simple idea, but an effective one.

Thinking about leaving customers with something extra leads us to the next strategy for maximizing your success.

Focus on Outrageous Service

If you expand on the simple idea of doing something extra for your customers to doing *lots* of special things, you arrive at a unique place we call outrageous service. Outrageous service is service that is so superior your customers will talk about it to other potential customers. You know outrageous service when you experience it. For outrageous service to really make a difference in your business, you must be able to deliver it consistently time after time. It must become a part of the very culture of your company.

Greg Hatcher of the Hatcher Agency went far beyond handing out cookies to his customers. He built his company on the concept of delivering outrageous service. He started his health insurance agency in 1990 with one employee, his secretary. Now if you are familiar with the health insurance business, you know it is quite boring and very hard to differentiate yourself from your competitors because there are a limited number of health insurance companies and all of their products are pretty much the same and competitively priced. Well, by the end of its third full year of operation, the Hatcher Agency was the largest health insurance agency in the state of Arkansas and the company was named Arkansas' Small Business of the Year by *Arkansas Business* newsmagazine. Today, the Hatcher Agency employs more than 30 people and has $100 million in annual sales. And Greg Hatcher has joined the exclusive ranks of multimillionaires. This outrageous service mentality was so important to Greg that he wrote a book on the subject (see Appendix A).

Here are just a few of the service ideas that the associates in Hatcher's firm have implemented:

- **Thank you notes.** This is not just for the salespeople; every employee must write five thank you notes per week! The administrative staff may write a note to a vendor while sales staff drops notes to customers. He's not concerned so much to whom the note is written, but that they are thanking someone. If you are a vendor, can you remember the last time a customer actually dropped you a note thanking you for the job you did? I'm sure you can remember and the answer is likely never! If you found yourself in a pinch and needed your vendor's immediate attention, what do you think his likely response would be?

- **Goodwill calls.** Every salesperson agrees to call every customer once per month just to say hello. This is not a sales call and the salesperson does not bring up any business issues. This is simply a care call just to let the customer know he is thought of as a person, not just a meal ticket. When was the last time a vendor called you just to say hello? And just to put this in perspective, the typical sales-person in the Hatcher Agency has 70 accounts!

- **Staff meetings at 7 A.M.** The typical sales organization (and many others as well) have a Monday morning staff meeting that is required attendance for all employees. You're at your office and anxious to get your week off to a fast start so you call your vendor only to find out that everyone is unavailable because of a company-wide staff meeting. At the Hatcher Agency, they have their company-wide meeting on Wednesday mornings, but to make certain they are available when their customers need them, they start the meeting at 7 and it is over by 8. Now that's outrageous service!

How do you create an outrageous service model for your company? The best thing to do is to sit down with your employees and brainstorm on the subject. Let the employees know what your goal is: to create an outrageous service model for your business. Ask each employee to come up with three ideas. Create a "safe" environment by offering a prize for the most outrageous idea. At your meeting, use an easel-size writing pad to list everyone's ideas. As people think of additional ideas, add them to the list. At this point, don't make any judgments about good versus bad ideas. To do so will stifle creativity.

After you've exhausted all of the ideas, have everyone vote on the top three. Place the vote count beside each idea. This will give you a sense of which ideas the group feels are the best. It's important that everyone feels like they are part of the decision-making process because you will be asking for their support for implementation.

Now you should carefully select the top one or two ideas and integrate them into your business processes and culture. Only when these first couple of ideas are firmly implemented should you go back to your list. Most people get excited and want to implement the top dozen ideas only to find that they have taken on too much change and everyone becomes discouraged by failures.

Focus on Marketing

When people start a new business, and often for their whole careers, all they want to do is do their work. For example, if you're a chef, you just want to cook. If you own a landscape business, you just want to do landscape designs and plantings. If you own a nail salon, you just want to do nails. To be successful, however, you must become a master marketer. You must constantly focus on building your business, especially in the first several years.

If people don't know about your products and services, you won't sell anything. If you don't sell anything, you won't make any money. If you don't make any money, you can't save any money. The value of your business will decline, and so will your wealth. Therefore, your business must have a marketing system that you know will bring in business. How do you develop one? Start with the following questions:

- Can you explain and identify the demand for your product or service?
- Who is your competition?
- What are the distinct characteristics of your product or service?
- Who exactly is your target market?
- Where does your target market live?

- How will you determine the price?

- How will you advertise and get the message out?

- How will you test your advertising on a small scale?

- Can you describe in detail your advertising budget for the first year?

- How will you deliver your product to your customer?

If the answers to these questions didn't come easy to you, don't be discouraged. Most new business owners focus on the "doing" and not on the planning related to their business.

Let us help you with some key marketing strategies:

- **Decide on the market you want to serve.** The more specialized the niche the better, as long as the potential customer base is large enough to satisfy sales growth now and in the future.

> **That Reminds Us ...**
>
> When I decided to start my own Wealth Management firm back in 1984, I chose physicians as my niche market for three reasons. First, they were in a business that had very little day-to-day exposure to matters of personal finance. They were typically spending 10 to 12 hours or more on medical matters so I knew many would seek professional help for their financial issues. Second, they were in a fee-only type of business so I knew they would appreciate the impartiality of fee-only financial advice. And third, they could afford to pay my fees. Birmingham, Alabama, was then, and is today, a major medical center with the state's largest employer being world-renowned UAB Health System (www.health.uab.edu). This meant that my target niche was likely to be growing in shear numbers of prospective clients. Today, fully half of our clients are health-care professionals. The other half includes retirees, business owners, and executives. Targeting a specific market allowed us to focus our marketing efforts.
> —Co-author Stewart Welch

- **Determine the pricing of your products or services.** Early on you will need to decide if you're going to compete on price. If that's going to be your approach, then your goal will be to be the volume leader. Sam Walton, founder of Wal-Mart, chose to do just this and became the largest retailer in the world. A better choice for most small business owners is to develop a niche market, then develop an outrageous service system so that you can create what we call pricing power.

◆ **Develop a marketing system.** After you've identified your target market and set your pricing, you need to develop a system for being constantly in front of your audience in an effective way. For every business it will be different. To arrive at the right strategy for you, initially go through the same process as you used to develop your outrageous service plan. Your answer need not require a lot of expensive advertising, although strategic advertising can be very effective. Just as your outrageous service system will differentiate you from your competitors, so should your marketing system.

In 1994, at the age of 29, Bill Phillips took the helm of Experimental and Applied Sciences, also known simply as EAS (www.eas.com). This obscure company sold supplements to bodybuilders. This was something Bill knew a lot about because he'd been a competitive bodybuilder. Bill believed strongly that the more you give, the more you will receive. He shifted the company's focus from traditional body builders to helping the average person build the best body possible. To this end, EAS offered a free easy-to-read 200-plus page book of scientific information on a variety of supplements (that his company sold, of course!). He sent out free motivational tapes, videos, workout routines, and nutrition plans. He even had a 24-hour free hotline where people could call and speak with a trained specialist in weight training and supplements. Bill gave and gave and gave until people finally bought. And buy they did. EAS became the largest seller of nutritional supplements in America. Bill then parlayed his success into a best-selling book, *Body for Life*, which sold more than 350 million copies! He sold EAS while still in his 30s for more than $100 million. What he gave free of charge to potential customers was information that they truly valued. In return he received their trust and loyalty.

What can you do for your potential customers to create trust and loyalty? If you can come up with the answer to this question, you will have a winning marketing system.

◆ **Monitor your results.** Whatever marketing system you decide to use, include in your system a periodic review of your actual results versus your target results and be prepared to adjust your strategy as needed. If you're always thinking marketing, then you will likely have an alternative strategy waiting in the wings.

Systematize Your Business

Let us ask you two questions. How many of you have had a McDonald's hamburger? We will presume that all hands are raised. Next question. How many of you believe that you can make a better hamburger than McDonald's? We again assume that all hands are raised. So if you can make a better hamburger than the number-one seller of hamburgers in the world, why aren't you rich? The answer lies in business systems. McDonald's has one of the very best business systems in the world. The company has broken down even the smallest task into a written procedure that is taught the same way to every employee all over the world. It works for them and it will work for you. You will be creating what we call a procedures manual that will detail the systems that make your business run successfully. If you take the time to do this, your business will not only run more efficiently, but it will also be better positioned to expand and grow. This in turn will help you build your wealth much more quickly.

Initially, this will be a lot of work, but it is the difference between building a business and owning a job.

That Reminds Us ...

Why do you think a little local hamburger franchise, such as a McDonald's restaurant, can sell for as much as $1 million? Sure, the profit margins are great, but the main reason is that the systems and procedures are so efficient and well maintained that anyone can manage the franchise. Every task in that franchise, from pouring a drink to turning off the lights at closing, is written down and delegated to an employee. That's what your goal should be. You should develop a procedures manual that everyone in your company can see and improve upon every day. That's what it takes to build a successful, profitable, and sellable business today.

Your job as a business owner initially is to identify and build your own systems. These systems must be designed and written in the form of a systems or procedures manual. Every segment of your business has certain procedures that make up the assembly line of your business. These procedures are initially developed out of goals that you set. Here are the steps to developing a written procedures manual:

1. Focus either on your goals or your biggest frustrations that you'd like to see eliminated.

2. Brainstorm the tasks necessary to achieve the goal or eliminate the frustration.

3. List the necessary tasks and resources you'll need.

4. Prioritize the tasks; develop the procedures and write them down.

5. Implement and test the procedures.

6. Measure the results.

7. Improve the procedures.

8. Implement and test the tasks again.

9. Measure the results.

10. Continue to improve the procedure as technology allows.

This process goes on forever. Any business not dedicated to constant improvement is doomed to eventual failure.

By the way, most small businesses don't have a procedures manual. By having one, you will stay ahead of your competition.

Written procedures do more than help you run your business. They will also …

♦ Enable you to develop new products and services.

♦ Enable you to train new and promoted employees.

♦ Help you find procedures you can outsource.

♦ Help you find ways to automate your business.

♦ Enable you to see inefficiencies in your business.

♦ Enable your employees to cross-train each other.

♦ Make your business more attractive to potential buyers.

The litmus test for a well-written procedures manual is if a competent stranger can come in and, using only the manual, complete a particular task without having to ask questions. This should be your goal. After the procedures are built, you must focus your efforts on making them as efficient and effective as possible. You should encourage everyone to come up with better ideas and be willing to test them.

At The Welch Group, co-author Stewart Welch's company, a portion of each associate's incentive compensation is tied to their maintaining their portion of the company's procedures manual. We have found that it saves a

> **Treasure Tip**
>
> One of the best ways to build your procedures manual is to have each employee responsible for writing their portion of the manual. After all, who knows the job or tasks better than they do?

tremendous amount of time when new associates come into the firm. It also tends to eliminate the employee who feels he or she can hold you "hostage" because of their unique skills and knowledge of your operations.

Sharing Management Responsibilities: Working with Your CPA

You really don't have to do this all by yourself, nor should you. In Chapter 11 we discussed who should be on your executive team, but here we would like to focus on how to use your CPA to help you co-manage your business.

Behind almost every wealthy person is a great CPA. Almost without exception, every wealthy individual we've ever met had a CPA. Many business people still don't understand the value of a good CPA. We think it's because most people don't understand the value of measurement and accountability, which are vital to the success of a business. Most people think a CPA is someone who will fill out your income tax forms.

Wealth Warning

You will want to hire a CPA who has experience in your field. However, if at all possible, don't do business with your competitor's CPA.

However, a good CPA can do so much more than your taxes. He or she can help you solve problems, plan for your future, maintain financial statements, set goals, offer second opinions, and refer you to other professionals who can help you. CPAs are, in essence, the coach and statistician in the wealth game. Best of all, they can be like silent partners in your business venture, assisting you with difficult financial decisions.

Measuring Your Way to Wealth

We've learned that whatever is systematically measured tends to improve. Close scrutiny of your financial statements leads to ways to improve your company. It's a natural result. If you want a successful company, you must measure your success at least every month. You can do this yourself with financial software, have someone in your office do it for you, or hire a CPA.

We prefer the last option. Why? First, CPAs are Orville Redenbachers. They do one thing, and (we hope) they do it better than anybody. You want someone who single-mindedly focuses on tax planning and financial statements. Second, there are too many tax code changes to keep up with on your own. Third, it's better to have someone outside your firm measuring your success because such a person is more likely to be objective and unbiased. Fourth, if you'll pay a CPA to do what he or she does best while you continue to do what you do best, you'll both make more money in the long run. Fifth, many creditors require audited financial statements prepared by a CPA. The basic set of statements a CPA should prepare for you include:

♦ Income statement (profit and loss statement)

♦ Balance sheet (assets, liabilities, and equity)

♦ Cash-flow statement

That Reminds Us ...

If you expect to build your wealth through your business, you need to understand the basics of financial statements. Take advantage of classes available at your local university. Some local banks also offer classes on cash management. If you can't find a class, go to the bookstore for help. This can be a boring subject, but it is vital to your success in business. If you can't read a financial statement, you won't know how well your company is performing.

A full-service CPA can also help you with additional services and measurements:

♦ Pro-forma financial statements

♦ Financial ratio analysis

♦ Personal financial statements

♦ Financial statement forecasting

♦ Depreciation schedules

♦ Payroll management

♦ Business valuation

In fact, a good CPA will teach you how to read and understand all of these statements.

If you don't understand financial statements or just hate working with them, it might be better to ask your CPA to do your financial statement forecasting for you. It's worth the money to have this done each year.

This kind of forecasting involves three steps. First, you make a few key assumptions such as future sales growth and expense projections for the next several years. Second, using financial statement forecasting software, you enter your assumptions as well as your last several years of financial statements. Third, you let the computer calculate the expected effect of the assumptions on your financial statements. If you don't like the desired effect, you can make certain changes in your assumptions. This kind of business forecasting not only allows you to find the optimal amount of sales growth for your company, but it also gives you the opportunity to project your company's profitability. If you can do this successfully, you can also measure, project, and keep track of your wealth.

Wealth Warning

How do you prepare for an IRS audit? The best tool you have before, during, and after your audit is a good CPA who has been with you for years.

When the IRS Calls

Sooner or later, you will get the dreaded letter from the Internal Revenue Service saying they want to audit your books. You're going to need someone who knows your business as well as or better than you. Who's going to know you better financially than your CPA?

Call your CPA and have him or her go over with you verbally what you can expect from an IRS audit. Discuss what you two can do together to make it less likely to happen and easier to handle if it does.

CPAs cannot do everything. If you need additional help in an audit situation, you might want to seek the council of a tax attorney with a lot of IRS audit experience. Find a firm with a good track record. Make certain that it has successfully defended clients who faced the IRS.

Second Opinions

A good CPA is someone who knows you and your business and is willing to give you advice whenever you ask. During your wealth-building journey, you are going to face many decisions. Some will be easy, and some will be difficult. Using a good CPA who knows your situation is like having a partner. Use this partner when you can to help you with the big decisions. Here is a list of the most common problems with which your CPA should be able to assist you:

♦ Business expansion

♦ Mergers and acquisitions

♦ Business deals with others

♦ Lease versus buy decisions

♦ Investment ideas and tax consequences

♦ Investment professionals

♦ Investment performance evaluation

Helping You with Your Banker

Most business owners don't think of their CPAs when it comes to banking. However, the banker does. Anyone who's ever borrowed money from a banker knows that good, accurate accounting is important to a banker. Before you visit your bank looking for a loan, visit your CPA. Make sure your personal financial statement is up-to-date. Get him or her to help you with your loan proposal. Get your financial statements in order, and consider bringing your CPA with you when your banker wants to discuss your loan proposal.

Treasure Tip

After you've started your business, you might want to send copies of your financial statements each quarter (or at least annually) to your banker—even if they're not required. This makes a banker feel good about you as a client.

Your Corporate Setup

A CPA can do most of the initial framework involved in helping you decide how to legally set up your company. However, you might want to get additional assistance from an attorney who is experienced with the different ways to incorporate. Most people who are starting a business don't give this much thought. However, this can be a very important decision due to complex tax laws and issues of personal liability.

> **Treasure Tip** _____
>
> One of the best ways to minimize the cost involved in hiring a good CPA is to provide him or her with accurate and organized records. We know people who show up on the CPA's doorstep with a box of unorganized invoices and canceled checks. This is no way to run a business and no way to build wealth. Wealthy people keep their records organized and automate their accounting. Automate your business accounting from the beginning by utilizing one of the many accounting software packages available such as Quick Books Pro (www.intuit.quickbooks.com).

When Things Go Wrong

Things are going to go wrong occasionally no matter how smart or hard you work. It's how you handle the problems that make you a good or bad businessperson. The wealthiest people we know make mistakes occasionally. They learn from every mistake they make and do whatever they can to avoid letting it happen again. You have to accept the fact that you will have failures in your business. No matter how much you plan, things are going to go wrong. If you're not experiencing some failure on a regular basis, you're probably not trying hard enough to succeed. As a business owner, you are under the constant threat of sudden changes in the economy, competition, customer needs, and employee needs. You can take some preventative measures, but you still have to be ready for surprises.

How do you plan for things that go wrong? How do you prepare for them? First, imagine the worst things that could happen in your business. Sit down and design measures that could prevent these things from happening. Second, develop a "damage control plan." The following is a damage control plan we designed to use when things go wrong. Every problem is unique and every suggestion might not apply, but it's a start:

- Separate the symptoms from the true problem.

- Describe the exact underlying problem in detail.

- Identify the true obstacles.

- Identify which elements can and cannot be controlled.

- Decide how you will change the things you can control.

- Identify the possible solutions. (List at least 10.)

- Prioritize the best solutions and implement the best.

- Describe how you can prevent this from happening again.

If you want some creative ways to solve your problem, get your employees involved. They may come up with ideas that you haven't even considered. If you don't have any employees, get a group of your friends or even your best customers if you have to. Don't give up without getting some ideas from other people.

The key is to anticipate the most obvious potential problems and design solutions for them. Then if the problem does in fact arise, you already have a solution that you identified when you were clear-headed and not under pressure.

Treasure Tip

Most business owners think that if you work hard all the time, you'll eventually be successful. This is not true! You have to work smart. This implies a lot of thinking and planning. Thinking and planning require time and a peaceful, relaxed mind. Without either of these two, your business cannot prosper. So don't forget to take some time off!

The Most Common Mistakes Business Owners Make

Most of the businesses that fail do so for similar reasons. Knowing why they failed is important to someone who might be considering starting a new business. Here are the 22 most common reasons business owners fail:

- No clear goals or objectives.
- They don't dream big enough.
- Failure to plan or don't know how to plan.
- Not enough discipline to follow the plan.
- Can't maintain their focus on the important issues.
- Not enough cash—cash-flow problems.
- Hiring ineffective employees.
- Forgetting to test on a small scale.
- Spending too much money personally.
- Spending too much money on the start-up.
- Starting a business just for the money.

- Not knowing how to work with a banker.
- Refusing to borrow money.
- Not testing a big-ticket item before buying.
- Making hasty decisions that could—and should—have been researched.
- Not making customer service top priority.
- Not listening to the customer and empathizing.
- Not listening to employees.
- Ignoring industry trends and new product developments.
- Starting a business in the wrong location.
- Letting the competition steal your market.
- Failure or the inability to delegate.

Don't get caught up in these traps. They are easy to avoid if you pay attention and plan properly. You may want to take each one and change it to a positive context. For example, you could take "Not listening to employees" and change it to "Listen to employees." Take this new list and pin it up somewhere. It just might help you avoid a lot of mistakes.

The Least You Need to Know

- To be wildly successful in your business, remember to be careful what you promise; do all that you promise; then do something *extra*.
- Use the goals you set and the frustrations you feel to build a set of systems and procedures that will enable you to run your business more efficiently.
- Build an outrageous service system to keep customers coming back and turn them into ambassadors for your company.
- If you plan to build serious wealth, you need a great CPA to watch after your company's finances, keep up with tax laws, give you an objective opinion, and give you the opportunity to focus on what you're the best at so you can build wealth more quickly.
- Plan on things going wrong with a damage control plan that will help you identify the problem, solve it quickly, and prevent it from happening again.

Chapter 16

Surround Yourself with Great Talent

In This Chapter

- Why you should consider the outsourcing option instead of hiring
- How to increase profit margins
- Where to find the best employees
- Why you should consider paying your new employee a little more than he or she expects
- How to design a bonus program that dazzles

This chapter has the single greatest potential for catapulting your business forward into profitability. That means that this chapter also has the greatest potential for getting you to Wealth Stages 4 and 5. Your associates truly can be your greatest asset or your biggest nightmare. It all depends on whom you hire and how you manage them.

Hiring vs. Outsourcing

Before you run out and hire someone, ask yourself first whether you can outsource the work. Outsourcing allows you to hire the best without taking them on your payroll. For example, unless you're a CPA, you're going to need accounting work done for your business. Instead of hiring a CPA and putting him or her on your payroll, you can outsource your accounting work by paying an independent CPA to do the job for you. Look at every procedure of your business and ask yourself whether it can be outsourced. Then, find someone willing to do the work. You can find help from …

Treasure Tip

If you can get payroll costs under control, you are well on your way to being more profitable and wealthier.

- Temporary services.
- Employee leasing companies.
- Vendors.

Keep Payroll Costs Under Control

If you want to make money, you must know how to control your biggest fixed cost, which is usually payroll. One other thing you need to be aware of before you hire is your total payroll costs. Many business owners hire what they think they need well before they look at the budget for payroll. The inevitable result is a poor profit margin or layoffs.

You should have a maximum target for your payroll costs that is a percentage of revenue. For example, a healthy payroll target for a general dentist practice is 22 percent. Talk to a number of business owners in a similar business to yours to get a feel for what is appropriate in your business. Another excellent source is your CPA. Our definition of payroll includes all costs associated with all employees (except the owner). A partial list of those costs would include salaries, payroll taxes, and insurance premiums such as health insurance, group life, and contributions to retirement plans. By establishing this standard, you will have a better sense of employee efficiency. For example, if our general dentist found that her payroll was 28 percent when the standard was 22 percent, she might want to check employee efficiency before hiring another employee. Something is probably wrong. She just needs to figure out what.

Master the Art of the 5-Minute Interview

Building wealth using your business is directly tied to the capacity of work your employees can handle. The amount of work they can handle is directly tied to their desire to achieve company goals. The level of desire they have will depend on their passion for the business and their belief that if they work hard in your company, they can achieve their own personal goals.

One of the best ways to find great employees is to do a lot of interviews. Most business owners make the mistake of refusing interviews when they have no openings. Instead, interview everyone. If you take this approach, you must develop what we call the "art of the 5-minute interview." What we've found is that generally within the first 5 minutes of meeting someone, we know whether he or she is a good fit for our company. In many cases the answer will be "no." When this is the case, you need to bring the interview to an end politely but quickly.

That Reminds Us ...

We make a habit of interviewing anyone interested in our business. To keep things simple, we set up a rating system. We are committed to having nothing but "A" rated employees at our company. When interviewing a prospective employee, we only have two files; the "A" file and the round file (waste basket!). When a prospective employee makes initial contact, we are up-front in saying we have no openings at the moment but would love to have her drop off her resumé and meet him or her. The applicant has no expectations that this will be a long or formal interview. If he or she is not a good fit, we keep the meeting short (5 minutes tops!) and the application goes in the "round" file. If we judge the applicant to be "A" quality, we extend the interview, set up a follow-up interview, or place his or her resumé in our "A" file for future reference. Whenever we have an opening, we typically have a handful of great resumés. We then track them down and hire them away from their current employers. I should mention that if the interviewee is sharp, we try to help them get a job if we don't have an opening.

—Co-author Stewart Welch

Master the Art of the Long Interview

After you've separated the wheat from the chaff and you've identified a top candidate for employment in your company, an in-depth interview is your key to determining if this person will be a productive team member. As with everything else in your business, the interview process should be part of a system. Here are some key points:

- **Be on time.** Obviously, you expect the prospective employee to be on time, and you should extend the same courtesy. Remember, you very likely will ask her to be a team member, and team membership demands a certain amount of dual respect and equality.

- **Be professional in your dress and demeanor.** This is a big decision for you and, hopefully, for the interviewee. You know the interviewee will be putting her best foot forward. You want to do likewise. Don't lose sight of the fact that you are selling yourself and your company.

- **Know the key skills you are looking for in the position you are filling.** You should have a list of these skills and build your questions around them.

- **Use mostly open-ended questions.** Your goal is to get the interviewee to expose her real self. Avoid leading questions. For example, let's assume that the job position requires someone who is very detailed-oriented. Don't say, "This job requires a great attention to detail. Do you consider this a strong suit of yours?" Instead, ask, "Do you enjoy 'big picture' work or detailed analysis work more?"

- **Closely observe the interviewee's body language and listen closely to her questions.** This can provide you with valuable insights into her personality.

- **Make notes immediately following the interview.** Include impressions, strengths, potential weaknesses, and so on. Do you still consider her an "A" prospect?

That Reminds Us ...

After we've gone through the initial interview process, we bring the top one or two candidates back in to meet all of our associates. They meet one on one and our associates begin with a brief description of what they do at our firm and then engage the prospective associate in a conversation about her interests both job and non-job related. We then ask our associates for their input and impressions as well as their vote in favor or against hiring each candidate. Our goal is a unanimous "yes" vote. If we can get it, everyone has a sense of ownership in the decision and is anxious to see her succeed in her new position. The new employee also knows that everyone wanted her there, which is a big confidence builder. If we get "no" votes, we pay close attention because our associates may have uncovered something we missed. This type of interview process gives us an advantage over large companies whose hiring is handled, by necessity, out of a centralized HR department.

—Co-author Stewart Welch

When the candidate has passed all of your tests, you should consider having her go through an industrial psychologist's screening process. We have found this process accurately pinpoints strengths and weaknesses that we missed. This can be done fairly inexpensively through various online services such as those offered by Kolbe Corporation (www.kolbe.com). For higher-level positions, you should consider using an industrial psychologist. You can find one through the Yellow Pages or a referral from another business owner or your CPA.

What to Look for in an Employee

As a business owner and manager, your most important role is putting together your team. If you get this right, you will be well on your way to financial success and the journey will be a blast. Get it wrong and you will struggle for reasons that will be unclear to you and the journey will feel like a root canal.

Hire for Attitude

First, let's set up a rating system so that we are all "singing from the same hymnal." Let's rate employees on a scale from 1 to 10, with 10 being a super employee and 1 being an employee you would rather burn the building down before hiring. Do yourself the biggest favor of your life and refuse to hire anything but 10s. Many magical things happen when you make this commitment:

♦ You get a great employee with a great attitude, who has initiative, is a team player, and is a corporate cheerleader.

♦ A group of "10" employees will run off all of the "1" to "8" employees you have and save you the trouble of firing them.

♦ The 10s are anxious to take on additional responsibility and can be counted on to do what they say they will do, making management unnecessary. As the business owner, your job will be to point, not drag.

♦ The 10 employees will require top dollar but will do the work of $1^1/_2$ to 2 average people.

Please don't take this recommendation lightly—it may very well be the most important commitment you accept.

Being a 10 employee is mostly about attitude. It's a bit hard for us to describe it to you but we suspect you will know it when you see it. In essence, you are looking for innate or natural skills that are difficult to teach. Such skills include a "can-do" attitude, good work ethic, customer focus, and conscientiousness. You can usually teach someone to do a job (use the computer software, answer the phone the way you want, and so on), but the attitude and work ethic–type skills are much more difficult.

Assuming you have all of your systems (procedures manual) in place as described in the previous chapter, your new 10 employee will have little trouble getting up to speed and will become a productive member of your team in a very short period of time.

Hire for Experience and Smarts

We've found from our own missteps that experience really does matter as long as the person has a great attitude (innate skills) as well. Many entrepreneurs have strong egos and often, unconsciously, hire people less sharp than themselves. On the surface, you can see where this approach would be less threatening. You are always the "brightest bulb on the tree" so everyone naturally looks to you for leadership. This approach strokes the ego but stifles the growth. So your second commitment is to try to find people who are smarter than you and who have business experience. After you've done this, your primary role will be to provide the vision for your company. Your team of "smarter-than-you" associates will help devise strategies you alone would have never considered. Better yet, they will take ownership of executing the strategies developed.

> ### That Reminds Us ...
>
> When I first started my company, I filled our ranks with inexperienced people with good attitudes. This left me carrying the ball with few blockers. I realized the importance of having experienced team members who are brighter than me. Today each of my partners comes from "Big 8" accounting backgrounds with 10 to 20 years of business experience under their belt. This has made all the difference in the world. They have the skill-set to run the company without me, which frees me up to focus on visionary thinking for the company rather than being bogged down in all the details.
>
> —Co-author Stewart Welch

Your ideal employee mix will include experienced talent along with young, enthusiastic people who are eager to learn. This gives you an opportunity to set up a mentoring program where the new upstarts work alongside experienced old guard. What you will find is that they learn from each other. Teaching others what you know is one of the best ways to advance your own learning because it forces you to articulate what you know so that it can be understood.

Exceed Your Employees' Expectations

If you plan to hire and keep top-quality employees, you will need to compensate them well. For each position, you need to do your research and determine the range of compensation for that position in the marketplace. This is not always easy to do but it can be done. One way is to always ask interviewees what their salary expectations are. You can also ask owners of your same type of business but who are not competitors (owners in a different geographical area, for example). When you know the salary range in your market, you have two goals for compensation for your employees. First, you want your total compensation package to be high enough so that it will be hard for a competitor to hire away any of your employees. This is very important because of the training costs associated with every employee. Second, when hiring a new employee, you want them to tell you what their salary expectation is, then pay them a little bit more than they are asking. This assumes their request is within the market range. It's a great way of telling your new employee that he or she is worth the extra money. This not only builds self-confidence in the employee, it also builds loyalty and trust. Show us a company with loyal, trustworthy, and confident employees, and we'll show you a wealth-building machine. Now that you have the base salary covered, give your employees a true sense of ownership with a bonus program.

How to Supercharge Your Employees

Wouldn't it be nice to get your employees to focus on things that will maximize company profits? If you've been in business at all, you know how tough this is to accomplish. The secret is to establish strategic incentive programs. This can be tricky because you're looking for both individual achievement and cohesive teamwork. It's imperative for you to understand how powerful this concept of incentive pay is for your business. Overnight, it can change your business forever.

The Team Incentive Program (TIP)

The goal of your Team Incentive Program (TIP) is to reward your employees for working together to maximize revenue and control expenses. It is an incentive pay program based on a certain percentage of the net profit from your business. It is one of the keys to motivating your employees to help achieve your company (and therefore your wealth-building) goals.

We will assume that you are producing monthly financial statements, so calculating your net profit should be easy.

The TIP program is designed to allow your employees to share a predetermined percentage of your net profit. After you've decided on the percentage and calculated the net bonus total, you then divide the bonus dollars according to each employee's percentage of payroll. One strategy is to calculate the bonus at the end of each quarter. Half is paid immediately, and half is placed in a pool to be distributed at the end of the year. However, an employee must still be employed on December 31 of the year to receive the other half. This discourages terminations during the year, particularly if you're having a good year.

You should include all employees in your bonus program because your goal is to reward them for working together as a team. Here's what the TIP system might look like:

Operating Income (Current Quarter)

Minus	**Operating expenses** (excluding depreciation)
Minus	**Loan payments** (principal and interest)
Minus	**Money for cash reserves** (5 percent of revenue, for example)
Equals	**Net income for bonus calculation**
Multiply by	20 percent
Equals	**Net bonus amount**
Multiply by	.5
Equals	**Immediate bonus**
Multiply by	**Each employee's percentage of payroll**
Equals	**Employee's bonus for the quarter**

By holding back one half of the quarterly bonus until the end of the year, you give yourself a cushion should you have losses in future quarters. In other words, the bonus is based on annual profit, not simply quarterly profits. Should second-half quarters turn negative, it will cause the deferred portion of the bonus to be reduced. This keeps the pressure up all year long rather than quarter to quarter.

A variation of this strategy is to have the bonus program come into play only after you've achieved certain predetermined profitability objectives. For example, you could say that after the company has made $100,000 in profit, employees would share in 25 percent of all additional profits. This strategy suggests financial rewards only for extraordinary team effort.

Treasure Tip

Do all you can to make your company an exciting and fun place to work. The results will amaze you. Your employees will be more efficient, effective, and loyal.

The Maximize Associate Productivity (MAP) Program

Okay, you have everybody working together as a team, paying attention to both gross revenue and expenses because their team bonus is based on *net* profit. Now we want to focus each associate like a laser on the things each of them can do to maximize their own productivity using our MAP strategy. You'll want to share the key goals of your business plan with your associates, and then their individual goals should "dovetail" into the business plan goals. What you want to reward here is not routine responsibilities, but extra activities that can really move your company to the next level of profitability.

There are several keys to making the MAP program a success:

♦ Review the broad and specific goals outlined in your business plan with your associates in a group meeting. Then outline the objective of the MAP program: an offer of a bonus of up to 10 percent of salary for extra effort. The employee and you will jointly define the activities of this extra effort.

♦ Have each employee write their own extra activity goals along with what they believe each one is worth in dollars (total to equal 10 percent of salary). Let them know you will challenge both the goal and particularly the value associated with it. They will need to be prepared to justify the cost-benefit of each goal. Let them know you will be tough in your judgment. This will make them think about how much a particular activity is really worth in dollar terms. In other words, they have to think like an owner! Make certain that each goal can, in fact, be accomplished. For example, avoid using a sales goal because a salesperson has little control over other people saying yes. Instead, use a sales calls goal because the salesperson definitely has control over the number of calls he or she makes. You want the goals to challenge your associates but you want them to succeed.

◆ You should also develop a list of activity goals for each associate—things that you know will lead to greater profitability. Don't be disappointed if they're not good at this. After all, they are not owners and making the transition to thinking like one will take time.

◆ Meet with each associate privately to have them present their activity goals and associated financial rewards. They are likely to come up with some great ideas that you have not thought of. Acknowledge them for these great ideas and then suggest some from your list. You must make certain each goal is clearly measurable. Place the burden of measurability on the associate. "How will I know when this goal has been completed?" Ask them to go back one more time and integrate your ideas with theirs and come back with a new combined list of activities and financial rewards. After you receive their final list, let them know you will review it and give them the final approval in a couple of days. Make your final adjustments as to the dollar value of each activity goal and get back with the associate for a final review to get their agreement on each goal and bonus amount. Now you have both their ideas and yours included in a list they helped designed so they will feel ownership of the program.

◆ After you've done this for all associates, have a group meeting and briefly outline the company goals one more time. Then have each associate briefly outline his or her individual activity goals (not the dollar incentives for each goal—this is confidential). This will create an even greater sense of commitment on their part.

◆ As goals are accomplished, celebrate by giving the associate a check at your weekly staff meeting. The associate will appreciate the instant reward and the recognition.

◆ At least once per quarter at a group meeting, have each associate outline where he or she is regarding accomplishing her goals. This will give some associates bragging rights and turn up the heat for others. You need to be aware of any associates who are falling off schedule for completing each of their goals and get with them to discuss how to get on track. This should be done privately, not during a group meeting. Don't allow them to fail!

If all of your associates accomplish all of their goals, not only will they feel great pride and earn additional income, but your company will be catapulted to a higher level of profitability.

Celebrate Your Success

Workdays quickly fall into a routine of everybody going about their business. This can easily become boring and make work less enjoyable. To break the boredom, you should celebrate your successes. What many companies do is celebrate employees' birthdays. A much better idea is to celebrate company successes. For example, if you close a big sale, do something to celebrate. Have gourmet desserts brought in one afternoon. If you have your best sales month in the history of the company, treat your associates to lunch at a restaurant of their choice. If someone does something note-worthy, drop him or her a handwritten note of appreciation. One week, come up with a group goal that if accomplished, everyone gets to leave at lunchtime on Friday. The ideas are endless, but what is important is that something is always going on. Keep them guessing. Keep it fun. You'll be amazed at what a difference it will make in the attitudes and raised spirits of your employees.

Delegate and Succeed

Most entrepreneurs will tell you that delegating is initially difficult to get accustomed to. However, if you can do it successfully, you dramatically increase your chances of achieving Wealth Stages 4 and 5.

The rule in delegation is this. You should do only those things that only you can do; delegate everything else. Do not assume that your employees cannot handle increased responsibility. We've found that the type of associates we're recommending you hire can handle just about anything you throw at them. Give them a chance to succeed but monitor their progress just in case they need support. Tell them the end result you are looking for, not how to do the task; then get out of their way. Require progress reports on intervals that will not allow them to get waist-deep in quicksand. This "delegate everything else" is a top-down strategy. After you do it for you, do the same thing for the next highest person in your organization. Keep doing this until you run out of people. This insures that everyone is always doing the highest level of work they are capable of.

Treasure Tip _____

The Delegation Rule: You should do only those things that only you can do. Delegate everything else!

When your business is operating this way, you'll have the necessary time you need to focus on strategic planning, which is really what you should be doing. Great books on this subject are *The E-Myth Revisited* and *The E-Myth Manager*, which are both written by Michael Gerber (HarperBusiness).

Because you will owe a big part of your business success to delegation, you need to give your employees permission to make mistakes. We all make them. Too often we will see business owners and managers berate an employee for a mistake. Never do this if you want to succeed. It's like cheating on your wife, then handing her a knife and turning your back. You are asking for trouble. Meet with the associate in private to discuss the error. Your demeanor should be calm with your goal to be to make sure the mistake is never repeated by anyone in your company. A mistake is usually indicative of a broken system. Figure out where the breakdown in the system is, fix it, and move on. The focus is on repairing the system, not the employee—unless, of course, the employee is not following the system. If this is the case, simply direct the employee back to the system.

Treasure Tip

While praise should always be given in public, mistakes should always be discussed in private.

Match People and Jobs

When you hire, make sure the responsibilities you want handled are properly matched with the personality of the prospective employees. Ask your prospective employees what they really enjoy doing. Ask about their strengths and weaknesses. Find out what they do best and make sure that it matches what you're looking for. If the person you need to hire is going to be in sales, find someone with excellent people skills. If you need an administrative person, make sure the person you hire enjoys working with numbers. This match game is an ongoing process, too. You have to stay abreast of your employees' personalities as they develop over time. Personalities do change sometimes, so be sure to meet individually with each employee on a regular basis.

Truly Get to Know Your People

If you really want to build wealth through the growth of your business, you need to know each of your employees' personal goals and aspirations. If you care enough to help them achieve these goals, they'll be loyal and dedicated to your vision. Help them and they'll help you.

That Reminds Us ...

I don't believe in the traditional employee review meeting. Instead, I get to know my employees' own personal goals, and I help them accomplish those goals through the success of my company. If I can show my employees how they can accomplish their personal goals by accomplishing the company's goals, we have all won. There's no need for me to be a motivator. If my employees see how their personal goals can be accomplished through the success of the company, then they'll naturally be motivated to produce. It's a simple concept.

—Co-author Larry Waschka

Conduct Regular Team Meetings

To build a successful and profitable business that can be sold later, you must hold regular meetings. Team meetings are vital to the success of a business. They hold together the people and the responsibilities of an organization. They develop and maintain a team spirit that is necessary for success. Weekly meetings should be how you monitor the progress of goals set each month. They shouldn't be any longer than one hour in length. The primary purpose of monthly meetings is to discuss the results of each goal in progress and to set new goals. At least once per year, hold an offsite retreat meeting to review the company business plan with your associates, receive their input, and adjust the plan as appropriate. You will get a different perspective on many issues and they will feel greater ownership in the company.

The basic weekly meeting agenda should at least include ...

- **Old business.** Items from the last meeting that need attention.
- **Goal review.** Reviewing the status and results of current goals.
- **New business.** New goals and any other items to discuss.
- **Calendar planning.** Reviewing everyone's calendar.

The "old business" section is a great way to keep everyone (including you) accountable for the projects that should be in process.

You must also encourage an open and flexible meeting where anything can be discussed. If your employees are intimidated or afraid to give their opinions, you may have problems for years before you ever see them. Your employees should be your greatest asset. Most employers don't realize their employees' full potential.

Let Your Employees Contribute

The key to long-term business success and the wealth-building process is getting employees involved in helping you develop the company vision and then letting them run with it. Your role should be to support these people while making sure everyone continues to be headed in the right direction ... toward your company goals. If you have a big vision, you need qualified, motivated employees. The only way to get truly motivated employees is to include them in your vision and in setting goals. The technical term for this type of management is participative management.

The Least You Need to Know

- Before hiring your first employee, examine the responsibilities of the job and find out whether you can outsource the position.

- Your employees can help you build wealth if you help them achieve their own personal goals, involve them in the company's vision and in setting goals, and pay them well.

- A company-wide bonus based on a percentage of net profits will encourage teamwork by your associates.

- A strategic individual incentive bonus program for your associates will help them stay focused on activities important to the success of the company.

- The secret to building a great business is to establish systems in your business that your employees can run so that you as a business owner can work *on* your business rather than *in* it.

- If you really want to build your business and your net worth, hire the best, match their work with their personality, give them responsibility, and get the heck out of the way!

Chapter 17

How to Sell Your Business

In This Chapter

- ♦ Learning strategies that will build wealth through your business
- ♦ Placing a value on your business
- ♦ Finding a buyer for your business
- ♦ Designing the smooth sale
- ♦ Achieving Wealth Stage 5 by taking your company public

The techniques used to prepare a business to be sold should simultaneously build wealth and cash flow. When you build your business, why not focus on possibly selling the business at a later date? It's like getting a two-for-one deal.

As you know from Chapter 3, where we introduced the Five Stages of Wealth, you've achieved Wealth Stage 4 if the market value of your business would produce (after capital gains taxes) enough proceeds to build a portfolio sufficient to support and substantially increase the level of your lifestyle, while at the same time keeping up with inflation. Regardless of whether you plan to sell your business in the future, if you plan to achieve Wealth Stage 4 using your own business, you need to understand the theory of preparing your company for a sale.

One of the benefits of owning your own business is the opportunity to build wealth at a much faster pace in relation to the traditional method of monthly investments in the stock market. Because the equity value of your business is tied to its growth and profitability, the key to building wealth is maximizing earnings growth. This not only makes you money, but it also makes your business worth more to a buyer. What we've learned is that what makes your business worth more to a buyer also makes you money in the process. Therefore, you should run your company as if you were going to sell it some time in the near future. Whether you can sell your business or not, you can at least save part of your earnings. If you actually sell your business in the future, your efforts will be further rewarded at the time of the sale.

This chapter teaches you how to build a company that will not only make you a lot of money, but will also make a buyer salivate.

24 Ways to Build Your Business and Get Rich

Are you ready to learn how to get to Wealth Stages 4 and 5? These are all common-sense measures to help you increase profits, build your equity value, and make your company more attractive to buyers. Every business is different, which means that a few of these might not apply to your situation. Use what you can and leave the rest.

◆ **Maximize your profit margin.** Take steps to improve your earnings enough to produce a profit margin that exceeds industry standards. Your trade organization should have data on this. You can achieve higher profit margins in one of two ways: cutting your overhead expenses and maximizing sales or gross income.

Many business owners try to minimize taxes so much that they inevitably forget about profits. If you plan to sell your business, you need to focus on maximizing profits because that's what the new owner is looking for.

◆ **Get *audited financial statements*.** Have your financial statements audited by a reputable CPA firm. The first thing a potential buyer will want from you is your company's financial statement. Accurate financial statements will build trust between you and your potential buyer. Plus, the buyer will want to have your statements

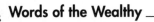

Words of the Wealthy

An **audited financial statement** is one prepared by an independent accounting firm using generally accepted auditing standards to determine that the financial statements can be relied upon. **A reviewed financial statement** is one whereby an independent accounting firm uses certain procedures to determine the reasonableness of the statements.

audited anyway. A less expensive alternative to an audited financial statement is a *reviewed financial statement.*

◆ **Maximize sales and earnings growth.** Focus on maximizing your company's sales and earnings growth. Your goal should be to achieve a growth rate that exceeds industry standards. Call your trade organization and ask about the average sales and earnings growth rates in your industry. You might also ask who the most successful firms are in your industry. Call them and ask if you can visit to share ideas. Many trade organizations publish benchmarking information and/or provide it on their website to members.

◆ **Show the potential for more growth.** Build a case that illustrates for the new buyer more potential for growth in sales and market share. If your company dominates the market with 60 percent market share, the buyer will be worried about the prospects for further growth. Show the buyer how your market may be growing. Even a declining market share in a rapidly expanding market can be viewed as a positive selling point. Make it easy for the buyer to visualize success.

◆ **Design written systems and procedures.** If you and your employees take the time to design and maintain written systems and procedures, your company will not only run more smoothly and efficiently, but your prospects for a sale will greatly improve as well. Empathize with a potential buyer, and imagine yourself making a buying decision between two businesses. If everything else is held constant, except that one had a written procedures manual for all operations and all employee positions in the company, which one would you choose? You'd choose the company that can operate the best with the least supervision—the one with written systems and procedures that anyone can follow. That's every businessperson's dream.

Treasure Tip

Trade shows and conventions held for your industry are one of the greatest learning tools available to you. Few people understand their value. The key to maximizing the return on your time is to ask a lot of questions ... of everyone!

◆ **Clean house.** Do you find yourself cleaning your house prior to company coming over? Well, you need to do the same thing when prospective buyers start to visit. Implement a procedure to keep your facility as neat and tidy as possible. You might even consider painting or other improvements that might be attractive to a buyer. If it were your house for sale, what would you do?

- **Smiling, happy people.** If you want to really impress your prospective buyer, show him or her a group of happy, enthusiastic, team-oriented employees. If you haven't taken the steps to create this positive work atmosphere, do it now. You can't produce this overnight, but you can at least get started.

> ### That Reminds Us ...
>
> We actually teach our associates how to act when we have a client or visitor at our office. They stop what they're doing, get out of their chair, smile, stick out their hand, and give a firm handshake. They say the person's name and introduce themselves. It's a simple concept. Just think of every visitor as a guest stopping by your home.
>
> —Co-author Stewart Welch

- **Keep it confidential.** You might not want to tell your employees about your interest in selling. It could create unwanted confusion and fear. If your employees think they might lose their jobs as a result of a sale, they will immediately begin to look elsewhere. Likewise, your competitors may use this information to their advantage.

- **Always take time to plan.** Few people take time to plan. They get so caught up in their work that they never have time to plan. It's like the lumberjack who was so busy sawing that he didn't take time to sharpen the saw. Commit to spending a minimum of four hours per week working *on* your business rather than *in* your business.

- **Identify owners or managers of "best practices" in your industry.** If you want to leap completely over your competition and experience exponential growth, find the best people in your business today and imitate them. Some people are reluctant to help others, especially if you're in their town. Therefore, focus on those who are out of your geographic area. Ask if you can visit with them about their business.

- **Do what you love to do, and delegate everything else.** We already covered this in Chapter 16, but it's important enough to repeat.

- **Always have a big vision.** To build a better business, you must have a vision of what you want to build. This vision must be big enough to drive you and challenge you. Employees are also motivated by a big vision. Note that most businesses either don't have a vision for their company at all or their employees don't know what it is. Having a vision that everyone embraces will create a competitive advantage for you.

That Reminds Us ...

When I was young, my friend Brandon and I built a tree house. We spent weeks building what we thought was the best tree house in the world, and in our little world, it was the best! It was our escape. However, within a week, we got bored. We thought of all the things we'd do differently and all the things that needed improvement. We wanted a bigger, better house—so we built another and then another. It took me many years to understand the moral of that adventure. I learned that you must have a dream big enough to challenge you all your life. Otherwise, you end up building one tree house after another.

—Co-author Larry Waschka

- **Focus on what you're good at.** What are you better at than most people? What do others say you're good at? If you'll identify your strengths and use them, you might find yourself with a natural competitive advantage that will speed you on to success. If you're really good at something now, just imagine how competitive you'd be if you focused on improving that skill even more. Use your natural strengths to build your business and beat your competition.

- **Eliminate the fear of failure.** Fear of failure will kill your business. You should always ask yourself, "What is the worst thing that can happen?" Next you should ask yourself, "Can I handle the worst thing?" If the answer is yes, then don't worry about it any more. Make plans to handle the worst thing, and then eliminate the fear.

- **You must work hard and smart.** Research indicates that the average self-made millionaire works 59 hours per week. However, if you have a compelling vision, you might find yourself wanting to work more than 59 hours. Although working hard is important, working smart is vital. Continually review every recurring process in your business and ask the question, "How can this be done faster, cheaper, or more efficiently?" Challenge your employees to ask the same question and reward them when they come up with money-saving answers.

- **Avoid negative people.** If you want to ruin your vision, spend time with problem-oriented, negative, and jealous people. If you want to build a better business, focus your social efforts on positive people who are also success-oriented. Successful business owners associate themselves with others who appreciate win-win relationships. They celebrate each other's victories and are eager to help after disappointments.

The same is true with business relationships. If you know that a potential or existing client is going to be a problem in the future, you might want to give the client to your competitor. Explain that you feel his or her objectives will be better served by the other company.

- **Be an information sponge.** In today's world of computers, the Internet, and fast-paced business transactions, you have to keep track of changes. If you want to learn new ways to improve your business, you must become a Curious George and ask a lot of questions. You also need to be able to read a lot of information in a short amount of time. Where should you focus your attention? The following list gives the most common fast-paced changes that will affect your business:

    - Improved computer systems that increase your efficiency

    - Internet software that can connect you to your customer

    - Changes in your industry and the economy

    - Changes in the needs of the customer

    - Changes in your competition

- **Keep a good attitude.** If you want to build a better business, you must develop an air of confidence, enthusiasm, and humility. For example, if you try to make a sale with a fearful or hungry attitude, the prospective buyer will probably run away. You have to be confident in yourself, your product, and your business. You also have to be optimistic and see the opportunity in every problem you encounter.

Treasure Tip

A good source of business information is *Audio-Tech Business Book Summaries* (www.audiotech.com). This company will provide you with audio cassette or CD summaries of business books each month.

- **Focus on helping others.** Customer service is simply the art of helping others get what they want and exceeding their expectations. The most successful companies in the world don't try to merely meet their customers' needs; they try to exceed them. This should be part of your company's core policy. One way to start this process is to examine your marketing efforts.

If you exceed the expectations of a prospective buyer, you increase the odds of the buyer becoming a client.

◆ **Develop your genius.** Genius is not knowledge. Our definition of genius is someone who can single-mindedly focus on one thing at a time. This might sound easy to you, but with all the hats you're going to wear as a business owner, it's not easy!

◆ **You must be a decision maker.** First, ask yourself this question: "Am I a decision maker?" If your answer is yes, then proceed. If your answer is no, ask yourself this question again until your answer is yes. To be a good decision maker, you must understand two things. First is the principle of the worst-case scenario. As we said earlier in this chapter, if you can handle it, then don't worry about it. Second, list all the pros and cons of the decision. Weigh each alternative and select the best alternative. Accept the fact that you'll be wrong some of the time.

◆ **Make sure you need it before you buy it.** Before you buy anything—especially a big-ticket item—think about it for a while and make sure you need it.

That Reminds Us ...

Within six months of starting my own business, I spent more than $10,000 on software that I never used. I honestly thought I needed it, but when I narrowed my focus from financial planning to money management, the software became obsolete. This was an expensive lesson in planning. I could have spent that money on so many other things. It still drives me crazy to know that I spent that much money on something that wasn't needed during a time when every penny counted. Learn from my mistake.

—Co-author Larry Waschka

◆ **Establish some barrier to entry.** Do whatever it takes to set up as many barriers to entry as you can. A barrier to entry is simply something that deters or prevents other people from competing against you. The best barriers are licenses, patents, copyrights, and professional degrees. If none of these apply to your business, then consider other tactics such as ...

  ◆ Advertising and dominating your market.

  ◆ Being willing to do what others won't do.

- Establishing yourself in the local media as the expert.

- Establishing an outrageous customer service program.

Treasure Tip

Before you sell your business, make sure you're ready. Spend some time imagining what you'll be doing after the sale. What will your goals be? What will you want to do next? Do you want to continue working with the new owner?

- **Build a company that runs without you.** The business should be able to run without you. If the business is built around you, the purchaser may be worried that the business will fail without the owner. Therefore, your goal is to put the right people in the right positions so that you become unnecessary in the day-to-day activities of the business. This will allow you to now spend the majority of your time working *on* the business rather than *in* the business. When you reach this point, your business should begin to flourish at a rapid rate.

Why Sell?

Everyone is different, and every business owner has his or her own reasons for selling. Your reason might be to build a liquid portfolio that would provide more than enough income for you to live—Wealth Stage 4. The most common reasons business owners sell their businesses (or a part of it) include the following:

- Retirement

- Desire to diversify into other businesses

- Need for additional capital to continue growth

- Strategic alliance with a larger company, allowing economies of scale and access to new markets

How to Value Your Company

To know when you've reached Wealth Stages 4 or 5, you need to know what your business is worth. Putting a price on a closely held business can be a difficult process.

To put it bluntly, the value of a business is equal to the largest amount of money anyone is willing to pay for it. It's rarely like selling a house where you have comparable sales transactions within the same neighborhood. In contrast, sale prices of closely held companies aren't usually public information, and that makes the valuation process difficult. Therefore, you often have to calculate an estimate of fair market value based on vague criteria. The fair market value is only an estimate. In the end, the real value is whatever price the buyer and seller agree upon at the time of the sale.

Some business owners jump to the conclusion that their companies are worth 16 times their earnings, just like some companies traded on the New York Stock Exchange. They fail to recognize that publicly traded companies have several advantages over most closely held companies, including the following:

◆ Easier access to capital

◆ Ability to use stock for acquisitions

◆ Highly scrutinized financial reporting to the SEC

◆ Diversified group of management and directors

◆ The company's success doesn't rely on one person

The most common methods of valuation involve mathematical models that take into consideration the company's assets, past and future earnings, industry outlook, strength of management, and uniqueness of the product or service.

There are a dozen different ways that a company can be valued. In Revenue Ruling 59–60, the Internal Revenue Service outlines a method that is widely used. Basically, it suggests that the value of a business is determined by how much a buyer would be willing to invest to achieve a given rate of return that results in an amount equal to the adjusted profit of the company. For example, take a 5-year average net profit of the business and divide your result by the return you would expect on your investment based on the risks you are accepting. If your 5-year average net profit was $50,000 and you expected to earn 20 percent based on the risk of investing in a private business, the price you would be willing to pay is $250,000 ($50,000 ÷ .20 = $250,000). A variation of this that is often used is called the Profit Multiple Business Valuation. Again, you determine your pretax profits and then multiply them by a factor typically ranging from 1 through 5, based on industry standards. In essence, these valuation methods focus on sustainable profits and an acceptable return on the purchaser's invested capital. If you have significant hard assets (plant and equipment), the valuation should take these into account as well.

The best way to determine the value of your company is to get some help. Many CPAs are trained in business valuations. What the CPA's valuation cannot tell you is the opportunity cost. What would the buyer obtain that is not in the numbers? Is there value to the additional market share? Is your company in a high-growth area? Also, check with your industry association. Not only will they likely be able to provide you with valuation "rules of thumb," but they are also a good source for companies that specialize in valuations for businesses of your type. For more information on business valuation methods, go to www.ventureline.com.

Finding a Buyer

Before you can sell your business and get to Wealth Stage 4 or 5, you must find a buyer for your business. Buyers can be hard to find if you don't know the players in the market. Even if you do know the players, will you know how to conduct the sale? Selling a business involves complex valuation methods, tax considerations, and strategic negotiations. Can you do all that alone?

Check in Your Own Backyard First

If you've truly been committed to hiring top-quality employees, it is likely that one or more of your key people is perfectly capable of buying and running your company. This is a great place to start, but it typically requires substantial lead-time for planning. You should always be mentoring your key people to take over the responsibility of running your company. As soon as you envision the sale of your company, you should begin exploring the possibility of a sale to key employees.

Think about it. Who understands the inner-workings of your company better than your key people? The biggest challenge will often be their ability to raise money for the purchase. This is why it is important to allow as much lead-time as possible, perhaps as much as several years. This gives the key employees time to line up their financing. It's also possible for you to provide the financing whereby the new owner-employees pay you on an installment basis from company cash flow. If you do this, make sure you have additional collateral above the company stock.

You could also consider an Employee Stock Option Plan (ESOP) whereby you sell your company to your employees over a period of years. ESOPs are a tax-qualified employee benefit plan, and as such, contributions are tax-deductible by your company. Effectively what you're doing is using company cash and cash flow to purchase your stock over time, thus allowing you to further diversify your assets. In other cases, you will contribute company stock instead of cash and use the benefits of the tax deduction to further increase your profits. The law even allows you to magnify the tax benefits by doing what is called a Leveraged ESOP. In a Leveraged ESOP, the ESOP Trust borrows money from a financial institution and uses the proceeds to either …

♦ Purchase the stock of the owner. In this case the owner sells stock for cash and can then use the cash to diversify his or her investment holdings or as he or she wishes.

♦ Buy new shares of stock. If the goal is to raise additional capital for the company, the company will sell new shares of stock to the ESOP.

For a more detailed look at the advantages and intricacies of ESOPs, go to www.esopassociation.org.

Looking Outside Your Company

If a sale to key employees is not a viable option, you will need to look outside your company. Here are some tips for beginning the search:

♦ **Identify people who can help you.** Depending on the size of your business, there are basically three types of people who can help you find a buyer and walk you through the sales process. They will also help you negotiate the sale. If you own a small business with less than $1 million in sales, you can hire a business broker. You can find business brokers in the Yellow Pages and from referrals by attorneys or CPAs.

If your business has $2 million to $50 million in sales, you're considered a middle-market business, in which case you want to hire an intermediary. Intermediaries are similar to business brokers but are accustomed to dealing with larger businesses and more sophisticated negotiations. Intermediaries are hard to find unless you live in a major metropolitan city. If your business grows to more than $50 million in sales, you might want to consider hiring an investment banking company. These companies are easy to find in the phone book.

Be sure to do your research before you hire one of these people. At the very least, ask for references and call them with questions. If you know of a company in your industry that has been sold recently, ask the seller and buyer who helped them. Most trade organizations also keep track of intermediaries that specialize in their industry.

◆ **Maximize your company's exposure to buyers.** Make sure your company is in all the local chamber of commerce listings. Confirm the way they categorize your company, whom they list as president, and all other pertinent information. This includes the membership list, as well as other directories that might apply, such as the book of local manufacturers.

Ask your state industrial development office for its guide to businesses in your state. Are you listed? Is the information up-to-date? Think of all the different services your company offers, and make sure you are properly listed in the phone book under these services.

◆ **Talk to local CPAs, attorneys, and bankers.** These people know others who might be looking for a business to buy.

◆ **Contact a venture capital firm.** Venture capital companies are in the business of providing funding to other operating companies. This can take the form of an outright purchase or of supplying needed capital in exchange for a percentage of ownership in the business.

◆ **Don't list your business in the local paper.** You might not want everyone to know you're selling, and you could have all kinds of people calling you, most of whom will not be qualified. If you do list locally, be anonymous and let your business broker or intermediary help you.

◆ **Talk to your competitors**. Assuming you have "friendly" competitors, they can be a great prospect for buying your company. After all, they fully understand the business. Obviously there may be a confidentiality issue with these types of discussions that you must consider.

Construct Your Business Profile

A business profile is similar to a business plan. It is used by your prospective buyers as they begin their research on your company. This profile will help maximize your sales price if you design it carefully. Given the right amount of profitability, it may be your ticket to Wealth Stage 5. Be accurate and honest. An outline of a typical business profile follows:

I. Introduction

   A. Summary of operations

   B. Financial summary

   C. History of company

   D. Ownership

   E. Reasons for sale

   F. Company strengths and opportunities

II. Description of business

   A. General business description

   B. Description of market and current market share

   C. Future growth potential

   D. Sales and marketing

   E. Competition

   F. Management and employees

   G. Current customers

   H. Suppliers and contracts

III. Business facilities

   A. Location and facilities

   B. Equipment

IV. List of exhibits

   A. Audited financial statements

   B. Marketing material and brochures

   C. List of major equipment and furniture

   D. Resumés and job descriptions of all key employees

   E. Results of recent client survey

   F. Business advisors and references

Complete the Deal

Many of the people we know who have achieved Wealth Stages 4 and 5 did so by selling their business. They knew what their company was worth, they negotiated with the buyer to agree on a win-win deal, and they had help along the way.

What's Important to You?

The following list of questions should help you decide exactly what you want out of the sale:

1. Would you be willing to finance the sale?

2. Do you want to continue to work with the company after it's sold?

3. If you were required to work for another year or two as part of the negotiation, would you be willing to? For how long?

4. If you did work, what hours would you want to keep? Do you need to continue your health insurance? What responsibilities would you want to focus on?

5. How will you structure the deal to achieve your financial goals?

6. Do you have key employees or your children in the business who want to continue working? Will the new owners keep them?

7. What would your employees do if they knew you were thinking about selling? Should you keep it confidential?

Treasure Tip

Selling is a lot like dating. If you badly need the buyer, he'll run away. If you don't need the buyer, he'll never leave.

After you know what you want out of the transaction, prioritize each item by its level of importance to you. This will make the negotiation much easier because you'll know what you can and cannot compromise. Be sure to let your attorney know these items and make sure he or she keeps the win-win concept in mind. Many attorneys will fight tooth and nail without compromising anything. Don't let this happen. You must be willing to compromise some things.

Suggestions for Peaceful Negotiations

The negotiation process takes time and a lot of patience. You and the buyer must both be willing to work hard to make the transaction go smoothly. Here are several tips that will make the process a little easier and less time-consuming:

- Know exactly what you're willing to compromise and what you're not.

- As long as you know your goals, be flexible as to their accomplishment.

- Don't insist on winning every argument.

- Empathize with the buyer and his or her needs.

- Don't get too excited if you get a better deal than you expected.

- Never hesitate to walk away from a sale that doesn't meet your goals.

- Never threaten to walk away unless you are serious about it.

- Listen for the buyer's goals.

- Listen and find out what exactly the buyer is willing to compromise.

- Be honest and strive for win-win.

Treasure Tip _____

Strive for a win-win deal where both you and the buyer are happy with the deal.

Treasure Tip _____

Be sure to research your buyer. Make sure you know who you're dealing with. Does he or she have adequate capital? Is this person capable of running the company? Make the research for the buyer easy. Do the homework for him or her in advance. Be honest, and don't hide anything that will surprise your buyer later.

How to Have a Smooth Sale

Make sure you understand, in advance, the tax liabilities of selling your company. Hire a tax lawyer who can help you structure the sale to minimize taxes.

Don't procrastinate or be unprofessional in the transaction. Be patient and understand that this is a difficult process. However, don't allow your buyer to stall for no reason.

The personality of the buyer is important, especially if you plan to continue working with the company. If you have more than one attractive offer, be sure to give a lot of consideration to the nature of the person or people you'll be working with. Spend some social time with the buyer and get to know him or her personally. This can improve the level of trust and rapport necessary for a good transaction.

Allow the new buyer to get to know your key employees on a social level. If your key employees are happy with the new owner, things will run more smoothly for both you and the buyer.

Make sure the buyer has enough money after the sale for working capital and emergencies. You might get your business back if he or she runs out of money. If the buyer says he or she plans to make up for the lack of cash through net earnings from the business, make sure your company is profitable enough to accomplish this. You also want to make sure you get enough money up front to cover three things: any commission you might have to pay your broker or intermediary; taxes due on your sale; and any expenses you might encounter if you happen to get the business back.

Make sure your company is profitable enough to cover the debt payments for the buyer. If your buyer can't pay the debt on the business, he or she will have to give it back to you.

Taking Your Company Public—the Initial Public Offering

If your heart is set on achieving Wealth Stage 5, you must understand how to take your company public. When you make an *initial public offering (IPO)*, you sell a certain percentage of your company's stock to the public for money. You usually sell only a minimal amount of stock so that you can still maintain control. The *underwriter* helps the company decide on the price of the new shares and the timing of the IPO. The reason behind an IPO is to raise money for expansion and growth in the business. If your company is growing fast and the amount of money you need for expansion is too large for a bank to consider, an IPO might be in order.

> **Words of the Wealthy**
>
> An **underwriter** is a brokerage firm that handles the process of offering a company's stock to the public through an **initial public offering.**

Taking your company public gives you the opportunity to cash in on your company's success without giving up control or selling your majority interest of the shares. The benefits of taking your company public include …

- You typically are selling only part of your company.

- Often you will remain the largest shareholder and therefore will maintain some control over your company.

- By taking your company public, you will have significantly increased its value.

- Your publicly traded stock is much more liquid than your privately held stock was.

- Publicly traded stock can be more readily used for collateral than privately held stock.

All these benefits come with a price:

- Most people do not realize the cost of going public in dollars and time. The change of focus of management from running the company to the public offering can hurt a company if you're not prepared to deal with the many changes.

- You have to give up some future profits.

- You must fully disclose financial information on your company.

- Your company will be highly regulated by the Securities and Exchange Commission.

- You must answer to shareholders.

- You must answer to your board of directors.

Additional Resources

If you decide to start you own business, be sure to check out *The Complete Idiot's Guide to Starting Your Own Business*. It is filled with great tips and all the ideas you need to get started. Your library and local bookstore might also have other titles that will help.

The Least You Need to Know

- Preparing your business to be sold in the future will not only help you get to Wealth Stages 4 and 5; it will also make your business more attractive to a buyer.

♦ If you take the time to find the most successful businesses in your industry and imitate them, your business will grow, completely dominate your competition, and increase your chances of achieving Wealth Stages 4 and 5.

♦ Recognize that the perfect buyer may be one or more employees of your company.

♦ Consider getting help with the preparation to sell, as well as the selling process.

♦ Reduce the chance of surprise by taking time to reflect upon what you want from the sale of your business.

Part 4

The Advanced Strategies for Building and Preserving Wealth

Whether you've chosen to seek your fortune as an employee or as the owner of your own business, you will need to become savvy when it comes to tax matters. We'll teach you basic as well as advanced strategies for using the tax laws to your advantage. We'll also introduce you to one final and very powerful strategy for building wealth fast: investment real estate.

As you embark on your journey down the road to riches, it's important that you protect your assets and employ strategies to prolong your wealth. We'll introduce you to these strategies and show you how to achieve greater balance in your life. Money has no meaning in and of itself. Its meaning is derived from your value system and how you use your wealth and influence to improve not only your world, but also the world around you.

Chapter 18

Building Wealth with Real Estate

In This Chapter

♦ Learning how to use leverage to magnify your returns

♦ Taking the risks out of owning investment real estate

♦ Making money in raw land

♦ Knowing how to cash in on the Baby Boomer generation

Investment real estate is a great way to achieve Wealth Stage 4 and even Wealth Stage 5, second only to owning your own business. What is particularly attractive about investment real estate is that you can do it in your spare time, as a hobby, or pursue it as a full-time business. There are also many, many ways to approach the business of investment real estate including residential housing, apartments, raw land, commercial real estate for retail businesses, office buildings, or industrial complexes. What makes real estate so powerful as a wealth-building strategy? Leverage!

Understanding the Power of Leverage

Investing in real estate offers you the opportunity to significantly magnify the power of your money, because lending institutions (and often individuals as well) will gladly loan you money to help with your purchase. If your goal is Wealth Stage 4 or 5, it is critical that you both understand and use the power of leverage. Let's look at two examples that will clearly explain the value of leverage.

Let's assume you've signed a contract to buy a duplex for $100,000 where the rents are $10,000 per year. If you paid cash for the building, your return on investment would be 10 percent annually. If instead you invested $20,000 and got a 7 percent loan for the $80,000 balance, you've significantly increased your return. After subtracting your interest payments from your rents, you would have $3,000 left. This $3,000 represents a 50 percent increase in your rate of return over a nonleveraged purchase (from 10 percent to 15 percent). Don't forget, you still have $80,000 of your cash left. If you repeated this process four more times, you would own $500,000 worth of real estate yielding 15 percent. Now if the value of your real estate increased in value 5 percent during your first year, or $25,000, what would be your return on your $100,000? Well, you would have received $50,000 in rental income plus $25,000 of appreciation (increased equity) less $35,000 in interest payments for a total net benefit of $40,000, which represents a total return of 40 percent! Okay, we've over-simplified our example by not including maintenance costs, property taxes, insurance, and vacancy losses, but we've also not included depreciation. At this point, we simply want you to understand the concept and value of using leverage to increase your returns. We'll get to the details of how to structure a winning transaction later in this chapter. For now, let's look at a little known strategy anyone can use that was developed by co-author Welch.

The Home Sale Strategy: The Biggest Tax Break You Never Heard About

During President Clinton's administration, passage of the Taxpayer Relief Act of 1997 provided one of the biggest tax breaks imaginable—that very few people understand or take advantage of. What if you could purchase an asset, have it appreciate up to $500,000, sell it, and avoid paying any taxes on your gain … forever? Although this may sound too good to be true, it gets even better! This law allows you to repeat this process every 24 months!

We're referring to the tax benefits from the sale of your personal residence. Under prior law, if you sold your home for more than what you paid for it (your cost basis), and you did not fully reinvest all your proceeds in a new residence, you were subject to capital gains taxes. The exception to this rule: if you were over the age of 55, the first $125,000 of gain was not subject to the tax. Under the new rules, if you sell your home, there is no tax on the first $250,000 of realized gain (i.e., profit) and there are no age limitations. The only requirement is that you must have owned and occupied the residence as a principal residence for an aggregate of at least 2 of the 5 years prior to the sale or exchange. If you are married, you and your spouse together can exclude up to $500,000 of realized gain assuming you file a joint tax return.

Here's the strategy. If your home has appreciated sizably since you bought it, consider selling it and realizing your profit. Keep just enough cash to cover a down payment on a new home. You should look for a "fixer upper" in a stable neighborhood and then start the process of rebuilding equity in your new home. Take your remaining cash profits and buy investment real estate as discussed in this chapter. This strategy will let you take advantage of the equity you have built up in your home. The added benefit is that you don't have to share any of this money with the IRS!

Let's look at an example:

Assume you paid $150,000 for your home 10 years ago and financed $120,000. You sell it today for $300,000 or a profit of $150,000. You take part or all your profit and invest it; you use your remaining home equity as a down payment on a new home. Maybe you are recently an "empty nester" and are taking this opportunity to downsize, or you are able to find a fixer-upper home that just needs some loving care (cosmetic surgery) to bring out its appreciation. Your old equity is now working hard for you in additional investment real estate while your new residence is now appreciating quickly due to your "sweat equity." Remember that you can do this once *every two years!* This process of periodically "retrieving" your equity and investing it is a strategy that should enhance your ability to accumulate wealth. Radical idea? Yes. Tax efficient? You bet! Should you do it? Only if you are anxious to get to Wealth Stages 4 or 5!

Rental Real Estate

Many people have achieved great wealth by investing in rental real estate. It's a compelling strategy whereby you come up with the down payment and your tenant then pays you enough rent to cover all future expenses including your mortgage payment.

Eventually, your mortgage is paid in full and your free cash flow from the property soars. Is it that simple? Yes and no. You absolutely can buy properties that will give you these results but finding them will require you to look at a lot of poor deals before you find the one that meets these criteria. As a matter of fact, the typical ratio will be about 100 to 1. In other words, you'll need to review, on average, 100 deals to find 1 that yields this result. Before we discuss the criteria for a "green light" deal, let's discuss the pros and cons of investing in residential real estate versus commercial real estate.

Residential Real Estate

Residential real estate includes single-family homes, duplexes, and apartment buildings. All these rental situations involve individual renters, and these rental transactions tend to operate on a very personal level. In addition, although you may have a very strictly drawn lease agreement, many state and local laws may take precedent over your contract. In fact, the law has tended to grant tenants broad rights, making getting rid of a bad one quite a hassle. This is not meant to discourage you, but rather to emphasize the need to have a well-executed screening process for finding tenants who are not likely to give you problems. One very big advantage of residential real estate is that you can start very small and get your feet wet without risking financial disaster. This advantage is also a disadvantage because it means that a lot of other people may be competing with you for a given property.

Commercial Real Estate

Commercial real estate includes a wide variety of properties including retail businesses, office buildings, industrial buildings, and hospitality properties. The focus here is on the business, and things tend to operate on a business level. The lease agreement tends to rule the day. A potential disadvantage of commercial property is that it often requires more money to buy, not only because the property is more expensive but also because the lending institutions tend to have stricter loan requirements. Instead of 90 percent loan-to-value, they may require 50 percent to 60 percent loan-to-value. This disadvantage may also be an advantage because fewer people will be looking at the same property. However, those who are looking are likely to be more astute investors.

Vitals of the Real Estate Deal

You can make your fortune in investment real estate or you can lose your shirt. The good news is that you can stack the odds in your favor by following a few simple rules:

♦ **Build in a profit when you buy your property.** The best way to make sure you make a profit on any particular deal is to make your profit when you buy the property. This might sound strange, but it is a perfectly sane objective. You see, unlike the stock market where the value of a stock is absolutely known from moment to moment, the real estate market is very imperfect. Values and sales prices vary widely depending on a number of factors including the number of buyers for a particular property, the sophistication of the seller (and buyer), and the particular circumstances surrounding the sale (divorce, bank foreclosure, property tax lien, and so on). Your goal is to find special situations where the seller is highly motivated to sell and will sell for less than the true value.

That Reminds Us ...

I was making an offer on a residential property that was listed for $135,000 but I knew the seller was highly motivated because he had already moved and the house was vacant. The hot water heater had burst over the winter and his property insurance company would cancel coverage after they knew the house had been vacant for what was now about nine months. I arranged my financing in advance, then took an offer to the seller for $80,000 and stated I could close for cash, next week. My explanation for the low price was that I believed the house really was worth what he was asking but $80,000 was all I could afford to pay. He accepted my offer without a counter. I sold the house two years later for $135,000.

—Co-author Stewart Welch

♦ **Never purchase real estate where going in you have negative cash flow.** Cash flow is the name of the game in rental real estate. *Positive* cash flow, to be more specific. Always, always make certain the property you buy is projected to produce a positive cash flow from day one. There may be a few exceptions, but they are rare.

> ### That Reminds Us ...
>
> A close friend of mine identified a four-story 40,000-square-foot office building that had been turned over to the bank. It was about 50 percent leased and all the bank wanted was to get their money out of the deal. At 50 percent occupancy, there was no way this deal would work. Our solution was to put together a small group of investors who would occupy the remaining 50 percent of the space. We got a great deal on the building and its value soared after it was 100 percent occupied. A couple of years later, we refinanced the building and were able to pull out our original cash investment while still maintaining a positive cash flow.
>
> —Co-author Stewart Welch

- Only buy property where the property stands alone as the collateral for your loan. One of the great things about real estate is that lending institutions love it so much, they will allow it to stand as the sole collateral for a loan. You don't have to personally guarantee the loan will be paid off. If the worst case happens, you can simply give the bank the keys to the property and you have no further liability. Sure, you lost your down payment and any other monies you put in the property, but you did not lose everything else you have. In fact, in many cases, instead of foreclosing, the bank will work with you to get the property back on its feet because the bank would rather have you doing the hard work than them.

- Minimize your down payment/maximize your loan. On the surface, this rule would seem to increase the risk of owning a property. This is definitely true if you don't strictly adhere to the previous rule that says the property must have a positive cash flow. Assuming your property has a positive cash flow, a low down payment allows you to own more properties and further diversify your holdings. Go back to our $100,000 example earlier in this chapter. By taking your $100,000 and buying 4 to 10 properties that are *all producing positive cash flow*, you have created greater diversification and effectively reduced your risks.

- Look for a higher and better use. Some of the very best deals are the ones where you can take a property, and use your creativity to immediately increase its value. For example, you might convert a 4-plex apartment building into condominiums.

- Never lose sight that the next great deal is just around the corner. Never fall in love with a particular property. Remember that this is a business of numbers.

The numbers must work from the very beginning. Don't do any deals based on your anticipation that the deal will turn positive cash flow in the future. If you can't get positive cash flow at closing, walk away.

How to Find Great Deals

Now that you know the rules that will reduce the risks of buying and owning real estate, how do you find great deals? Did you ever notice that when you bought a new car, suddenly you see your make and model everywhere? It's the same with investment real estate. When you get in the game, deals will begin to come out of the woodwork. It is critical that you understand that you must look at a lot of deals and make a lot of offers before you'll actually land a deal that fits the criteria (our rules) just described. If you are easily frustrated, this is not the game for you.

Consider setting some goals for yourself. Why not set a goal to buy one property per year? Don't be concerned with how big the deal is, just focus on getting one deal done each year. Investment real estate expert Dolf de Roos (www.dolfderoos.com) uses the following success formula: 100:10:3:1. He says that, on average, you will need to look at 100 deals, make 10 offers, and try to finance 3 deals to end up with one that you actually buy. Looking at 100 deals sounds like an awful lot of time and trouble but this is what it takes. We never said you could get rich without effort! Let's see if we can break it down and make the job less daunting. 100 deals a year is 8.33 per month or 1.9 per week. Okay, round up to 2 deals per week. Now this seems manageable.

Where to Look

So where do you start your search? Here are some typical sources:

- **Classified ads.** This is perhaps the easiest place to get started because the listings are concentrated under the real estate or investment property section.

- **Real estate agents.** Call a local real estate office, ask for the manager or owner, and then ask to talk to the best agent to help you find investment property. Meet with the agent and tell her what the general parameters are of the type of deal you're looking for. In most cases, the realtor handles the actual negotiation of offers. You will need to decide if this is okay or if you want to do that yourself. If you do, let her know you want to handle the negotiations.

- **Real estate magazines.** In most cities, someone publishes a free magazine of listings in the area, typically complete with photographs. This can be an excellent source. You'll often find them outside of retail stores and restaurants.

- **Banks. Banks often end up owning properties due to foreclosure.** Because banks are in the business of lending money, not managing foreclosed property, their goal is to sell these properties as quickly as possible. Contact your local banks and ask if they currently hold any properties they wish to sell. Also, let them know you are an interested buyer of properties that they might hold in the future.

- **Run your own ad.** It is relatively inexpensive to run a small classified ad in the real estate section of your local newspaper indicating your interest in buying investment property. Be specific about the type of properties you are seeking.

- **Call on property owners.** If you see a property that interests you, contact the owner to see if he or she is interested in selling. Every now and then, they will be. Just as important, leave her your contact information in case the owner changes his or her mind at a later date. If you really like the property, touch base with the owner every 6 to 12 months. This will not offend most people. If the owner ever does decide to sell, you are likely to be his or her first call.

- **Check the Web.** The Internet can provide you a wealth of information about properties available for sale. Do a Google search (www.google.com) and type "investment properties (your town and state)" in the search engine or check your area's multiple listing service.

What to Say

If your goal is to look at 100 deals over a 12-month period, you can save yourself a lot of time by doing a good bit of your screening over the phone. For your initial call, consider these questions:

- **I noticed your property for sale (in the paper, sign in the yard, and so on). What can you tell me about it?** This is a good open-ended question, and the seller's response will tell you a lot about the seller's motivation. Your goal is to continue to ask probing questions. You want to hear him or her talk, not you.

- **What kind of return should I expect on this investment?** The seller's response to this question is likely to focus on appreciation versus cash flow and yield. This is because his or her asking price is probably more than the property is worth.

◆ **What were the rents and expenses for the past 12 months?** Now you're focusing on cash flow. If the returns are negative, you may have just found out why he or she wants to sell. Follow up with questions about current occupancy. If the property is full and still not making money, follow up with questions about market rents for that area and type of property. Are the rents you are receiving typical for this area? The seller will likely suggest that they are low and could easily be raised. Ask why he or she has not raised the rents. You will need to follow up with your own research for market rents in the area. Call the property manager of several similar properties in the area and ask what the rents are.

◆ **Why are you selling?** Listen closely to the seller's response and ask follow-up questions that probe deeper into why he or she is selling. You might uncover a divorce situation, health situation, moving out of town, and so on. You are looking for signs of a motivated seller.

◆ **Tell me about the condition of this property.** Take good notes here. Your follow-up questions should discover if there have been substantial improvements recently or if there are any major repairs pending. If repairs will be needed, ask the seller what he or she estimates they will cost. If the seller suggests that the new roof will cost $15,000 but it turns out it will cost $21,000, you can use this as a negotiating point.

◆ **How flexible is your price?** Here's where the rubber meets the road. Do not be surprised if the seller lowers the price right over the phone. This conversation may also give you additional insight as to whether he or she is a motivated seller. Never, never make the first offer! Let us repeat this. Never, never make the first offer.

◆ **Would you be willing to hold the mortgage?** If the seller is willing to hold the mortgage, you might be able to avoid a trip to the bank. More often than not, the seller will want cash. If the seller is truly motivated, he or she may be willing to hold a second mortgage allowing you to have little or nothing in the property. You won't know until you ask.

Remember, rarely is a great deal going to simply fall in your lap. Most great deals are great because you made them that way. It is your counteroffer to a motivated seller that turns a poor deal into a great one.

Raw Land

If you decide to buy raw land, you are typically doing so with the primary objective being capital appreciation because there is typically no cash flow. However, you should always be alert to possibilities for generating cash flow. For example, a small group of friends purchased 192 acres of wooded land for $115,000, in what was then way outside of Birmingham, Alabama, with the intent of holding it long-term for capital appreciation. About a year after the purchase, lumber prices spiked up to their highest levels in years. One of the investors, who was a forester, suggested they have the property surveyed to see what the timber was worth. They did, and it turned out they could do a "select cut" and make $100,000! They still own the property, but today it is in the center of the major growth-way for Birmingham and is worth approximately $10,000 per acre.

If you're going to buy raw land, maximizing your rate of return will be more challenging than rental real estate. This is because you will have cash outflows until it is sold, including property taxes, and possible insurance and interest payments. This negative cash flow must be part of your calculation in your total return. You have to have a lot of capital appreciation to overcome negative cash flow. If you do have negative cash flow, it creates opportunity costs as well. In other words, what could you have done with the cash you are using to carry your raw land investment? If you could have bought more investment real estate, the costs could indeed be very high. Most of these land deals are purchased with the intention of holding the property for years, even decades, so you need to make certain you have the staying power to handle negative cash flow for a long time.

Vacation Real Estate

One of the true dynamic phenomena of the next several decades is the Baby Boomer generation. The Baby Boomer generation is defined as those Americans born between 1946 and 1964. A bit of simple math will tell you why this is important now. Most people retire between the age of 60 and 70. By adding 60 years to the above birth dates we see that the leading edge of the Baby Boomers begin retiring in 2006 and will continue retiring until the trailing edge retires sometime around 2034. Don't lose sight of the fact that Baby Boomers represent 80 million people out of a total U.S. population of approximately 300 million; a full quarter of our population! They are also expected to inherit more than $10 trillion from their parents. And what do you think they are going to do with all that money? What would you do? We think they will want to spend their retirement years, or at least part of them, living in resort areas. The ocean comes to mind. The mountains come to mind. Lake front properties also come to mind. Anywhere you would like to vacation, they are likely to want to live or at least have a second home. So what is the best way to take advantage of this opportunity? Let's review several strategies.

The Flip Strategy

This strategy involves signing a *letter of intent* to purchase a property that is in the pre-construction phase. Normally, you will be required to also put up a down payment that may be as small as a few thousand dollars up to 20 percent of the expected price of the property you are buying. Typically, your down payment is refundable if you decide not to go through with the sale based on final construction. What the developers are looking for is pre-construction sales, which indicate an interest in the project and also help the developers when raising money from their financial institutions. Your goal with this strategy is to sell your contract to another buyer before you are required to close on your property. Some people refer to this as real estate speculation, and to some extent it certainly can be. One key way to take the speculation out of the strategy is to be prepared to close on the property and use it as a vacation home until you have an opportunity to sell for a profit.

The Own and Rent Strategy

If you end up owning a vacation property either because your flip strategy didn't work or you simply wanted to own a vacation home, you could consider placing the property in a rental pool. Obviously, before you buy you should make certain that the property is eligible for a rental program. Some projects don't allow rentals, while others prohibit rentals in certain buildings. Typically, having your property in a rental program will reduce your ongoing costs of owning but will not eliminate them because rarely is the rental income sufficient to cover all your costs. One big reason is that the rental management company will take a hefty fee (25 percent to 50 percent) for handling all the duties associated with managing the program (booking rentals, cleaning units, and so on). There is also a wear and tear issue because renters tend to not take as good care of your property as you would. Often you can research the mathematics of how this might work for a particular property if the project has several years of rental experience.

You need to be aware of the tax rules regarding renting out your vacation home. People tend to think that the expenses associated with renting a vacation home are deductible and that any income after the rental expenses, including depreciation, is taxable income. Not so. The rules can be divided into several categories:

- **Minimum rental use.** If the property is rented for 14 days or less, you receive no deductions for expenses or depreciation but the rental income is not includible as income.

- **Maximum personal use.** If you personally use the property less than the greater of 14 days or 10 percent of the total number of days the property is rented, you may treat the property as straight investment property for tax benefit purposes.

- **Additional limitations on deductions.** If you use the property personally for more than the greater of 14 days or 10 percent of the number of total days rented and the total days rented exceeds 14 days, then your deductions may not exceed your rental income.

Whew! Complicated. It's even a bit more complicated than this, so be sure to speak with your tax advisor for specific details about your property.

The important thing to remember with this strategy is that rental income tax benefits may help cover some of your ongoing costs but not all.

The Capital Appreciation Strategy

If you don't want to fool with the hassles of renting your vacation property, you can simply own it and enjoy using it while it's appreciating in value. Obviously this is not a get-rich-quick strategy and it will negatively impact your cash flow, but it can help build wealth.

If you use this strategy, consider going in with one or more friends to share the expenses and get greater use out of your vacation property. Realistically, how often do you think you would be able to use the property in a given year? Three weeks? That leaves 49 weeks that it is vacant. Seems a shame for you to pay all the ongoing expenses by yourself but get so little use from the property. By time sharing you get the same amount of use at a fraction of the costs. For the same money of owning by yourself, you could own an interest in several resort properties around the country.

If you go this route, it's a good idea to set up a partnership and formalize as many of the details as possible: how the use weeks are chosen; how much and how often each member will make deposits into an escrow account for repairs, mortgage payments, and so on; how someone sells his interest; what the voting requirements are for changes to the partnership agreement.

That Reminds Us ...

When I first started out in business, I knew nothing about investing but had a strong desire to build my net worth. I decided the best way to do this was to buy real estate. Being single at the time, I thought, "Why not buy vacation property? I get the benefit of owning real estate while having some great places to vacation." To be able to afford to implement my strategy, I bought properties with small groups of friends so we could split the various expenses. At one time, I owned interests in a condo on the beach in Florida, a condo in the ski resort town of Breckenridge, Colorado, and a cabin on a lake. I had a blast and made money on all the properties.

—Co-author Stewart Welch

College Funding Strategy Using Real Estate

Your son or daughter just graduated from high school. You almost can't believe that your child is an adult, heading off to college. Of course, you're delighted but also nervous. With graduation from high school, the rites of passage have begun for your child. This is an exciting time for your child but also a challenging financial time for you as parents. The average annual cost to fund public college for one child is $13,000 to $15,000 for tuition, fees, and so on. Private universities cost, on average, roughly $34,000 annually. These figures don't include housing.

Fortunately, there is one way you can reduce your overall expenses and get some tax benefits. Consider buying your child a home to live in for the next four (or five?) years while he or she completes the coursework for an undergraduate degree. Although this concept may seem strange, especially if your child has never lived on his or her own, there are some key benefits. Not only does your child get to live in more comfortable surroundings than a crowded dormitory, you are also making a sound investment. Of course, as with any real estate purchase, you have to do some homework. You should spend some time exploring the college neighborhood. Remember, you're not looking for a house for you. You want to find a house that works for students. You'll want to find a home located near campus, preferably within walking distance. You also want to buy a home with at least three bedrooms, ideally four bedrooms. You'll want to rent out the extra rooms and have your child act as the "property manager." Your child will be responsible for finding and keeping tenants. Usually this is very easy because they will have friends who are excited about the freedom of being "on their own" in a real house!

As a result, several very positive things happen for both you and your child:

♦ You receive all the tax benefits of owning rental property. Your interest payments are deductible; you receive a depreciation deduction for the property; and all repairs are either deductible or depreciable. In fact, this is one big tax write-off!

♦ Your child learns some valuable lessons about business, dealing with people, and responsibility.

♦ Your property management "payments" to your child are tax-deductible. This is money your child can then use to pay personal expenses and/or college expenses.

♦ When you go to visit your "property," part or all of your travel expenses are deductible. Now that's a nice thought! You go to visit your child for parents' weekend, and you deduct your airline, hotel, and food costs!

♦ When your child graduates, you can sell the home to another parent with similar goals and, hopefully, realize a nice profit.

As the property owner, you may want to consider charging a higher rent but then continue paying for such items as utilities, lawn care, and so on. Not only will this create additional deductions, but this will also insure that these expenses are paid and the home is properly maintained.

Here's how to create financial incentives for your child. First, he or she would receive a percent of rents (typically 10 percent) as a fee for their management responsibilities. This encourages them to keep the property fully rented at the highest possible rental rate. Second, you could offer to share the profits from the home sale after they graduate. This will encourage them to keep the property in good condition.

This strategy produces the possibility of significantly reducing the cost of funding college and the possibility of helping create another entrepreneur!

The Least You Need to Know

◆ Investment real estate is one of the most powerful wealth-building tools because you can use financial leverage to purchase properties.

◆ An easy way to get started in investment real estate is to use up to $500,000 of tax-free appreciation in your home using our Home Sale Strategy.

◆ When buying rental real estate, always make sure you will have positive cash flow including your mortgage payments from the inception of the deal.

◆ There are a number of different strategies for turning vacation real estate into investment real estate.

◆ Turn your child into an entrepreneur and cut the cost of college funding by buying campus investment real estate for him or her to live in and manage.

Chapter 19

Tax Planning Can Make You Money!

In This Chapter

- Avoiding the most common tax-related mistakes
- Finding the last of the great tax shelters
- Reducing taxes through real estate
- Having your own business may be your best tax deduction

As you build wealth, just how important is the subject of taxes? Consider this: The process of minimizing taxes is directly related to the size of your wealth and the amount of taxes you pay. The theory sounds simple: the more you can reduce your tax burden, the more income you'll take home. All you need to do is know the basics and hire a good CPA to help you. Unfortunately, most people wait until they have a tax problem before they do anything. By then, it's often too late. This chapter focuses on the habits and strategies that do help, as well as the habits that don't. There aren't a lot of tax shelters or loopholes left any more; however, this chapter does cover several strategies you can still use.

The Most Common Tax-Related Mistakes People Make

One of the most common characteristics we see among wealthy people is their knowledge of taxes and their tenacity to eliminate tax-related mistakes. They hate mistakes, especially when it means paying more taxes than they should. They do everything in their power to pay the least amount of taxes. A large part of this effort is eliminating the unnecessary mistakes most people make.

> **CAUTION**
>
> **Wealth Warning** _____
>
> If you are a small business owner you are responsible for a slew of withholding taxes, unemployment taxes, and other important requirements. A CPA is indispensable for meeting these tax deadlines in a timely fashion.

Is Saving Taxes Priority #1?

For those people who make building wealth a priority, a common tax-related mistake is maintaining the belief that saving taxes is more important than making money. Don't let this happen to you. Always use due diligence before you attempt to save taxes. Remember that your first goal is to build wealth. Saving taxes must be, at best, your second goal.

Silly Mathematical Errors

One of the best ways to reduce your taxes is to reduce mistakes. In fact, a number of CPAs have told us that the most common mistakes people make when preparing their taxes are simple mathematical errors. These mathematical errors can continue to affect your numbers, especially if you've designed your own spreadsheets for estimating your taxes and financial statement projections. After the mistake is made, it can continue to be a problem until it's detected.

Treasure Tip _____

Don't be afraid to question your CPA's work, ideas, or actions. Remember, she's human and can certainly make mistakes, too.

Poor Recordkeeping

Failing to keep good records is by far the number-one mistake we find people make. Set up a system of records and maintain it well. Keep track of all contributions to charity, cost basis of investments, confirmations of buys and sells from your brokerage firm, and all check registers. Otherwise, you are going to overlook deductions, lose important records, and pay your CPA and the IRS more money than you should.

Wealth Warning

A classic example of poor recordkeeping is the mutual fund buyer who purchased a mutual fund several years ago but has no statements or records of all the dividends that have been reinvested. Every reinvestment of dividends creates a new cost basis for the purchased shares.

Trying to Do It All Yourself When You Know You Need Help

We see this all the time—people trying to do their own taxes and financial statements just to save a dime. Why not hire a specialist who can do all this for you? Here's a list of reasons why:

- A CPA is a specialist who knows the tax code.

- One person dedicated to this task will do a better job.

- Other people may be more objective than you.

- Hiring help should eliminate any possibility of procrastination.

- The cost is nothing compared to the potential mistakes and sleepless nights of worry.

Failing to Understand the Alternative Minimum Tax (AMT)

It's bad enough that figuring how much income tax you owe is so complicated. After you get all the way through the process, the government makes you go back and calculate your taxes again using a different method called the Alternative Minimum Tax, or AMT. In essence, you must calculate your tax liability twice using two different methods and pay the higher of the two answers. The government's goal in creating this rule was to prevent the wealthy people from avoiding paying taxes altogether. The AMT calculation disallows certain deductions that you are able to take under the regular tax calculation method. Certain nontaxable income becomes taxable as well. Because of the complexity of the AMT laws, it is beyond the scope our discussion in this book. Suffice it to say that you need to have at least a basic working knowledge of AMT to avoid its pitfalls.

Overlooking Deductions

Many people make the mistake of not taking all of the deductions that are allowed. Most of the time this is due to poor record keeping or not understanding what is deductible. The following is a list of some of the most overlooked deductions:

◆ Fees for tax preparation services, IRS audits, and investment and financial planning advice

◆ Amortization of taxable bond premiums

◆ Appreciation on property donated to charities

◆ Business gifts of $25 or less

◆ Cellular telephones and charges when used for business purposes

◆ Cleaning and laundering services when traveling on business

◆ Commissions on sales of property

◆ Contact lenses

◆ Depreciation of home computers when used for business purposes

◆ Fees for a safe-deposit box to hold investments

Incorrect Withholdings or Estimated Tax Payments

If your tax refund is large, you are withholding too much money, and consequently, the IRS is getting a tax-free loan from you. Don't let this happen. You'll lose the power of compounding over time that's so important to building wealth. However, be careful not to withhold too little money. Have your CPA calculate your estimated quarterly taxes for you each year, and adjust your withholding or quarterly tax payment accordingly. A penalty for underpaying your taxes is a total waste of money.

Not Capitalizing on Qualified Plans

Retirement plans continue to be one of the best tax deductions available, yet we continue to run into people who are not taking advantage of them. It's a bit of a mystery—even they cannot explain why they fail to take advantage of this important tax benefit.

Using the Wrong Kind of Debt

You can use a home equity line of credit of up to $100,000 for any purpose and the interest is deductible. Too often, when we review the finances of a prospective client, we find that they are paying high interest rates on large balances where none of the interest is deductible. If you're committed to avoiding new debt and reducing your current debt, then a home equity line of credit is a much better choice. In other cases, we find that someone has borrowed money to invest but failed to take a deduction for the interest. It is important to note that when you borrow money to invest, your interest is deductible only to the extent that you have investment income. The one exception is if you use up to $100,000 of a home equity line of credit, then all of your interest is deductible regardless of the amount of investment income.

Improper Use of Bonds

Municipal bonds are IOUs issued by city, state, and local municipalities. The interest they pay is not taxable at the federal level. Because the federal government doesn't tax muni interest, munis don't have to pay the bondholder as much interest as other taxable bonds to be attractive. Sometimes, we see investors in the lowest tax bracket buy these bonds. However, they aren't in a high enough tax bracket to make the tax break worthwhile. This is an easy mistake to make if you don't know your tax bracket or don't understand how municipal bonds work. The flip side of this story can also be a mistake. Sometimes we'll find people who are in the highest tax bracket buying taxable bonds when they would benefit from buying municipal bonds.

> **CAUTION**
>
> **Wealth Warning**
>
> Don't fall victim to the tax-free sales hype associated with municipal bonds. Typically, munis are only appropriate for those people in the highest tax bracket.

Before you buy a municipal bond, take the time to estimate your income and tax bracket if your income has increased this year, or simply look back at your tax forms from the prior year. If you are not in the highest tax bracket, be cautious of buying municipal bonds.

Sheltering money from taxes is one of the classic ways the rich use to enhance wealth accumulation. Even as you begin the wealth accumulation process, you can make use of some of the same strategies the rich use.

The Best Tax Shelters

Back in the late 1970s and early 1980s, limited partnerships were the hottest tax shelters around. Many of these partnerships promoted $2, $3, or even $4 of deductions for every $1 you invested. They lured billions of dollars from investors who were looking for tax breaks. What the majority of these investors got instead were big losses, most of which were not deductible, along with interest and penalties after the IRS disallowed the tax shelter. The investors who thought tax savings were more important than making money were in for a rude awakening.

Things are different now, but there are still opportunities to keep the taxman at bay. Here's the best of what is available.

Retirement Plans

We have already covered this topic a number of times in this book, but we do want to make certain that you understand the distinction between your *marginal tax rate* and your *effective tax rate*. Understanding the difference will help you understand why investing in retirement plans is such a powerful tax strategy.

Words of the Wealthy

Your **marginal tax rate** represents the highest tax rate paid on any of your taxable income, while your **effective tax rate** represents the average tax rate paid on all of your taxable income.

We've often been asked whether it makes sense to invest in tax-deductible retirement plans or if it's preferable to pay the taxes now and invest personally. This would allow someone to avoid the retirement "tax trap" whereby all distributions from retirement accounts are subject to income taxes. Some advisors also advance the argument that …

- Income tax rates have gone down, so the tax deduction for contributions to retirement accounts are worth less. Over the past few years, the maximum federal income tax rate has dropped from 39.6 percent to 35 percent.

- Long-term capital gains rates have declined, reducing the taxes on gains from sale of personal investments, making personal investments more valuable. In recent years the tax rates on long-term capital gains have dropped from 20 percent to 15 percent.

- Tax rates on corporate dividends have been reduced, making personal investments in U.S. corporations more attractive. Corporate dividends were taxed as ordinary income, but are now taxed at a maximum federal rate of 15 percent.

All of the above pronouncements are correct, but does this necessarily lead to the conclusion that tax-deductible retirement plans are no longer advisable?

We have examined numerous scenarios of people in various income tax brackets, both before and after retirement. We concluded that, in all but the most extreme case facts (very low tax bracket during contribution years and very high tax bracket during retirement years), you significantly benefit from investing in tax-deductible retirement accounts. The reason is because of the difference between your marginal tax rate as contributions are made during earnings years and your effective tax rate as funds are withdrawn during retirement years.

Let's look at an example of this concept. Assume a married couple has a gross income of $85,000. After the standard deduction and personal exemptions, they have a taxable income of $69,300, which puts them in a marginal tax rate of 37 percent (including federal, state, and local taxes plus Social Security and Medicare taxes). This marginal tax rate means that if they earned one additional dollar, they would owe 37¢ in various taxes on that dollar. This also means that if they invested $1 in a tax-deductible IRA, they would receive a 37-cent tax refund. Thus, they are rewarded for their contribution by a tax deduction that creates a 37 percent tax benefit.

At retirement, this couple begins withdrawing $100,000 per year from their IRA account. After the standard deduction and personal exemptions (same taxable income of $69,300), they owe federal taxes of $13,400 or an effective tax rate of only 13.4 percent. In effect, this couple received a tax deduction of 37 percent for their contributions but only paid 13.4 percent in taxes on their withdrawals. If you compare the actual dollars ahead for a 50-year-old couple contributing $20,000 per year to their 401(k) plan versus paying the tax on the $20,000 and investing the remaining balance personally for a 15-year period at 10 percent, the retirement account would be tens of thousands of dollars ahead on an after-tax basis (approximately $605,000 versus $397,000).

Based on multiple scenarios, we get similar results. Time and time again, we find that investing in tax-deductible retirement accounts yielded better long-term results both before and after taking taxes into account. For your long-term investment strategy, focus on the power of tax-deductible retirement accounts. We should add that the perfect scenario is to max out retirement plan contributions *and* invest personally each year. At retirement, this allows you to draw funds from either or both of your personal investment account and retirement account. This added freedom allows you to exercise much greater control over your income taxes from year to year during your retirement.

There are many different types of retirement accounts, each with its own restrictions and limitations. Let's look at several of the more common ones for your consideration:

- **IRAs.** Current tax law allows you to contribute $4,000 each year to either a Traditional IRA or a Roth IRA ($5,000 for 2008 and after and indexed for inflation). If you are over age 50, you also qualify for an additional $1,000 "catch-up" contribution. Don't forget that with the Traditional IRA, you receive a tax deduction for your contribution and tax deferral of income and capital gains until you begin withdrawing money during retirement, at which time all proceeds are taxable as ordinary income. With the Roth IRA, you don't receive a tax deduction for your contributions but your earnings and capital gains are tax-deferred and distributions at retirement are tax-free. Each has different rules you must comply with to be eligible to contribute so check with your tax advisor.

- **SEPs.** Simplified Employee Pension plans were designed with the small business owner in mind. These plans allow you to put a lot of money into what is essentially an IRA account, and therefore you avoid administrative hassles typically associated with a qualified retirement plan. The SEP allows you to contribute up to 25 percent of net income to a maximum of $42,000. You must include all eligible employees. $5,000 catch-up contributions apply.

- **SIMPLE plans.** These plans were also designed with the small employer in mind. The Savings Incentive Match Plan for Employees (SIMPLE) allows employees to contribute to the plan while you make a matching contribution.

Currently, the contribution limits are 100 percent of pay up to $10,000 (indexed for inflation). Plan administration hassles are minimal. $2,500 catch-up contributions apply.

♦ **401(k) plans.** These are now the most common retirement plans provided by employers. A 401(k) allows employees to contribute 100 percent of pay up to $15,000. Although employer matching contributions are not required, many employers will match 50 percent of the employees' contribution up to 6 percent of salary. The administrative hassles with these plans are significantly higher than for previous plans mentioned. $5,000 catch-up contributions apply.

♦ **Single-person 401(k) plans.** Relatively new, the single-person 401(k) plan is designed to allow self-employed people with no employees the opportunity to put away the kind of money big companies allow through their regular 401(k) plans. Administration is streamlined. In addition to the profit-sharing contribution of 25 percent of the profit in a sole proprietorship, you can contribute 100 percent of your compensation up to $15,000. $5,000 catch-up contributions apply. The overall maximum contribution is $42,000.

♦ **Profit-sharing plans.** This is an "employer pay all"-type of plan that allows you to decide what percentage of compensation to make on behalf of your employees and yourself. The percentage you choose (0 percent to 25 percent) must be applied to all eligible employees, although you can integrate your plan contributions with the contributions you are making to Social Security (FICA) on behalf of your employees. The maximum contribution allowed for any participant is $42,000.

We should note that Congress wants to encourage taxpayers to save for their retirement and has actively sought to increase the contribution limits under the various retirement plans discussed. Be sure to check with your financial advisor for the applicable limits based on your facts.

♦ **Health Savings Accounts**. Not technically a form of retirement account, Health Savings Accounts (HSAs) allow you to invest additional money on a tax-deductible basis. The purpose of HSAs is to empower individuals to proactively seek to reduce their health-care expenses. Here's how it works:

You start by electing a health insurance plan with a very high deductible. For single-only coverage, the minimum deductible is $1,000 and for family coverage it is $2,000. You are then allowed to set up a "side fund" or HSA equal to your deductible amount, not to exceed $2,650 for single coverage plans and $5,250 for family coverage plans. Taxpayers age 55 and older are allowed to contribute an additional $700 per year ($1,400 for family coverage where both spouses are age 55 or older). The contribution limits and catch-up limits are adjusted for inflation.

You receive a tax deduction for your HSA contribution and your distributions are tax-free when used for qualified medical expenses. If you take a distribution for anything other than qualified medical expenses, that distribution will be subject to ordinary income taxes plus a 10 percent penalty if you are under age 65. Investing in an HSA does not interfere with your ability to invest in a Traditional IRA or Roth IRA.

Qualified medical expenses include copayments, coinsurance, prescription and over-the-counter drugs, dental services, vision care, and other typical medical related expenses. Funds can also be used to pay for long-term care insurance premiums (limitations may apply), COBRA premiums, and health insurance premiums if the applicant is receiving unemployment benefits. If you are age 65 or older, you do not qualify for an HSA. For more information, go to www. treas.gov and enter "health savings accounts" into the search engine.

Investment Real Estate

Investment real estate offers many opportunities to reduce taxes. Obviously, many of the expenses associated with operating your property are deductible, but there are two additional benefits that make real estate an outstanding investment:

♦ **Depreciation.** Imagine buying an apartment building and immediately getting a tax deduction for its declining value when in fact you know that it is increasing in value! This is exactly what the government allows, and the result is a "paper" loss that you can use to shelter income. "That seems wonderful," you say, "but won't that increase your taxable gain when you sell the property?" Very astute of you. And you are correct until you consider the next strategy.

♦ **Like-kind exchange.** When you decide to sell your property, the law allows you to avoid paying taxes on your gains by way of a like-kind exchange (also known as a 1031 exchange). You can, in effect, swap your property for another property of the same or higher value and continue to postpone your gains. The cost basis (what you've invested in the property, including capital improvements less depreciation) of the original property is carried over to the new property.

Owning Your Own Business

Starting a business and expensing your hobby might seem like a great tax shelter. However, the IRS says you must have a profit motive. How do they determine this? The *Federal Tax Handbook* says that you must show a profit for any three or more out of five consecutive years. There is one exception: If you breed, show, or race horses, you have to be profitable only two out of seven years. This is often referred to as the Hobby Rule.

However, when you get past the Hobby Rule, owning your own business opens a whole new world of possible tax deductions and tax benefits. Depending on the type of business, many people you know and meet are potential customers and therefore many entertainment activities are potential tax deductions. Travel expenses become potentially fully or partially deductible if you conduct business a portion of the time.

A great example is Sam Walton, founder of Wal-Mart. Wherever Sam was on vacation he always made a point to visit retail stores as part of his ongoing research. One critically important factor is that he kept meticulous notes on all of his visits. This is important because you will need to be prepared to defend all of your deductions when the IRS audits you. The better you are at recordkeeping, the more deductions you will get to keep.

Treasure Tip

When you do your own tax work or financial statement projections, remember the carpenter's rule: Measure twice; cut once. That is, double-check your work!

Municipal Bonds

For people who are in the highest income tax bracket and who need bonds as part of their investment allocation, municipal bonds are often the best choice. They are not subject to federal taxes, and if the municipality is located in your state of residence, they are not subject to state income taxes either. We recommend that you stick with high-quality bonds to reduce the risk of default. Review our bond strategy in Chapter 9.

Dividend-Paying Stocks

Dividends paid by corporations are now taxed at a maximum federal tax rate of 15 percent. This significantly boosts their competitiveness when compared to short-term and intermediate-term treasuries and high-quality corporate bonds on an after-tax basis. You also get the benefit of long-term growth and likely rising yields; something you won't get with bonds.

The Least You Need to Know

- There are still many ways to reduce your taxes, including retirement plans, health savings accounts, investment real estate, and owning your own business.

- Just because an investment product offers tax-free or tax-deferred income doesn't make it suitable for you or worth investing in.

- Careful and complete recordkeeping is one of the key elements in securing maximum tax deductions.

- If you take a personal loan, consider using mortgage debt first because it's usually cheaper and you can write off the interest expense.

Chapter 20

Protecting the Goose

In This Chapter

- Buying the right amount and type of life insurance at the best price
- Insuring yourself in the event of a disability
- Protecting yourself against lawsuits
- Planning your estate

There are many ways in which your wealth game plan can be sabotaged, including premature death, permanent disability, lawsuits, and death taxes. Each of these contingencies can and should be handled through pre-planning. Our goal is to make certain your wealth is guaranteed no matter what the circumstances. This chapter offers simple solutions to some of the biggest risks to your wealth.

Life Insurance

The younger we are, the more invincible we feel. Intellectually, we all know that one day we will die. We simply assume it will be many decades into the future. The obvious solution to being "wrong" about our timing is to own adequate life insurance. In reviewing finances of hundreds of people, we find most are improperly insured for premature death. Most

often we find people paying too much in premiums for too little life insurance. We suspect the reason is that life insurance is one of the most complex and confusing products sold. Life insurance does not have to be complicated, so let's demystify this product and help you decide exactly how much life insurance you need, what type you should buy, and where you can get the best deals.

What Type of Life Insurance Is Best?

Although life insurance policies come in many shapes and sizes, all life insurance falls into one of two categories:

◆ **Term Insurance.** Term insurance is pure insurance. You pay a premium that covers you for a certain period of time. If you die during that period of time, your beneficiary collects the face amount of the policy. If you don't die during the term of the policy, you don't get any money back, and you must renew the insurance by paying an additional premium if you want the coverage to continue. The typical policy is level term insurance whereby the insurance company "levelizes" the premium for a stated period of time, typically 5, 10, 15, or 20 years. The longer the time period, the higher your premiums. At the end of the term, you must take (and pass) a physical exam and buy another level term policy or your coverage will lapse. Most policies will guarantee you the right to convert to a cash value policy if you can't pass the physical exam. The premiums for cash value insurance are much higher than for term insurance.

◆ **Cash Value Insurance.** Cash value insurance is nothing more than term insurance with a savings feature. In addition to the term premium, called mortality reserves, you give the insurance company "extra" money which it "invests" for you. Later those savings can be accessed through loans or in some cases, withdrawals. At the time of your death, your beneficiary receives the term insurance plus the "savings account." There are a number of different types of cash value policies including whole life, universal life, variable life, and survivorship life.

In Chapter 8, we discussed why you do not want to use life insurance as an investment. If your primary purpose is to provide your family with a source of income should you die prematurely, then level term insurance is your best bet. It assumes that you have a wealth accumulation plan in place as outlined in Chapter 5. In working with our

clients, we normally recommend either 15-year or 20-year level term policies. This is because we've implemented a wealth accumulation plan that is expected to achieve total financial independence by the end of that period. For example, let's say you determined in Chapter 5 that you need to accumulate $3 million of investment capital to be financially independent. After you've accumulated that sum, you no longer need life insurance as a source of income protec-
tion for your family. It is possible that you might need "permanent" life insurance for other reasons, such as estate liquidity, which we'll discuss later in this chapter. Keep in mind that if you purchase a term insurance that is convertible to permanent insurance without having to pass a new physical exam, you have left your options open.

Wealth Warning

Not all term life insurance is convertible to permanent life insurance for the full term of the policy. Make certain that yours is before you buy.

How Much Life Insurance Is Enough?

Ask 10 people and you are likely to get 10 different answers. The three-step process that follows takes you through a simple yet logical approach to answering this important question. First, if you're single and have no children or other dependants, you do not need life insurance. Second, if you are married and have no children, you only need enough life insurance to pay off any joint debts. If, on the other hand, you have young children, your need for life insurance increases substantially. Use the following three-step process to determine your life insurance needs:

1. If you're the sole income provider, multiply your annual income by .80. (Note: if both you and your spouse work, combine both incomes and multiply by .80.) This results in reducing your income by 20 percent. The reason you do this is because if you die, there is one less spender in the household (you!).

2. Divide your answer in step 1 by the rate of return you would reasonably expect to earn on the life insurance proceeds after they are invested. Your answer here indicates how much money you will need to continue the necessary income stream to your surviving family.

3. Subtract any savings or investments you already have from your answer in step 2. The result is the amount of life insurance you should own.

Look at two examples:

John and Mary Smith have two children. John earns $50,000 a year and Mary stays home to raise the children. The couple assumes that they could earn 7.5 percent on investments; they have $25,000 in personal investments.

1. Multiply John's income by .80: $50,000 × .80 = $40,000.

2. Divide $40,000 by their expected rate of return on invested money (7.5 percent): $40,000 ÷.075 = $533,333. This amount of money invested at 7.5 percent will provide the needed $40,000 per year for Mary and the children.

3. Subtract their current savings and investments ($25,000) from $533,333: $533,333 – $25,000 = $508,333. This is the amount of life insurance John needs to buy on his life.

If both John and Mary work, the example changes. Their total income is $65,000, but John's earnings are $30,000 and Mary's earnings are $35,000. To see how much life insurance John needs, do the following calculation.

1. Multiply the family income of $65,000 by .80: $65,000 × .80 = $52,000. Again, the survivors' income need is reduced because John is no longer a spender. Because Mary plans to continue working, also subtract her income: $52,000 – $35,000 = $17,000. This $17,000 represents the income that needs to be replaced upon John's death.

2. Divide $17,000 by their expected rate of return (7.5 percent): $17,000 ÷ .075 = $226,667.

3. Subtract their current investments ($25,000) from $226,667: $226,667 – $25,000 = $201,667. This is the amount of life insurance needed on John.

Note: because the family also depends on Mary's income, you now need to complete this exercise for her! See the following table.

Life Insurance Needs Worksheet

1. Your annual family income	$_____
Discount factor	× .80
Total income needed by surviving family	=_____
b. Subtract surviving spouse's annual income	–_____
Surviving family income need from outside sources	=_____

2. Divide your estimated rate of return on invested
   assets into answer in step 1b   _____

   Equals the total amount of money needed to
   provide for your survivors   _____

3. Subtract your current savings and investments   –_____

   Equals total life insurance needed   =_____

The answer arrived at using this three-step process should only be used as a rule of thumb. Then you should personalize the solution to your particular situation. For example, you may want to increase the amount of insurance to help cover the costs of funding college expenses for your children. Or, you may want additional insurance that would be used to pay off some of your debts. If your goal is to provide a lifetime income for your dependents, additional insurance will be needed to offset the ravages of inflation.

Treasure Tip _____

Our government provides a Social Security Survivors Benefit to help surviving spouses with young children. To determine the level of income for which you are eligible, review your Social Security statement, which the Social Security Administration sends out each year. You can access your statement by going to www.socialsecurity.gov/mystatement or by calling the Social Security Administration (1-800-772-1213). View these benefits as "extra" money and not as part of your calculation for life insurance needs. Remember, these benefits end when your youngest child reaches age 18.

If you have young children, replacing the services of a homemaker can be quite expensive. Ask yourself this question: If my homemaker spouse were to die, could I afford to pay someone to perform those services out of my current income? You might be lucky enough to have a family member who could step in. In such a case, no life insurance would be necessary. On the other hand, if you decide life insurance on a homemaker is necessary, a $200,000 to $400,000 term policy should provide adequate coverage. By buying a 10- to 15-year level term insurance policy, you will provide coverage until the children are old enough to assist with their own care.

Where to Get the Best Deals?

So far you've decided how much insurance you need and what type to buy. Now you want to make certain you get a great deal. You are in luck because term life insurance is very competitive, and with a minimal amount of homework on your part, you should be able to find a great deal. After you've decided on the plan (say 15-year level term) and the amount of coverage (say $1 million), simply go to the Resource Center at www.welchgroup.com and click on Life Insurance Quotes. By completing a short questionnaire, you'll receive about a dozen quotes from some of the most competitive companies available. For example, a 31-year-old nonsmoker in excellent health could purchase $1 million of 15-year level term for $370 per year! That's a lot of protection for a little money. If you have a local agent, ask her for an "apples-to-apples" quote—a simple comparison will ensure that you get the best deal. Personally, we prefer to work with a local agent because you will receive more personal service.

> **Wealth Warning**
>
> Whether you're buying life insurance, disability income insurance, or long-term care insurance, make sure the insurance company is rated AA or higher by one of the top rating services such as Moody's, AM Best, or Standard & Poor's.

Disability Income Protection

Your single most important asset is your ability to earn a living. We all worry to one degree or another about becoming disabled. From a financial perspective, being disabled is a fate worst than death. With death, at least you are no longer a financial burden on your family. With disability, not only do you continue to consume financial assets, in many cases, family members must abandon their normal routines—in some cases work—to provide for your assistance. Disability can be very expensive, costing tens of thousands, hundreds of thousands, and even millions of dollars. Take the well-publicized case of Terri Shiavo, who was in a vegetative state for more than 15 years. Her medical bills reportedly exceeded $1 million. Also, the likelihood of being disabled is about 4 to 5 times greater than dying during your working years, so it is a topic to which you need to give some attention. The solution that we recommend is to buy long-term disability income insurance. Disability income insurance is a contract provided by an insurance company whereby they agree to pay you a certain income for a specified period of time should you become disabled through an accident or illness and be unable to work.

Many people live paycheck to paycheck. If your paycheck stops, where would the money come from to pay your bills for the next six months, year, or five years? If you don't have an answer, most likely you need disability income insurance. However, there are two possible instances when you may have little or no need for disability income insurance:

♦ Your spouse has a substantial income that is enough to cover the family expenses.

♦ As a couple, you've accumulated enough income-producing assets that disability income insurance is not necessary.

How much disability income insurance do you need? A policy that insures from 60 percent to 70 percent of your income is sufficient because when you become disabled, many expenses are significantly reduced. For example, you won't have to pay income taxes or buy clothes for work. Also, most insurance companies will not insure you for more than this amount because they want you to have a financial incentive to go back to work. Two types of disability coverage may be available to you, which we'll cover in the following sections.

Group Disability Insurance Coverage

Many employers provide group disability income coverage. Others make it available through payroll deductions. However, don't assume your employer's coverage is always adequate. Often group coverage provides limited benefits for a very limited period of time. Compare your group coverage to the policy features we recommend later in this section. If no employer group coverage is available, see if you have access to group coverage through your trade or professional organization. The premiums are usually very reasonable but, again, you will need to make sure that the coverage is adequate.

If you can find good group coverage, it will be your cheapest route. Be sure that the group policy pays 50 percent to 70 percent of your total pay and that benefits are payable to age 65. Even if it meets this criteria, you may also want to supplement it with additional coverage.

Wealth Warning

If you're relying on employer-paid group disability benefits, you may need higher coverage because the benefits are subject to income taxes.

Individual Disability Income Coverage

Although the cost of an individual disability income insurance policy is significantly higher than a group policy, it does have some advantages. First, it is portable. If you change jobs, it goes with you. With group insurance, if you terminate or are terminated, you lose your coverage. Secondly, if you become disabled, the benefits you receive are tax-free. Group benefits are taxable if the premiums are paid by your employer. Finally, individual policies offer optional riders such as cost of living increases for benefits.

After you've decided how much insurance you need, you should choose your policy features. Disability policies often have options that you don't need and should not pay for. The following are features that you *do* want:

♦ **Non-Cancelable, Guaranteed Renewable.** This provision guarantees that the insurance company cannot terminate your policy for any reason, nor can your rates be raised.

♦ **Partial Disability Benefit** (also called Residual Benefit). This provision generally pays a partial benefit if a disability prevents you from working full-time. For example, you have a heart attack and are only able to work part-time, resulting in a 50 percent pay loss. Your policy would pay you a 50 percent benefit.

♦ **90-Day Waiting Period.** The waiting period is the time from the date of disability to the date when the insurance company begins making payments to you. Waiting periods are generally 30 days, 90 days, 180 days, 360 days, or 730 days. Naturally, the longer the waiting period the lower the premiums. Your premiums will be greatly affected by the waiting period you choose. Generally, we recommend a 90-day waiting period.

♦ **Definition of Disability.** The definition of disability will vary depending on your occupation classification. In other words, a physician will get a better definition than a bricklayer will. For example, the physician's policy may provide benefits if he is unable to perform his specialty, say surgery, whereas the bricklayer may only receive benefits if it is determined that he is unable to do any type of work. Most policies will pay the benefit for a period of 2 to 5 years if you're unable to do the main duties of your current occupation. After that, the benefit is paid only if you are unable to work in *"any job for which you are reasonably qualified based on your education, training, and experience."* To determine what definitions are available to you, your best bet is to get quotes from several of the major insurance carriers. Companies to consider include Unum, Guardian, Mass

Mutual, The Principal, Met Life, and Standard Life of Portland, Oregon. You can look these companies up in your phone book or speak with your life insurance agent.

♦ **Benefit Period.** The benefit period determines how long you will be paid by the insurance company. Typical choices include 2 years, 5 years, to age 65, or lifetime benefits. Generally, we recommend your policy pay benefits until age 65.

♦ **Cost of Living Adjustments (COLA).** If you become disabled, this feature increases the benefit you will receive based on a cost of living index such as the Consumer Price Index (CPI). This rider is expensive. If your spouse earns a reasonable income, pass it up. If insurance will be your main source of income, consider a cost of living rider that will increase your benefits 3 to 4 percent annually.

♦ **Future Insurance Option.** This feature allows you to increase your coverage periodically without having to prove you are in good health. If you expect your income to continue to rise (we hope you do!), this is a relatively inexpensive way to guarantee your ability to buy more coverage regardless of your health status.

Treasure Tip

If you have a family history of serious medical illness such as diabetes or a heart condition, you should seriously consider adding the Future Insurance Option.

♦ **Social Security Rider.** Under certain conditions you are eligible to receive Social Security payments for disability. With this rider, the insurance company must pay you the Social Security benefit in the event that Social Security rejects your claim. Because Social Security rejects more than 70 percent of the claims presented, this rider is an excellent way to provide you with needed coverage at a reduced cost.

Wealth Warning

Many people mistakenly think they are insured for disability because they are covered by Workers Compensation. This state-mandated program only covers injuries sustained while on the job. It doesn't cover illness or nonjob-related injuries.

The preceding options and features represent the core of what you want to consider as part of your disability income insurance plan. Skip other riders offered by insurance companies.

If no group insurance is available to you, you will need to shop the more expensive individual insurance market. Begin by deciding how much monthly income you want, your waiting and benefit periods, and what other options and features you want included.

> **Wealth Warning** _____
>
> Some auto loan, mortgage loan, and installment loan companies will try to sell you a disability income plan that will make your payments should you become disabled. These are overpriced policies and should be avoided unless you cannot get any disability insurance through the programs discussed in this chapter.

Many companies write competitive disability income policies. Locally you can contact your health or life insurance agent or get an online quote through the Resource Center at www.welchgroup.com.

Get two or three quotes from different carriers and choose the lowest premium.

Long-Term Care Insurance (LTC)

Long-term care (LTC) insurance is nothing more than a specialized disability income policy designed specifically to cover costs associated with nursing care. Under most contracts, to qualify for benefits, an insured person must be unable to do two of six of the "activities of daily living." These include walking, bathing, using a toilet, dressing, remaining continent, and being able to get from a bed to a chair.

When, if at all, should you consider buying coverage? The answer to this question is two-pronged. The first relates to your age and the second relates to your financial circumstances:

◆ **Your age.** Many agents recommend the purchase of long-term care insurance at the earliest age possible because premium costs rise with age. Generally, we recommend that you begin to consider buying long-term care after you turn age 50. Consider your general state of health and that of your spouse as well as your family medical history. For example, if you are relatively unfit and have a family history of heart disease, LTC insurance may be appropriate. If you and your spouse lead a healthy lifestyle and have good family medical histories, consider postponing the decision until age 65 or later. Research indicates that most of the benefits are paid after the age of 85, so you will likely be paying premiums for a long time.

◆ **Your financial circumstances.** LTC insurance is most appropriate for people who have a total net worth of between $200,000 and $2 million (excluding their home). If your net worth is less than $200,000, you may not be able to afford LTC premiums and you would quickly become eligible for *Medicaid*. With a net worth greater than $2 million, you can probably afford to self-insure.

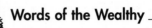

Words of the Wealthy

Medicaid is a program jointly funded by the federal government and states to provide medical assistance for certain individuals and families with low incomes and resources.

If you decide to buy LTC coverage, you will need to decide how much benefit you need. LTC benefits are expressed in the daily benefit paid by the insurance company. For example, you may choose a $100 per day benefit. A recent national survey indicates that the average cost of nursing care is approximately $200 per day, or about $73,000 per year. Depending on your net worth, you may decide to partially self-insure by buying, say, a $125 per day benefit. Key provisions that we recommend include the following:

◆ **Cost of living protection.** In most cases, you will be paying premiums on your policy for decades before you ever receive the first dollar of benefit. Health-care costs are expected to continue to rise 5 percent per year or more into the foreseeable future. If purchasing a policy before age 65, you should consider buying an inflation rider that increases the benefit based on 5 percent per year *compounded.* If you are age 65 or older, a 5 percent *simple rider* should be sufficient and will cost much less than the compound rider.

Words of the Wealthy

A **compounded inflation rider** provides that the daily benefit amount you purchase will increase each year on a compounded basis. For example, if you purchased a $100 daily benefit with 5 percent compound rider, the subsequent years your benefit would automatically rise to $105, $110.25, $115.76, and so on. Compare this to a 5 percent **simple inflation rider** where the subsequent increases would be $105, $110, $115, and so on.

◆ **Lifetime coverage.** Although statistics indicate that the average nursing home stay is less than three years, there's no way to predict the length of your stay, and you don't want to run out insurance benefits and begin depleting your personal assets. After all, this is the reason you bought

LTC insurance in the first place. The premiums for lifetime benefits are notice-ably higher, but that is because the potential payouts are much higher. If you can't afford the higher premiums, choose a policy that pays benefits for at least five years. Also, consider increasing your waiting period from the standard 20 to 30 days to 90 to 100 days to cut premium costs. Remember, the purpose of buy-ing insurance is to insure against catastrophic loss, such as, in this case, an extended need for nursing care.

◆ **Homecare coverage.** It is estimated that 80 percent of nursing care costs are incurred somewhere other than nursing homes. Most people prefer to have their care administered in their homes or at an assisted living facility. Make sure your policy covers care received outside of a nursing home.

◆ **Indemnity agreement.** If you're eligible for benefits, an indemnity policy pays you the full daily benefit regardless of the actual costs of the services. This puts you in the best position to negotiate costs and services and decide what to do with any excess benefits. Most policies limit benefits to the actual costs of services (reimbursement policy). The indemnity plan may cost a bit more, but generally it is our preference if you can get it.

Sifting through the language and various options offered by the insurance companies is a daunting task, even for someone well schooled in the subject. We recommend that you work with an independent agent who specializes in LTC insurance. To find a specialist near you, log on to www.ltc-cltc.com or call 1-877-771-2582. This website lists the contact information for people who have obtained the Certified in Long-Term Care (CLTC) designation. In the LTC business, most agents receive a com-mission for selling this product. You should work with an agent you are confident is looking out for your best interest or get quotes from more than one agent.

Personal Liability Protection

At no time in our history has there been such an epidemic of litigation. It seems that the slightest provocation elicits the response, "I'm gonna sue you!" And in many cases, they're not kidding. What you don't want to do is spend a lot of hard-working years building up your wealth only to have a lawsuit wipe it all out. This is not far-fetched. It is a true risk, one that you need to take steps to protect yourself from. Here are some of the basic solutions:

◆ **Personal umbrella policy.** This policy covers you for liability over and above your automobile and homeowner's liability. It also includes additional coverage for slander. Although this policy is inexpensive—typically under $300 per year for $1 million of coverage—it requires that you raise your automobile and homeowners liability coverage to $300,000 or $500,000. If your assets exceed $100,000, you should definitely consider adding an umbrella policy.

◆ **Business liability insurance.** If you own your own business, you will need to carry business liability insurance, sometimes called Errors and Omission insurance or simply E&O insurance. This policy will cover a number of business risks related to mistakes made by you or your employees. It can be fairly complex and is typically customized to your particular business. You will need to work with a property and casualty agent who specializes in commercial insurance. You can find one in the Yellow Pages under "insurance" or get a recommendation from a fellow business owner.

> **Wealth Warning**
> When buying a personal liability umbrella policy, be sure to talk to your automobile and homeowner's agent(s). The requirements for underlying limits vary from company to company.

◆ **Business entity.** If you own your own business, even a part-time business, you need to give serious consideration to the type of entity you will operate under. Most people start out as a sole proprietor because it requires no legal fees and the least effort on your part. This can be a big mistake because it offers no liability protection for you personally or your business. For a small amount of effort and relatively small legal fees, you can set up an entity for your business that will shield your personal assets from business lawsuits. The most prevalent entities include an S-corporation, C-corporation, Limited Liability Corporation (LLC), and a Limited Liability Partnership (LLP). Which is best for you depends on your particular facts and circumstances. A CPA or a good corporate lawyer can advise you.

◆ **Retirement plans.** In the past, creditor protection for Traditional IRA, Roth IRA, Simplified Employee Pensions (SEPs), and SIMPLE plans was determined by state law. The Bankruptcy Abuse Prevention and Consumer Protection Act of 2005 provides federal protection for all retirement plans. Traditional and Roth IRA assets are creditor protected under federal law for up to $1 million. Most importantly, assets in an IRA account as a result of being rolled over from qualified plans such as a 401(k) or profit-sharing plans receive unlimited creditor protection. For example, let's say you are a recently retired physician and that you made annual contributions to your IRA account each year for the past 25 years and it is now worth $325,000. Now you roll over $1.5 million from your profit-sharing plan, bringing your total IRA account value to $1,825,000. You are sued and the plaintiff receives a judgment of $3 million. What is the risk to your IRA account? None. Your regular contributions to your IRA are protected up to $1 million while your rollover contributions are protected without limit. This is true whether the IRA is a Traditional IRA or a Roth IRA. This is great news because it resolves one of the long-standing concerns held by many IRA owners. It also draws attention to two issues:

- ◆ Investing in retirement plans, whether it's your company 401(k) or your personal IRA, is more important than ever. It's a place you can confidently invest assets without concern about future creditors.

- ◆ It is vital that you maintain complete and accurate records because you will now want to be able to distinguish between personal contributions to your IRA versus rollover contributions from qualified retirement accounts such as 401(k) and profit-sharing plans.

Estate Planning

Estate planning is the process of controlling your assets both during your life and after death with three primary objectives in mind. First, you want to ensure that your assets will always be sufficient to provide for the lifestyle needs of you and your family. Second, you want to make certain that your assets go to the people and/or organizations of your choosing. Finally, you want to minimize the amount of taxes, fees, and court interference associated with settling your estate.

The following sections outline three basic elements you should consider.

Last Will and Testament

Research suggests that 80 percent or more of adult Americans either don't have a will at all or their existing will is out of date. As you begin to accumulate assets, you will want to make sure that they go to who you want, in the form you want (in trust, for example), and with a minimum of taxes. As with everything else we discussed, this requires some planning on your part. If you die without a will (called intestate), assets not passing by beneficiary designation (for example, beneficiary of your IRA account) or by title (such as joint checking account) will pass based on the laws of your state of residence. State laws can be very convoluted. It is especially important to have a will if you have children who are minors.

Although we hear of cases where people write their own will, download a fill-in-the-blank form from the Internet, or buy a form will from the office supply store, we highly recommend that you use a qualified attorney. Estate laws are complex and you need someone skilled to help you.

Power of Attorney

Picture this. You handle the family's finances and pay all the family bills. In addition, you own a small business. Among the assets held solely in your name are bank accounts, investment accounts, and real estate. You are in control and life is good, until tragedy strikes. You're in an automobile accident that leaves you in a coma. Financial decisions need to be made. Checks need to be signed. But you are unable to do so. What is going to happen? Someone is going to have to hire an attorney, go to court, and get a power of attorney that will permit him or her to act on your behalf. This can be expensive and time-consuming. A better solution is for you to be pro-active and have your attorney draw a power of attorney *before* you need one.

A power of attorney is a vital document that every adult should have. This document allows you to appoint another person as your "attorney-in-fact," which gives that person the authority to act on your behalf in legal matters should you not have the capacity to do so. A power of attorney can be drafted in several forms.

- The springing power of attorney only becomes effective under certain conditions, usually due to your incapacity. One significant disadvantage of the springing power of attorney is that when someone attempts to use it on your behalf, he or she may be required to prove that you are actually incompetent. This can create both inconvenience and significant delays.

- With a general power of attorney, you give your attorney-in-fact the authority to act on your behalf in all matters at any time. However, if you become incapacitated, this document is null and void. To solve this problem, you can draft a general *and durable* power of attorney which allows your attorney-in-fact to continue acting on your behalf in the event of your incapacitation.

- The Limited Power of Attorney allows someone to act on your behalf only under very specific circumstances. One possible reason might involve the signing of a specific legal agreement by your attorney-in-fact while you are out of the country.

First, you need to decide which type of power of attorney is most appropriate for your circumstances. Then you need to decide whom you would appoint as your attorney-in-fact. If you are married, a natural choice might be your spouse. But you should also have at least one successor attorney-in-fact. It should be noted that if you die, any and all power of attorney documents you have executed become null and void. Also, you should redo this document every four to five years. Many institutions, including banks, are reluctant to accept a power of attorney document that is older than that. These are powerful legal instruments, and care should be taken to keep them up-to-date.

Although you can get power of attorney standardized documents in books and various software programs, we recommend that you have it drawn up by an attorney or at least reviewed by one. Most attorneys will do this for a modest charge. Your attorney will make sure that the document conforms to your state law and will be able to help you decide which type of power of attorney is best for you.

Advance Healthcare Directive

Imagine this. Your spouse is in an auto accident and left in a comatose state. You are desperate to know what his condition is as well as the options that need to be considered for his cure. You are astonished to discover that the physician refuses to give you important details regarding his condition. Sound impossible? You might be further surprised to find out that the law may prevent the physician from talking to you under penalty of civil and criminal sanctions. The doctor could even lose his license to practice medicine.

In 1996, Congress passed a law called the Health Insurance Portability and Accountability Act, also known as HIPAA, which took aim at protecting the privacy of patients. What the law basically says is that physicians cannot release information about a patient without that patient's written permission. The HIPAA law does permit the doctor to release information if the doctor believes it is in the best interest of the patient, but with the current litigious society we find ourselves in today, some doctors are unwilling to chance landing in the middle of a lawsuit and therefore choose the more conservative position of not releasing information.

Dr. Rick Brown, an internal medicine specialist in Birmingham, Alabama, related this story. "One of my patients was in an auto accident and ended up in the emergency room in an out-of-town hospital. The attending physician would not release medical information to my patient's wife until I called him from my office and faxed him medical records on our company stationary."

The solution to this problem is to sign a HIPPA document whereby you indicate to whom you authorize medical personnel to release information.

In February of 1990, Terri Schiavo collapsed in her home and was rushed to the hospital. She was diagnosed as having minimal brain function and was in a persistent vegetative state, being kept alive on life support. This was the beginning of what became a very public story that brought world attention to the need for Advance Healthcare Directives and inspired the Vatican, the governor of Florida, and the president of the United States to weigh in on the heated debate. Ultimately, this story was about who had the right to decide about life or death. After 15 years in and out of court, her husband won the right to take her off life support, and she passed away in March 2005. The combination of medical costs and legal fees was well over $1 million. Although this was a high-profile story, the circumstances surrounding it are not unusual. In fact, similar scenarios play out hundreds of times every day in hospitals across America.

What you should ask yourself is, "What would I want done for me if I was in a similar situation?" After you have your answer, your next question should be, "What can I do about it?" You see, the problem with the Terri Schiavo case is that Terri should have taken steps to ensure that her wishes were well documented. You can do this by completing a Living Will and Advance Healthcare Directive. This is a straightforward document in which you indicate the level of medical care you would want under various severe circumstances. It also allows you to appoint an individual as your agent for health-care decisions. Make certain that your Advance Healthcare Directive includes HIPPA language that allows the attending physician to release information to those people that you have chosen. Most state legislatures have adopted a sample document for your use, making this an easy task for you to accomplish. To review information about the Advance Healthcare Directive laws and sample forms for your state, go to the Resource Center at www.welchgroup.com and click on "Living Will—State by State."

Estate Taxes

It is natural for us to think that we are free to give our assets to whomever we wish without interference from the government or additional taxes. After all, we have been paying taxes all our working life: taxes on our income, real estate property taxes, sales taxes. Surely we don't owe taxes when we die! Unfortunately, the government (both federal and state) wants to take one more "cut out of your financial apple" if you've managed to be financially successful before you die.

Making matters even worse, the estate tax laws are complex and subject to change based on the whims of Congress. Currently, if your net worth including life insurance (including spouse's net worth and life insurance) exceeds $2 million, your heirs may be responsible for paying estate taxes. Estate tax rates are very high (up to 45 percent to 46 percent), so this is serious business. Fortunately there are many strategies for reducing or eliminating these estate taxes, but you will need expert advice from an attorney who specializes in estate tax law. It goes without saying that this process of estate planning is something that you are doing to benefit your heirs, not you.

> **Treasure Tip**
>
> One source of information on estate planning is co-author Stewart Welch's book, *J.K. Lasser's New Rules for Estate and Tax Planning* (John Wiley & Sons, Inc., 2005).

Because some of our wealth-building strategies involve building or acquiring highly illiquid assets such as investment real estate or a private business, you may need to own permanent rather than term life insurance as discussed earlier in this chapter. Term life insurance can become too expensive to keep long term. The insurance industry has developed a solution for this situation with a product called a second-to-die or survivorship life insurance policy. This policy insures two lives, yours and your spouse's, and pays only when the second person dies. It is structured this way because the estate tax laws allow you to leave an unlimited amount of assets to a spouse free of estate taxes. In other words, the taxes are postponed until the death of the surviving spouse. This means that if Bill Gates, founder of Microsoft, died and left everything to his wife, there would be no estate taxes. But at her death, all of the taxes would be due, typically within nine months of the date of death. A second-to-die policy is a cash value policy, and while considerably more expensive than a term policy, it is typically much less expensive than purchasing a whole life, universal life, or variable life policy. This is because it will only pay off after the second of the two people die. All in all, second-to-die life insurance can be a good strategy for providing liquidity to pay estate taxes just when your heirs need the money.

The Least You Need to Know

- If you have dependants, you need life insurance.

- Your ability to earn a living is your greatest asset and needs to be insured.

- Lawsuits are a threat to your wealth. Proper use of insurance and entity selection can help build a shield of protection around your assets.

- Estate planning is for everyone. The basic tools include a will, power of attorney, and Advance Healthcare Directive.

Chapter 21

The Final Chapter ... Or Is It?

In This Chapter

- Finding the formula for success
- Learning how to guarantee you are a financial success
- Achieving massive financial success with the Trifecta Strategy
- Creating the life you always wanted

Well, you made it! You now have all the knowledge you need to achieve the level of wealth you desire. If you're in debt, we've shown a strategy for getting completely out of debt fast. If you haven't been a good saver in the past, we've outlined ideas that will help you become a great saver. If you've never really done any investing, you now have a specific recommendation of what to invest in according to how much money you have available. If investing is not your passion, that's okay. We've outlined an investment program that requires only minimal attention and monitoring. If you're excited about being an active investor, we've discussed many of the advanced investing strategies that will allow you to squeeze more return out of your portfolio if you have the "knack" these strategies require. If you want to start your own business, we've outlined the key elements that will help you succeed. You may have chosen investment real estate as your path to riches. If so, we've given you the basics you need to be a successful real estate investor. You now know the importance of minimizing taxes as part of your wealth accumulation plan along with tricks that the wealthy use to reduce taxes. And finally, you know what you need to do to protect your family and your wealth from potential external threats. So, with all of this newfound knowledge, tell us, what's holding you back?

Unleash Your Mental Power

What is it that holds people back from taking the action they know they must take to accomplish something that they have a strong desire to accomplish? As this question relates to this book, we have broken the answer down into three reasons:

- **Inaction.** You read the book but never did the exercises. You are what we call a passive reader. Throughout the course of this book, we asked you to complete a number of exercises. We asked you to calculate your target portfolio goal (TPG) and target savings goal (TSG) (Chapter 5). If you have not done this exercise, then you do not have any well-defined financial goals. Without well-defined goals, it will be hard to get or stay motivated to invest systematically because you will be constantly barraged with reasons to spend your money *now*. If you have an abundance of consumer debt, we asked you to use the Debt Pyramid Reduction Strategy to systematically eliminate your debt quickly (Chapter 4). We outlined some key actions that you need to take now to begin saving systematically (Chapter 5). We told you where and how to make your first investment (Chapters 7, 9, and 10). There are many other exercises and actions for you to take throughout this book that will set you on the road to riches. But it all begins with basic blocking and tackling; doing the basic exercises that form a solid foundation of any financial plan.

- **Procrastination.** We call procrastination "the great killer," for it is the culprit of a wasteland of unfulfilled goals, objectives, and dreams.

- **Fear.** Many people fail to act because of fear. Fear of failure. Fear of ridicule of others. And in some cases, fear of success.

If you find yourself locked into one of these reasons and unable to take the necessary actions to begin your journey to financial freedom, then review the following formula for success:

1. Make a Decision (to succeed). Make a decision that you are going to be a success. Decide, *now*. Nothing is going to get in your way. Picture in your mind exactly what success looks like for you. Picture that you are 90 years old and are looking back over your life. Picture how satisfying it will be to know that you made up your mind to succeed on this day ... and you followed through on that decision.

2. Get the Knowledge. After you've made the decision to achieve massive financial success, get the knowledge you need to accomplish your goals from someone you trust. Someone who is not selling you something. Yes, we're happy you bought this book and hope you'll recommend it to others, but our goal is to see you succeed. And to that end we've laid out a simple step-by-step road map for success. Knowledge will help reduce fear, but not eliminate it. The only way to defeat fear is to face it. Push through it and as a result, you will be a stronger person.

3. Exercise Discipline. When you've made a decision to become totally financially free and you've acquired the knowledge you need, all you have to do is exercise the discipline to begin your journey. Stop now and make a list of the first three things you need to do to get started. Maybe it's as simple as contacting your human resources department and having them begin withholding and investing in your 401(k) plan. Whatever it is, commit to do number one on your list today. Not tomorrow. Today. Next commit to do numbers 2 and 3 before the week is out. After you've done 1 through 3 on your list, make a new list of the next three things you must do. Set timelines for all your goals and action items. Each and every day ask yourself, "What can I do *today* to move me toward my financial goals?" Then do at least one thing each and every day. It could be as simple as saving money by bringing your lunch to work and sending a check for the difference to your investment account or paying against your number-one priority debt. Even if it's only $5 or $10, do it. You will *feel* the progress you are making. Remember the story of "How do you eat an elephant?" If you stumble, get up. If you lose your way, retrace your steps and get back on track. No matter what happens, continue to focus and move toward your goals. If you haven't done the exercises in this book, go back and complete them now. They are the beginning building blocks of your success.

Never, never, never give up. If you follow this three-pronged formula, you cannot fail. Remember, success is a state of mind. If you focus your mind each day with an unfaltering gaze on succeeding, you will succeed.

Automate Your Way to Success

One of the surest ways to guarantee your financial success is to place your key goals on automatic pilot. There are any number of ways to do this. Here are a few ideas to get you started:

◆ Have your employer automatically withhold a portion of your salary and invest in the company 401(k) plan.

◆ For emergency reserves, have your bank or employer set up an automatic transfer to a savings or credit union account.

◆ Set up an automatic debit from your checking account to a mutual fund.

◆ To reduce your debts, set up an automatic repayment plan that accelerates the payoff on a high-interest credit card.

Action for you to take right now: Think of your two most important financial issues and figure out how to set up an automated system for solving them. Then do it today.

The Trifecta of Wealth Accumulation

We know that you've gone through all of the exercises outlined in the various chapters of this book and now have written financial goals including your target portfolio goal and your target savings goal, right? Well now is a good time to take a moment and review those goals. When you review the list, how does it make you feel? Do you get excited? Do you feel inspired and powerful? Hopefully, the answer is "Yes." If not, you need to go back and create a truly compelling vision for your financial future. Don't be afraid to be outrageous with your vision and dreams. One of the worst mistakes you can make is to set the bar too low. If on the other hand you set the bar really high, the worst thing that can happen is that you achieve a lower level of success. This lower achievement of a really high goal is very likely to be higher than your original modest but uninspiring goal.

As we've emphasized in this book, there are three broad investment tracks you can take to achieve your goals: systematic investing using stocks or stock mutual funds, investment real estate, or starting your own business. If you really want to increase your chances of becoming rich, why not do all three? This is what we call the Trifecta of Wealth Accumulation. Done to perfection, this is what it would look like:

♦ Begin by setting up automatic maximum contributions to company retirement plans and IRAs (using primarily stocks or stock mutual funds).

♦ Set a goal to purchase one investment real estate property each and every year. Don't be concerned with how big or small each property is. If you find a great deal that is too big for you to handle, you should have little trouble finding other investors.

♦ While continuing to work at your current job, start your own part-time business. If the business you have in mind is not suitable as a part-time business, then begin to build your business plan and line up finances. In other words, get all your ducks in a row.

By attacking wealth accumulation on all three fronts, you will be amazed at how things will begin to fall into place. Expect it to take about 12 months to see noticeable results. Don't let the burden of activity overwhelm you. Rather, adopt the feeling of a business tycoon. This attitude will empower you and you will find that you are having a blast!

Now that you've made the decision to succeed, obtained the knowledge you need, and begun to systematically implement your action plan, financial success is all but guaranteed. But why would you settle for only being a financial success when you could have incredible success in every area of your life? Couldn't you use the same methodology we're using to achieve financial success to create success for your physical life, spiritual life, family life, intellectual life, and social life? The answer is "yes."

Beyond Financial Success

As we close the final chapter of this book, we want to make it perfectly clear that we don't think money is the most important thing in life. Far from it. It's not about "things" either, although things can make life more fun. It's really about your life's journey. About how you live your life. What kind of difference you make in the world. How you impact the lives of the people you come into contact with each day. By now you should know that we firmly believe you can have it all. Whatever your heart desires. All you need to do is crystallize your thoughts so clearly that you can write a detailed description of what you want. Then you need to write a simple but detailed step-by-step game plan that will lead to accomplishing your goals. Then take the first step ... then the next ... then the next, until you reach your goals or realize you need to make some modifications to your game plan. It's that simple.

So how is your life? Do you feel you are leading a balanced life? Take a moment to take our LifeWheel test.

First, make a copy of our LifeWheel below. Next, beginning at the center, color each section according to where you are today versus where you would like to be ideally. For example, picture your ideal physical health. Everybody's ideal will be different. Your ideal may be 20 pounds thinner and able to jog two miles. Whatever it is, draw that picture in your mind. Now think about where you actually are today. If you judge you are at 70 percent of your ideal, color in 70 percent of the section. By the way, it is possible to be at more than 100 percent. For example, if you are working to the exclusion of just about everything else in your life (workaholic), then your coloring may burst through the outside of this section. Do this coloring for each section of the LifeWheel. In group settings, we usually use crayons. It's fun to go back to our childhood roots every now and then!

The LifeWheel.

After you've completed this exercise, take a step back and admire your artwork. Does it have a lopsided appearance, as seen in the following picture?

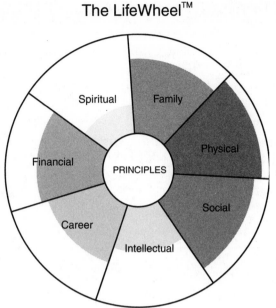

The LifeWheel™

The LifeWheel (example).

Imagine that this is a tire on your car but that the tire has seven separate air chambers with each chamber filled as depicted in your drawing. Is it any wonder that your life seems like a bumpy road? How would you like to create perfect balance in your life? Here's how to do it.

My Guiding Principles

At the core of your LifeWheel should be the principles that guide your life. Start by writing a statement about the principles that guide your life.

Write down the principles that guide your life:

_____

_____

_____

You can make your guiding principles as simple or complex as you desire. The most important thing is that you remember them and that you use them to guide all of your life decisions.

That Reminds Us ...

My guiding principles are as follows:

- ♦ I live my life with total integrity, in both my personal and business environments.
- ♦ I am my word.
- ♦ I make my decisions based on a win-win philosophy.
- ♦ I run my life from my spiritual center.

After writing this statement in the early '80s, I became motivated to leave the high-income world of selling products and start a fee-only Wealth Management firm. For me, the inherent conflict of making financial planning recommendations and then receiving commissions for selling a product solution was incongruent with my guiding principles. At the time, it was a scary decision, but one I knew I had to make.

—Co-author Stewart Welch

My Spiritual Goals

Whoa! We are not going to talk about the 'R' word are we? Whether you consider yourself religious or not, we believe everyone has a spiritual side of their nature. Many express it through their religious beliefs and affiliations. Others sense it in the natural world. However you express it, we want you to write a goals statement that reflects where you would like to be ideally.

My spiritual goals:

_____

_____

_____

An example might be, "I seek God's guidance in everything I do." Or, "I contribute to the improvement of the lives of the less fortunate."

Now that you've written your goals statement, you need to develop a brief action plan to connect specific actions to your goals.

Sample action plan (for spiritual goals):

- ♦ I will spend 30 minutes a day in Bible reading and prayer.

Or

◆ I will become active in Habitat for Humanity.

The actions you choose are those that will help you fulfill your corresponding goal. You can choose to keep them brief or outline very detailed goals and action plans. Under your action plan, be sure to list at least the first step you can take right away to begin moving toward each goal.

My action plan (spiritual goals):

_____

_____

_____

My Family Goals

In some ways family goals can be very easy. Typically you will want to spend more quality time with your family. Examples might be to establish a weekly date night with your spouse or a once-a-month one-on-one day with a child. Where it gets difficult is where families have dysfunctional members. If you are estranged from a family member or a family member is estranged from the rest of the family, what will your goal be? The point of this exercise is to think of what you want your family life to be like *ideally*. If ideally, you would like a normal relationship with an estranged family member, you should include this in your goals statement, then develop an action plan that will move you toward your goal. Recognize that all you can control are your actions. You can take the appropriate action, even if their response (or lack of) is not appropriate. We have found that most people respond (eventually!) in kind.

My family goals:

_____

_____

_____

Examples might include, "I will contact my parents once per day (week, month)." Or, "I will write a supportive letter to my (estranged) sister." Include specific actions that will lead toward accomplishing goals you have for each of your family members.

My action plan (family goals):

_____

_____

_____

My Physical Goals

With the current state of medical technology, we are likely to be on this planet for a very long time. This is a wonderful thing as long as our health remains good. You probably have a pretty good sense of your ideal state of physical health: what your ideal weight would be, the general ideal condition of your heart, your ideal nutrition program, and so on.

Treasure Tip _____

If you would like to jumpstart your physical transformation, we recommend you pick up a copy of the best-selling book *Body for Life* (HarperCollins Publishers, Inc., 1999). Author Bill Phillips outlines a complete nutrition plan that is healthy and will not let you go hungry, plus detailed exercise programs that are easy to follow.

My physical goals:

_____

_____

_____

A sample action might be as simple as, "I will walk 20 minutes per day." You may want to start small, get some successes under your belt, and then get more ambitious with your goals.

My action plan (physical goals):

_____

_____

_____

My Social Goals

Our lives are so busy that we often find our circle of activities narrows to the point that we rarely have time for our friends, especially those who don't live in our community. Yet we know that one of life's greatest rewards are our enduring friendships.

My social goals:

_____

_____

_____

A sample action might include making a list of friends that you want to stay in touch with and committing to make two calls per week (or send two e-mails) to out-of-town friends while committing one night every week to gathering with local friends socially.

My action plan (social goals):

_____

_____

_____

My Intellectual Goals

For many of us, when we finished our formal schooling, there was a sense of relief that we were done. By now you have probably figured out that you are never done learning. Goals might include higher education, specialized training, or simply being educated on current affairs.

My intellectual goals:

_____

_____

_____

Action plans might include enrolling in an MBA program, signing up for a training course, or subscribing and reading a current affairs publication such as *The Wall Street Journal* (the *National Enquirer* doesn't count!).

My action plan (intellectual goals):

_____

_____

_____

My Career Goals

Think about where you are currently in your career and where you would like to be. Write down your ideal career position and then ask yourself what actions you need to take to make this dream a reality. After reading this book, you may have already decided to start your own business.

My career goals:

_____

_____

_____

Can you achieve your career goals with your present employer? Have you ever communicated to your employer your career goals? This might be one of your action steps.

My action plan (career goals):

_____

_____

_____

My Financial Goals

Financial goals are what this book is all about. You should have these goals firmly locked in your mind. This is a good place to re-state those goals in a precise way along with the action steps you have decided on.

My financial goals:

_____

_____

_____

If you've performed all of the exercises we've asked you to do along the way, filling in your action plan should be a piece of cake.

My action plan (financial goals):

_____

_____

_____

Good Luck!

There you have it! We've enjoyed sharing this part of your journey with you and we would like to continue to be a resource for you as you travel down the road to wealth. Log on to www.welchgroup.com and access our Resource Center, where you will find links to numerous resources that will help you achieve your goal of getting rich!

The Least You Need to Know

- ◆ Success is a state of mind, and your mind gives you the power to succeed if only you will unleash its power.

- ◆ To guarantee your success, place your investment plan on autopilot!

- ◆ If you want to achieve massive wealth, consider our Trifecta Strategy: maximum contributions to retirement plans, investing in real estate, and starting your own business.

- ◆ Using the goal-setting and action-planning methodology you have learned in this book, you can create success in every area of your life!

Appendix A

Resources to Help Make You Rich

Websites

ABC's of Small Business   www.abcsmallbiz.com

This site offers tutorials for developing your business plan, as well as many articles on the subject of running a business.

Bank Rate Monitor   www.bankrate.com

A lot of useful news, calculators, and up-to-date interest rate quotes for mortgages, credit cards, auto loans, home equity, and banking.

Dollar Stretcher   www.stretcher.com

This site offers helpful suggestions on how to reduce expenses, as well as general tips for financial success. It offers stories, tips, searchable archives, and a newsletter.

Investopedia.com   www.investopedia.com

This website is full of free information and tutorials on investing, a dictionary with more than 4,500 investment terminology definitions, and numerous articles about investing.

Investor Guide   **www.investorguide.com**

This site has research, news, quotes, charts, and a lot of great links.

iShares   **www.ishares.com**

This site has a wealth of information about ETFs. Another site worth checking out is www.etfconnect.com.

Kelly Blue Book   **www.kbb.com**

Here is all the information you will need for buying, selling, and pricing new and used cars and trucks. Use this site to figure out what your car is worth or how to negotiate the best deal on your next auto purchase.

Microsoft Investor   **www.investor.com**

A huge site offering an online portfolio monitor, MSNBC and Reuters news offerings, and company information research.

Morningstar   **www.morningstar.net**

This site offers statistics on more than 6,500 mutual funds, information on more than 8,000 individual stocks, and a portfolio analyzer.

Quick Quote   **www.quickquote.com**

This site allows you to get a quote for term life insurance or health insurance from multiple top-rated insurance companies. Use this site to compare your current coverage, get quotes from prospective agents, or buy direct from Quick Quote.

SmartMoney.com   **www.smartmoney.com**

A major website with lots of free financial information. To appreciate its full value, you'll want to be a subscriber. For great information on basic investing, check out SmartMoney University at www.university.smartmoney.com.

The Welch Group   **www.welchgroup.com**

The Resource Center of co-author Stewart Welch's website offers access to a vast array of financial data. His "Stewart's Weekly Column" link offers more than 50 articles on financial matters, with a new article added each week.

Yahoo! Finance   **www.yahoo.com**

Provides free services that other sites charge for, as well as a Market Monitor, an excellent portfolio tracker, and Reuters news on individual companies.

Software

Deal Maker's Resource Center   www.bizbooksoftware.com

This center includes extensive software materials, and books and articles on buying, selling, and valuing your business.

Easy ROR (Rate of Return)   www.hamiltonsoftware.com

Exact calculations of time-weighted return on investment using minimal data input. Shows your true investment performance in just minutes. Monthly, quarterly, annually, and cumulative returns can be reported before or after tax and gross or net of fees.

Fundbuilder   www.fundbuilder.com

Shows how to take advantage of price fluctuations in your mutual funds to maximize returns. Calculates cost per share, compares it to the current fund price, and makes specific management recommendations based on the investment parameters you set.

Kiplinger's Home & Business Attorney www.kiplinger.com

This software program offers a comprehensive legal library including answers to your most important legal questions and more than 150 legal forms.

Kiplinger's Your Family Records   www.kiplinger.com

This software program will allow you to completely organize your records and important papers and documents.

Microsoft Money   www.microsoft.com

Allows users to manage accounts, track expenses against a budget, prepare tax information, and print checks. Includes online banking services, financial planning wizards, and investment management.

Quickbooks   www.quickbooks.intuit.com

For invoicing: Software does the math and calculates sales tax, creates customer statements, and displays old invoices onscreen instantly. For accounts receivable: Always knows what customers owe and for how long. Prepares deposits and reports overdue accounts. For accounts payable: Shows what you owe for each vendor and when and reminds you when bills are due.

Quicken **www.quicken.intuit.com**

Load this software onto your computer and you will do your future bill paying in one third of the time. Quicken also allows you to easily set up a budget-tracking system and print budget reports.

TurboTax **www.turbotax.com**

If you would like to do your own taxes, TurboTax is the #1 software on the market. It's very user-friendly.

Value Line Investment Analyzer **www.valueline.com**

If you're doing individual stock research, this CD-ROM software will help you analyze more than 1,700 stocks like a pro. Detailed information includes a "timeliness" and "safety" rating as well as three- to five-year projections for companies.

Books

The Intelligent Investor by Benjamin Graham

Originally published in 1949, this book is the classic "must read" for investors. The most famous follower of Benjamin Graham's teachings is self-made billionaire Warren Buffett. This is very advanced reading, but it will give you a very good understanding of how to choose great company stocks.

J.K. Lasser's New Rules for Estate and Tax Planning by Harold Apolinsky and Stewart Welch, III

As you achieve financial success, you will need to know how to protect and preserve your assets for yourself and your heirs. This book provides both simple and complex strategies for planning your estate and minimizing taxes.

The Millionaire Next Door by Thomas J. Stanley, Ph.D., and William D. Danko, Ph.D.

If you want to know what the typical self-made millionaires are really like, what they think, what they buy, and what they're interested in, then reading this book based on ground-breaking research will clue you in.

Richest Man in Babylon by George S. Clason

Originally written in 1926, through a riveting story this book reveals the timeless secret to achieving personal wealth.

The Seven Spiritual Laws of Success **by Deepak Chopra**

This book will challenge your intellect and stimulate your mind. If you can comprehend the universal laws that Deepak Chopra reveals, you will have unlocked the gates to abundance in your life.

Think and Grow Rich **by Napoleon Hill**

Originally published in 1960, this book has sold millions of copies because it reveals, in a "page turner" style, how to use your mind to accomplish anything you desire in life.

Who Moved My Cheese? **by Spencer Johnson**

If there is one thing constant in our world, it is change. If your goal is to become rich, you will have to master the art of change. This best-selling book will help you do just that.

Magazines and Newspapers

Barron's   www.barrons.com

A weekly publication for serious investors. It is so full of market information that it would be impossible for us to describe. Our suggestion is for you to pick up a copy at your local newsstand and read it from cover to cover. You'll then know if you want to be a regular reader.

Berkshire Hathaway Annual Report   www.berkshirehathaway.com

The "down home" wisdom of Warren Buffett is delivered every May in his annual report to shareholders. You can order a printed copy or download the report directly from the website.

Business Week   www.businessweek.com

This weekly magazine covers a wide range of current business topics.

Consumer Reports   www.consumerreports.org

Whatever you spend your hard-earned money on, you want it to last. *Consumer Reports* is the definitive magazine for identifying quality products and services.

Forbes   www.forbes.com

This monthly magazine offers great short articles on a wide variety of companies and the people who run them.

Fortune   **www.fortune.com**

This weekly magazine is full of interesting and inspiring stories of people and business. *Fortune* is famous for the Fortune 500 list and the list of the richest 500 people in America. Maybe one day you'll find your name on the list!

Kiplinger   **www.kiplinger.com**

This monthly publication takes a no-nonsense approach to bringing you top articles on a variety of life-improving subjects.

Kiplinger Retirement Report   **www.kiplinger.com**

This monthly publication is full of bite-size information that can help you better manage your money. It has an easy-to-read style and will keep you informed about the latest tax law changes that affect you. Your CPA will be amazed at your knowledge!

Morningstar FundInvestor   **www.corporate.morningstar.com**

Morningstar is the leader in mutual fund research. In *Morningstar FundInvestor*, the analysts at Morningstar search through more than 11,000 mutual funds to identify 500 of the best, divided by asset class. This monthly publication will greatly simplify your research efforts.

The Wall Street Journal   **www.online.wsj.com**

This daily newspaper is the most widely read financial periodical in America. You'll find daily stock and mutual fund prices, current articles on a wide variety of financial subjects, and much more. If you want to be up-to-date on what's happening in the financial world, you need look no further than the WSJ.

Worth   **www.worth.com**

This "all topic" monthly magazine is geared to high-net-worth individuals as well as those who aspire to become high net worth.

Words of the Wealthy—
the Whole List

12(b)1   A securities regulation that allows mutual funds to charge a fee in addition to the management fee for such things as marketing expenses, distribution expenses, or sales expenses. These expenses, in essence, disguise a commission. Be sure to avoid 12(b)1 fees in excess of .25 percent.

Asset   Property with a market value that can be sold for cash. This can include stocks, bonds, real estate, and privately held stock. Liquid assets can be sold quickly, whereas illiquid assets, such as real estate or a small business, usually take some time to sell.

Capital Ratio   A ratio that is calculated by dividing the bank's capital by its total assets. This ratio measures the bank's availability of capital and financial strength.

Certified Financial Planner™ (CFP®)   A financial planning professional who has been licensed by the CFP® Board of Standards by virtue of having passed a comprehensive national exam; has a minimum of three years of experience in the field of financial planning; has agreed to abide by a strict code of ethics; and receives continuing education of 30 hours every two years.

Collateral   Something of value that is pledged against a loan in case of default such as real estate you own.

Contrarian   Someone who invests contrary to everyone else, buying when the market is correcting and selling when the market reaches new highs. Contrarians welcome bad news because they know investors will overreact, and as a result, certain stock prices will fall lower than they should.

Depreciating Asset   When the value of an asset declines over time.

Discount Rate   The interest rate charged to commercial banks and other depository institutions on loans they receive from the Federal Reserve Bank. It is often used as a predictor of the future direction of interest rates.

Doodad   An asset that typically loses value over time and does not produce cash flow.

Effective Tax Rate   The *average* tax rate paid on all of your taxable income.

Estate Planning   The art and study of preserving wealth for family and future generations to come. It involves planning tools and techniques that can not only reduce estate taxes, but also make things a lot simpler after your death.

Fear Paradigm   The mindset and belief that when everyone is afraid of an investment, it should be avoided. The opposite is the contrarian paradigm, which is based on the belief that if everyone hates an investment, it should definitely be considered.

Fee-Only Advisor   A money manager or financial planner who receives a fee for service, which is usually based on a percentage of assets under management or time. Fee-only advisors do not receive any commissions for recommending products.

Fiduciary   An advisor who is also a fiduciary must place the interests of the client ahead of his own interests. All Registered Investment Advisors (RIAs) are fiduciaries when managing client investments.

Financial Asset   An asset that is expected to appreciate over time and that can produce cash flow for you either now or in the future.

Fixed Annuity   A contract with a life insurance company whereby you give a sum of money, and based on your age, life expectancy, and current interest rates, you'll eventually receive monthly payments for as long as you live. You decide when you want to receive payments, and until then, the money grows tax-deferred.

Full Service Brokerage Firm   A firm that offers its clients securities as well as advice. The firm is compensated by commissions, which are paid at the time transactions are made. A discount brokerage firm offers the same selection of securities, but because it does not offer advice, the commissions are usually lower.

Fundamental Analysis   The study of the basic facts that determine a security's value. A fundamental analysis of a mutual fund includes the study of the securities within the fund, the manager, the philosophy, expenses, and average P/E ratio.

Gross Domestic Product (GDP)   The total value of goods and services produced by a country during a year. The GDP's rate of growth is more popular in the news than the actual total GDP number.

Growth-Oriented Manager   Someone who searches for stocks with high earnings growth. Investors are willing to pay relatively higher prices for growth stocks for the chance that they may rise even higher later.

Haggle   From the Old English term *heawan*, meaning "to beat or cut." Haggling is the process of negotiating the lowest price possible in a purchase transaction.

Harvesting   An unconventional way of deriving income from a portfolio that includes not only dividends and interest, but also capital gains.

Hodaddy   Describes people who are generally fake or phony. A hodaddy is someone who puts on appearances of being someone he's not.

Inflation   An increase in the volume of money and credit relative to available goods, which results in a substantial and continuing rise in the general price level. Inflation is not a simple rise in prices, as most people believe. The rate of inflation is measured by the month-to-month percentage change of the consumer price index (CPI).

Investment Policy Statement (IPS)   A written document between the investment advisor and the client that outlines how the investment account will be managed. It details such restrictions as the allocation between stocks, bonds, and cash; cash distributions; and so on.

Junk Bond   An IOU issued by a company whose ability to repay its interest and principal in a timely manner depends on the economy and the company's ability to sell its products or services. It is also known as a high-yield bond. Standard & Poor's as well as Moody's offer corporate bond ratings, and a junk bond is any bond with a rating below BBB or Baa.

Law of Recency   Investors believe that the most recent market conditions will likely continue indefinitely, whether it is a bull market, bear market, or flat market.

Letter of Engagement   A document prepared by a professional advisor that outlines in detail what he or she will do for you. The letter should also illustrate how the advisor will be compensated and at what rate.

Liquid Assets   Those assets that can be instantly converted into cash. Illiquid assets are just the opposite; they are not easily converted into cash.

Marginal Tax Rate   The *highest* tax rate paid on any of your taxable income.

Money Manager   Another name for a fee-only investment advisor.

Multi-Level Portfolio Management   A term we use to describe the use of many different mutual funds in a portfolio. These funds add additional layers of diversification and together produce a certain synergy unachievable by any one investor alone.

Net Asset Value   The actual true value of each individual security held in a mutual fund.

No-Load Funds   Mutual funds that can be purchased, sold, and owned without any commission sales. The only charges involved are management fees.

No Transaction Fee (NTF)   A program started by Charles Schwab & Co. that gives investors the ability to buy hundreds of different no-load funds within the same account without paying any transaction fees. The program is so popular that many full-service brokerage firms now follow in their footsteps.

Outsource   A term that simply means to pay someone outside your firm to do a job for you. It's an alternative to directly putting someone on your payroll.

Over-the-Counter Market   A secondary market where securities are traded by phone and computer. The NASDAQ market is the largest and most popular over-the-counter market.

P/E Ratio   The price of a stock divided by the yearly earnings per share. It compares the price of a stock relative to its earnings, which is important to know when you compare one stock to another. It is also important in determining whether a stock is underpriced or overpriced relative to other stocks.

Paradigm   From the Greek word "paradeigma," which means model or pattern.

Past-Performance Paradigm   The past-performance paradigm is the belief that the past performance of an investment should be the primary justification for purchase.

Privately Held Company   A company whose shares are not publicly traded.

Pro-Forma Financial Statements   Used to project the estimated financial results of a new company. They consist of an income statement, balance sheet, and cash-flow statement.

Qualified Plans   Plans such as 401(k)s and SEPs that allow employees and/or employers to deposit part of their salary into the plan. The deposit is made pretax and the account grows tax-deferred.

Quantitative Analysis   The study of numerical information for the basis of decision making. Under the idea of quantitative theory, everything is expressed in measurable form and therefore is also predictable. Investors who use this theory believe that by studying specific market data, they can accurately predict the market's movements.

Relative Strength   A graphic illustration of the percentage (or fractional) difference between the price of a security and an index (or any other security).

Required Minimum Distributions   The law requires that you begin taking distributions from all retirement plans (except Roth IRAs) by April 1 of the year following the year that you turn age 70½.

Return on Equity (ROE)   Calculated by dividing the net income by the amount of capital invested in the company. This is perhaps the single most important measurement for stockholders and for judging the performance of management.

Rich Individual   A person who has cash flow from his or her investment portfolio of at least five times what it costs to pay for their lifestyle.

Rule of 72   By dividing your expected investment rate of return into 72, you can determine how long it will take for your investment to double in value. For example, if you expect to earn 10 percent on a particular investment, it will double in value in 7.2 years (72 divided by 10).

Secondary Market   Any market where previously issued securities are traded. The New York Stock Exchange (NYSE) is the most well-known example. There, investors can buy and sell stocks from each other through the designated traders on the floor of the exchange.

Soft Dollars   An indirect way many advisors are paid a commission for using the services of a particular brokerage firm or mutual fund. The brokerage firm or mutual fund company usually provides the advisor with research, software, or quotation machines that are normally part of the advisor's overhead expenses.

Standard Deviation   A statistical measure of varying distributions around the historical return of a specific security or group of securities.

Stock   What you hold when you invest in and become part owner of a company. Shares of stock can build your wealth by paying you dividends and by rising in price.

Target Savings Goal (TSG)   The amount of investment required each year to build a portfolio large enough to support your preferred standard of living at retirement.

Technical Analysis   Using charts to read the price history and other statistical patterns of stocks or mutual funds. Many investors and most professionals use these charts to make investment decisions. A technical analyst is also known as a "chartist."

Total Return   The percentage return of a portfolio, which includes dividends, interest, and capital gains. Total return is also known as portfolio performance.

Underwriter   A brokerage firm that handles the process of offering a company's stock to the public through an initial public offering.

Value-Oriented Manager   A manager who searches for undervalued stocks that are priced below what he actually thinks they're worth. The goal of the value manager is to sell at a profit after the market realizes the stock's true value.

Variable Annuity   Similar to a fixed annuity except that your investment choices include a limited number of stocks, bonds, and money market mutual funds.

Wealth   Defined by *Webster's Dictionary* as an "abundance of valuable material, possessions, or resources." The word *wealthy* is defined as "extremely affluent." The definition of affluent sounds even better: "having a generously sufficient and typically increasing supply of material possessions." However, your own definition of wealth is whatever you choose.

Wealthy Individual   A person who has cash flow from his or her investment portfolio of at least double what it costs to pay for their lifestyle including inflation.

Zero-Coupon Treasury Bonds   U.S. government bonds where the interest payments have been stripped out—for example, no interest is paid to the bondholder. They are sold at a discount of their face value so that the yield is based on the difference in what you paid for the bond and its value when it matures.

Appendix C

Sample Investment Policy Statement

Investment Policy Statement

For

John Q. & Mary J. Smart

Dated

January 1, 2006

Investment Accounts:

John Q. (IRA)—Charles Schwab & Co.	4276-xxxx	$57,962
John Q. (personal)—Charles Schwab & Co.	4792-xxxx	$10,433
Mary J. (IRA)—Vanguard	V6954R	$11,565
Mary J. (personal)—Vanguard	V6390P	$3,232

Investment Objectives: Long-term growth

Distribution Requirements: None expected until retirement

Time Horizon: Retirement at age 55 (15 years)

Investment Strategy: Modern Portfolio Theory (MPT)

Target Asset Allocation:

Cash (Money Market)	**2%**
Fixed Income	**18%**
U.S. bonds (investment grade)	10%
U.S. bonds (high yield)	3%
International bonds	5%
Equity	**80%**
U.S. large company stocks	45%
U.S. small company stocks	10%
U.S. real estate (REITs)	10%
International stocks	12%
Emerging markets stocks	3%

Target Returns:

Total Portfolio*	**9%**
Cash (money market)	3%
Fixed Income	6%
Equities	10%

Rebalancing Strategy: Rebalance to Target Asset Allocation every 12 months. Begin increasing fixed income allocation 5 years prior to retirement.

Market Correction/Bear Market Strategy: Remain invested. Historically, there are bear markets once every 3-5 years.

*Based on a 7-year market cycle

Annual Target Savings Goal Factor

By dividing your Target Portfolio Goal (Chapter 5) by the factor in this table, which represents the intersection of the number of years until you plan to retire and your expected rate of return on investments, you will determine the amount of money you must save annually to achieve your goal.

Annual Target Savings Goal Factor

Expected Rate of Return

# Yrs Until Retirement	4%	5%	6%	7%	8%	9%	10%	11%	12%
1	1.00	1.00	1.00	1.00	1.00	1.00	1.00	1.00	1.00
2	2.04	2.05	2.06	2.07	2.08	2.09	2.10	2.11	2.12
3	3.12	3.15	3.18	3.21	3.25	3.28	3.31	3.34	3.37
4	4.25	4.31	4.37	4.44	4.51	4.57	4.64	4.71	4.78
5	5.42	5.53	5.64	5.75	5.87	5.98	6.11	6.23	6.35
6	6.63	6.80	6.98	7.15	7.34	7.52	7.72	7.91	8.12
7	7.90	8.14	8.39	8.65	8.92	9.20	9.49	9.78	10.09
8	9.21	9.55	9.90	10.26	10.64	11.03	11.44	11.86	12.30
9	10.58	11.03	11.49	11.98	12.49	13.02	13.58	14.16	14.78
10	12.01	12.58	13.18	13.82	14.49	15.19	15.94	16.72	17.55
11	13.49	14.21	14.97	15.78	16.65	17.56	18.53	19.56	20.65
12	15.03	15.92	16.87	17.89	18.98	20.14	21.38	22.71	24.13
13	16.63	17.71	18.88	20.14	21.50	22.95	24.52	26.21	28.03
14	18.29	19.60	21.02	22.55	24.21	26.02	27.97	30.09	32.39
15	20.02	21.58	23.28	25.13	27.15	29.36	31.77	34.41	37.28
16	21.82	23.66	25.67	27.89	30.32	33.00	35.95	39.19	42.75
17	23.70	25.84	28.21	30.84	33.75	36.97	40.54	44.50	48.88
18	25.65	28.13	30.91	34.00	37.45	41.30	45.60	50.40	55.75
19	27.67	30.54	33.76	37.38	41.45	46.02	51.16	56.94	63.44
20	29.78	33.07	36.79	41.00	45.76	51.16	57.27	64.20	72.05
21	31.97	35.72	39.99	44.87	50.42	56.76	64.00	72.27	81.70
22	34.25	38.51	43.39	49.01	55.46	62.87	71.40	81.21	92.50
23	36.62	41.43	47.00	53.44	60.89	69.53	79.54	91.15	104.60
24	39.08	44.50	50.82	58.18	66.76	76.79	88.50	102.17	118.16
25	41.65	47.73	54.86	63.25	73.11	84.70	98.35	114.41	133.33
26	44.31	51.11	59.16	68.68	79.95	93.32	109.18	128.00	150.33
27	47.08	54.67	63.71	74.48	87.35	102.72	121.10	143.08	169.37
28	49.97	58.40	68.53	80.70	95.34	112.97	134.21	159.82	190.70
29	52.97	62.32	73.64	87.35	103.97	124.14	148.63	178.40	214.58
30	56.08	66.44	79.06	94.46	113.28	136.31	164.49	199.02	241.33
31	59.33	70.76	84.80	102.07	123.35	149.58	181.94	221.91	271.29
32	62.70	75.30	90.89	110.22	134.21	164.04	201.14	247.32	304.85
33	66.21	80.06	97.34	118.93	145.95	179.80	222.25	275.53	342.43
34	69.86	85.07	104.18	128.26	158.63	196.98	245.48	306.84	384.52
35	73.65	90.32	111.43	138.24	172.32	215.71	271.02	341.59	431.66
36	77.60	95.84	119.12	148.91	187.10	236.12	299.13	380.16	484.46
37	81.70	101.63	127.27	160.34	203.07	258.38	330.04	422.98	543.60
38	85.97	107.71	135.90	172.56	220.32	282.63	364.04	470.51	609.83
39	90.41	114.10	145.06	185.64	238.94	309.07	401.45	523.27	684.01
40	95.03	120.80	154.76	199.64	259.06	337.88	442.59	581.83	767.09

Expected Rate of Return

13%	14%	15%	16%	17%	18%	19%	20%	21%	22%
1.00	1.00	1.00	1.00	1.00	1.00	1.00	1.00	1.00	1.00
2.13	2.14	2.15	2.16	2.17	2.18	2.19	2.20	2.2	2.22
3.41	3.44	3.47	3.51	3.54	3.57	3.61	3.64	3.67	3.71
4.85	4.92	4.99	5.07	5.14	5.22	5.29	5.37	5.45	5.52
6.48	6.61	6.74	6.88	7.01	7.15	7.30	7.44	7.59	7.74
8.32	8.54	8.75	8.98	9.21	9.44	9.68	9.93	10.18	10.44
10.40	10.73	11.07	11.41	11.77	12.14	12.52	12.92	13.32	13.74
12.76	13.23	13.73	14.24	14.77	15.33	15.90	16.50	17.12	17.76
15.42	16.09	16.79	17.52	18.28	19.09	19.92	20.80	21.71	22.67
18.42	19.34	20.30	21.32	22.39	23.52	24.71	25.96	27.27	28.66
21.81	23.04	24.35	25.73	27.20	28.76	30.40	32.15	34.00	35.96
25.65	27.27	29.00	30.85	32.82	34.93	37.18	39.58	42.14	44.87
29.98	32.09	34.35	36.79	39.40	42.22	45.24	48.50	51.99	55.75
34.88	37.58	40.50	43.67	47.10	50.82	54.84	59.20	63.91	69.01
40.42	43.84	47.58	51.66	56.11	60.97	66.26	72.04	78.33	85.19
46.67	50.98	55.72	60.93	66.65	72.94	79.85	87.44	95.78	104.93
53.74	59.12	65.08	71.67	78.98	87.07	96.02	105.93	116.89	129.02
61.73	68.39	75.84	84.14	93.41	103.74	115.27	128.12	142.44	158.40
70.75	78.97	88.21	98.60	110.28	123.41	138.17	154.74	173.35	194.25
80.95	91.02	102.44	115.38	130.03	146.63	165.42	186.69	210.76	237.99
92.47	104.77	118.81	134.84	153.14	174.02	197.85	225.03	256.02	291.35
105.49	120.44	137.63	157.41	180.17	206.34	236.44	271.03	310.78	356.44
120.20	138.30	159.28	183.60	211.80	244.49	282.36	326.24	377.05	435.86
136.83	158.66	184.17	213.98	248.81	289.49	337.01	392.48	457.22	532.75
155.62	181.87	212.79	249.21	292.10	342.60	402.04	471.98	554.24	650.96
176.85	208.33	245.71	290.09	342.76	405.27	479.43	567.38	671.63	795.17
200.84	238.50	283.57	337.50	402.03	479.22	571.52	681.85	813.68	971.10
227.95	272.89	327.10	392.50	471.38	566.48	681.11	819.22	985.55	1,185.74
258.58	312.09	377.17	456.30	552.51	669.45	811.52	984.07	1,193.51	1,447.61
293.20	356.79	434.75	530.31	647.44	790.95	966.71	1,181.88	1,445.15	1,767.08
332.32	407.74	500.96	616.16	758.50	934.32	1,151.39	1,419.26	1,749.63	2,156.84
376.52	465.82	577.10	715.75	888.45	1,103.50	1,371.15	1,704.11	2,118.06	2,632.34
426.46	532.04	664.67	831.27	1,040.49	1,303.13	1,632.67	2,045.93	2,563.85	3,212.46
482.90	607.52	765.37	965.27	1,218.37	1,538.69	1,943.88	2,456.12	3,103.25	3,920.20
546.68	693.57	881.17	1,120.71	1,426.49	1,816.65	2,314.21	2,948.34	3,755.94	4,783.64
618.75	791.67	1,014.35	1,301.03	1,669.99	2,144.65	2,754.91	3,539.01	4,545.68	5,837.05
700.19	903.51	1,167.50	1,510.19	1,954.89	2,531.69	3,279.35	4,247.81	5,501.28	7,122.20
792.21	1,031.00	1,343.62	1,752.82	2,288.23	2,988.39	3,903.42	5,098.37	6,657.55	8,690.08
896.20	1,176.34	1,546.17	2,034.27	2,678.22	3,527.30	4,646.07	6,119.05	8,056.63	10,602.90
1,013.70	1,342.03	1,779.09	2,360.76	3,134.52	4,163.21	5,529.83	7,343.86	9,749.52	12,936.54

continues

Annual Target Savings Goal Factor (continued)

Expected Rate of Return

# Yrs Until Retirement	23%	24%	25%	26%	27%	28%	29%	30%
1	1.00	1.00	1.00	1.00	1.00	1.00	1.00	1.00
2	2.23	2.24	2.25	2.26	2.27	2.28	2.29	2.30
3	3.74	3.78	3.81	3.85	3.88	3.92	3.95	3.99
4	5.60	5.68	5.77	5.85	5.93	6.02	6.10	6.19
5	7.89	8.05	8.21	8.37	8.53	8.70	8.87	9.04
6	10.71	10.98	11.26	11.54	11.84	12.14	12.44	12.76
7	14.17	14.62	15.07	15.55	16.03	16.53	17.05	17.58
8	18.43	19.12	19.84	20.59	21.36	22.16	23.00	23.86
9	23.67	24.71	25.80	26.94	28.13	29.37	30.66	32.01
10	30.11	31.64	33.25	34.94	36.72	38.59	40.56	42.62
11	38.04	40.24	42.57	45.03	47.64	50.40	53.32	56.41
12	47.79	50.89	54.21	57.74	61.50	65.51	69.78	74.33
13	59.78	64.11	68.76	73.75	79.11	84.85	91.02	97.63
14	74.53	80.50	86.95	93.93	101.47	109.61	118.41	127.91
15	92.67	100.82	109.69	119.35	129.86	141.30	153.75	167.29
16	114.98	126.01	138.11	151.38	165.92	181.87	199.34	218.47
17	142.43	157.25	173.64	191.73	211.72	233.79	258.15	285.01
18	176.19	195.99	218.04	242.59	269.89	300.25	334.01	371.52
19	217.71	244.03	273.56	306.66	343.76	385.32	431.87	483.97
20	268.79	303.60	342.94	387.39	437.57	494.21	558.11	630.17
21	331.61	377.46	429.68	489.11	556.72	633.59	720.96	820.22
22	408.88	469.06	538.10	617.28	708.03	812.00	931.04	1,067.28
23	503.92	582.63	673.63	778.77	900.20	1,040.36	1,202.05	1,388.46
24	620.82	723.46	843.03	982.25	1,144.25	1,332.66	1,551.64	1,806.00
25	764.61	898.09	1,054.79	1,238.64	1,454.20	1,706.80	2,002.62	2,348.80
26	941.46	1,114.63	1,319.49	1,561.68	1,847.84	2,185.71	2,584.37	3,054.44
27	1,159.00	1,383.15	1,650.36	1,968.72	2,347.75	2,798.71	3,334.84	3,971.78
28	1,426.57	1,716.10	2,063.95	2,481.59	2,982.64	3,583.34	4,302.95	5,164.31
29	1,755.68	2,128.96	2,580.94	3,127.80	3,788.96	4,587.68	5,551.80	6,714.60
30	2,160.49	2,640.92	3,227.17	3,942.03	4,812.98	5,873.23	7,162.82	8,729.99
31	2,658.40	3,275.74	4,034.97	4,967.95	6,113.48	7,518.74	9,241.04	11,349.98
32	3,270.84	4,062.91	5,044.71	6,260.62	7,765.12	9,624.98	11,921.95	14,755.98
33	4,024.13	5,039.01	6,306.89	7,889.38	9,862.70	12,320.98	15,380.31	19,183.77
34	4,950.68	6,249.38	7,884.61	9,941.62	12,526.63	15,771.85	19,841.60	24,939.90
35	6,090.33	7,750.23	9,856.76	12,527.44	15,909.82	20,188.97	25,596.66	32,422.87
36	7,492.11	9,611.28	12,321.95	15,785.58	20,206.48	25,842.88	33,020.70	42,150.73
37	9,216.30	11,918.99	15,403.44	19,890.83	25,663.23	33,079.88	42,597.70	54,796.95
38	11,337.05	14,780.54	19,255.30	25,063.44	32,593.30	42,343.25	54,952.03	71,237.03
39	13,945.57	18,328.87	24,070.12	31,580.94	41,394.49	54,200.36	70,889.12	92,609.14
40	17,154.05	22,728.80	30,088.66	39,792.98	52,572.00	69,377.46	91,447.96	120,392.88

Expected Rate of Return

31%	32%	33%	34%	35%	36%	37%	38%	39%	40%
1.00	1.00	1.00	1.00	1.00	1.00	1.00	1.00	1.00	1.00
2.31	2.32	2.33	2.34	2.35	2.36	2.37	2.38	2.39	2.40
4.03	4.06	4.10	4.14	4.17	4.21	4.25	4.28	4.32	4.36
6.27	6.36	6.45	6.54	6.63	6.73	6.82	6.91	7.01	7.10
9.22	9.40	9.58	9.77	9.95	10.15	10.34	10.54	10.74	10.95
13.08	13.41	13.74	14.09	14.44	14.80	15.17	15.54	15.93	16.32
18.13	18.70	19.28	19.88	20.49	21.13	21.78	22.45	23.14	23.85
24.75	25.68	26.64	27.63	28.66	29.73	30.84	31.98	33.17	34.39
33.42	34.90	36.43	38.03	39.70	41.43	43.25	45.14	47.10	49.15
44.79	47.06	49.45	51.96	54.59	57.35	60.25	63.29	66.47	69.81
59.67	63.12	66.77	70.62	74.70	79.00	83.54	88.34	93.40	98.74
79.17	84.32	89.80	95.64	101.84	108.44	115.45	122.90	130.82	139.23
104.71	112.30	120.44	129.15	138.48	148.47	159.17	170.61	182.84	195.93
138.17	149.24	161.18	174.06	187.95	202.93	219.06	236.44	255.15	275.30
182.00	198.00	215.37	234.25	254.74	276.98	301.11	327.28	355.66	386.42
239.42	262.36	287.45	314.89	344.90	377.69	413.52	452.65	495.37	541.99
314.64	347.31	383.30	422.95	466.61	514.66	567.52	625.66	689.56	759.78
413.18	459.45	510.80	567.76	630.92	700.94	778.51	864.41	959.50	1,064.70
542.27	607.47	680.36	761.80	852.75	954.28	1,067.56	1,193.89	1,334.70	1,491.58
711.38	802.86	905.88	1,021.81	1,152.21	1,298.82	1,463.55	1,648.56	1,856.23	2,089.21
932.90	1,060.78	1,205.81	1,370.22	1,556.48	1,767.39	2,006.07	2,276.02	2,581.16	2,925.89
1,223.10	1,401.23	1,604.73	1,837.10	2,102.25	2,404.65	2,749.31	3,141.90	3,588.81	4,097.24
1,603.26	1,850.62	2,135.30	2,462.71	2,839.04	3,271.33	3,767.56	4,336.83	4,989.45	5,737.14
2,101.28	2,443.82	2,840.94	3,301.03	3,833.71	4,450.00	5,162.55	5,985.82	6,936.34	8,033.00
2,753.67	3,226.84	3,779.45	4,424.38	5,176.50	6,053.00	7,073.70	8,261.43	9,642.51	11,247.20
3,608.31	4,260.43	5,027.67	5,929.67	6,989.28	8,233.09	9,691.97	11,401.77	13,404.08	15,747.08
4,727.89	5,624.77	6,687.81	7,946.76	9,436.53	11,198.00	13,278.99	15,735.45	18,632.68	22,046.91
6,194.53	7,425.70	8,895.78	10,649.65	12,740.31	15,230.27	18,193.22	21,715.92	25,900.42	30,866.67
8,115.84	9,802.92	11,832.39	14,271.54	17,200.42	20,714.17	24,925.72	29,968.97	36,002.58	43,214.34
10,632.75	12,940.86	15,738.08	19,124.86	23,221.57	28,172.28	34,149.23	41,358.17	50,044.59	60,501.08
13,929.90	17,082.93	20,932.64	25,628.31	31,350.12	38,315.30	46,785.45	57,075.28	69,562.98	84,702.51
18,249.17	22,550.47	27,841.42	34,342.94	42,323.66	52,109.80	64,097.06	78,764.89	96,693.55	118,584.52
23,907.41	29,767.62	37,030.08	46,020.54	57,137.94	70,870.33	87,813.97	108,696.55	134,405.03	166,019.33
31,319.70	39,294.26	49,251.01	61,668.52	77,137.22	96,384.65	120,306.14	150,002.23	186,823.99	232,428.06
41,029.81	51,869.43	65,504.84	82,636.81	104,136.25	131,084.12	164,820.42	207,004.08	259,686.34	325,400.28
53,750.05	68,468.64	87,122.44	110,734.33	140,584.94	178,275.41	225,804.97	285,666.63	360,965.02	455,561.39
70,413.57	90,379.61	115,873.85	148,385.00	189,790.67	242,455.55	309,353.81	394,220.95	501,742.38	637,786.95
92,242.77	119,302.08	154,113.21	198,836.91	256,218.40	329,740.55	423,815.72	544,025.91	697,422.90	892,902.73
120,839.03	157,479.75	204,971.57	266,442.45	345,895.84	448,448.15	580,628.53	750,756.76	969,418.84	1,250,064.82
158,300.13	207,874.27	272,613.19	357,033.89	466,960.38	609,890.48	795,462.09	1,036,045.33	1,347,493.18	1,750,091.74

Index

J-K-L

Check Out These
Best-Sellers

Grammar and Style
SECOND EDITION

Laurie E. Rozakis, Ph.D.

1-59257-115-8 • $16.95

Buying and Selling a Home
FOURTH EDITION

Shelley O'Hara and Nancy D. Lewis

1-59257-120-4 • $18.95

Being a Groom
SECOND EDITION

Jennifer Lata Rung and Mark Rung

0-02-864456-5 • $9.95

Learning Spanish
THIRD EDITION

Gail Stein

0-02-864451-4 • $18.95

Personal Finance in Your 20s & 30s
SECOND EDITION

Sarah Young Fisher and Susan Shelly

0-02-864374-7 • $19.95

Organizing Your Life
FOURTH EDITION

Georgene Lockwood

1-59257-413-0 • $16.95

Total Nutrition
FOURTH EDITION

Joy Bauer, M.S., R.D., C.D.N.

1-59257-439-4 • $18.95

Positive Dog Training

Pamela Dennison

0-02-864463-8 • $14.95

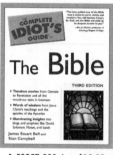

The Bible
THIRD EDITION

James Stuart Bell and Stan Campbell

1-59257-389-4 • $18.95

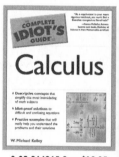

Calculus

W. Michael Kelley

0-02-864365-8 • $18.95

Music Theory
SECOND EDITION

Michael Miller

1-59257-437-8 • $19.95

The Perfect Resume
THIRD EDITION

Susan Ireland

0-02-864440-9 • $14.95

Playing the Guitar
SECOND EDITION

Frederick Noad

0-02-864244-9 • $21.95

Manga Illustrated

John Layman and David Hutchison

1-59257-335-5 • $19.95

Knitting and Crocheting
SECOND EDITION
Illustrated

Barbara Breiter and Gail Diven

1-59257-089-5 • $16.95

More than *450 titles* available at
booksellers and online retailers everywhere

www.idiotsguides.com

ALPHA